WHAT HAVE WE GOT?

Also by Simon Spence

A Likely Lad: Peter Doherty
(Little, Brown, 2022)

All Or Nothing: The Authorised Story of Steve Marriott
(Omnibus, 2021)

The Stone Roses: War and Peace
(Penguin, 2012)

When The Screaming Stops: The Dark History of the Bay City Rollers
(Omnibus, 2016)

Stoned: Andrew Loog Oldham
(Research & Interviews, Random House, 2000)

2Stoned: Andrew Loog Oldham
(Research & Interviews, Random House, 2002)

Happy Mondays: Excess All Areas
(Aurum, 2014)

Just Can't Get Enough: The Making of Depeche Mode
(Jawbone, 2011)

Still Breathing: True Adventures of the Donnelly Brothers
(Black and White, 2013)

Fuck 'Em All – Immediate Records
(Backstage, 2023)

Mr Big: Don Arden
(Research & Interviews, Chrysalis, 2004)

Staying Alive: Disco Inferno of the Bee Gees
(Jawbone, 2017)

WHAT HAVE WE GOT?

OMNIBUS PRESS
London / New York / Paris / Sydney / Copenhagen / Berlin / Madrid / Tokyo

(A division of the Wise Music Group
14–15 Berners Street, London, W1T 3LJ)

Cover designed by Amazing15
Front cover image © Virginia Turbett/Getty Images
Back cover image © Derek Ridgers
Picture research by the author

ISBN 978-1-913172-85-5

Every effort has been made to trace the copyright holders of the photographs in this book but one or two were unreachable. We would be grateful if the photographers concerned would contact us.

A catalogue record for this book is available from the British Library.

Typeset in Baskerville by Palimpsest Book Production Ltd, Falkirk, Stirlingshire

Printed in Poland by Hussar Books.

www.omnibuspress.com

'Punk rock – a loud, fast and deliberately offensive style of rock music'

Webster's New World Dictionary, Fourth Edition, 2003

'Oi! – a violent, tough, ugly music made for and by people from that background'

Trevor Taylor, Crown Court

Contents

Foreword

I am honestly of the opinion that the Oi! scene always was and still is a true working-class movement. In fact, it's the only working-class rock'n'roll movement. When I say working class, I mean exactly that – not people who think it's a cool thing to affect being working class. I'm talking about the people, no matter their colour, creed or sexual orientation, who are not from moneyed, privileged backgrounds.

Oi! came about because no other people other than the working class have been, and still are, so ignored and so excluded from power within society. The benefits of modern society, inclusiveness, equal rights and equal opportunity are now all around – as it should be. how come that equal rights and opportunity isn't also inclusive of the working class? What's going on?

When society continues to ignore a certain section then sooner or later those ignored people will begin to do their own thing, and that's exactly the place Oi! originally came from.

The working class were always there to help society, always there to go the extra mile, but were never genuinely called on unless it was as cannon fodder or as factory workers. The working class were always used by the ruling classes and viewed as expendable. When society continues to ignore, overlook or fails to give acknowledgement to a certain group of people then it is society that is at fault.

I was an original member of Cock Sparrer when they were first known as Janus. I joined in 1974 and was there until 1979. I wrote, among other songs, 'Runnin' Riot' and 'Chip on My Shoulder'. Those songs were about the working-class struggle, a struggle that is as old as time itself. If society truly wants to create a better place for all, then make it exactly that: For All.

Gary Lammin
November 2022

Author's Note

A definitive history of Oi!? Yes and no. I've discovered there's a lot more Oi! bands out there and a lot more to the story than I initially thought. Right to the last I was discovering contemporary bands from various parts of the world who were putting out good stuff, such as Clobber, Hard Wax and The Enforcers, bands adding twists to the Oi! template. I even fell down a 'hipster Oi!' rabbit hole thanks to Vanity's *Vain in Life* album.

Among the newer UK bands who I saw play live during the twelve months I spent researching Oi!, I especially want to mention Watford's Tear Up, Belfast's Takers & Users and the new young pups from Stoke-on-Trent, Rise Up; all three bands are undoubtedly part of the modern scene but I never did get round to speaking to them for one reason or another.

Most of the big hitters of the early original Oi! scene, however, are all here: Sham; Menace; Upstarts; Rejects; Bushell; Last Resort; Blitz; Business; Combat 84 and Cock Sparrer. I never really got close to getting the 4-Skins, which is a glaring omission on my part given that 'Chaos' is perhaps the definitive Oi! song.

I also steered clear of The Exploited, who featured on the first ever, genre-defining Oi! compilation album, *Oi! The Album*, released in 1980. They quickly made a scene for themselves separate from Oi!, known as a 'UK82', with liberty spikes prevalent among bands such as GBH, Discharge, Conflict, Chron-Gen and Anti-Nowhere League. Oi! and UK82 share some musical and cultural parallels, but it's really another world.

Oi!, in its very early days, *did* have a skins and punks united mission statement, but once the UK82 bands detached themselves, Oi! became all about skinheads. And, frankly, if you examined the roots of Oi! it was always all about skinheads, specifically a brutal and shocking post-punk, second wave of skinheads. A cult started by a smallish group of London lads circa 1977, who gained numbers and notoriety through '78 as part of the so-called 'Sham Army'.

But this isn't a book about skinheads; a little disingenuous to say that as the majority of people who I interviewed for this book were skinheads. What I mean is there's no deep exploration of the origins of skinhead culture to be found in these pages: music, clothes, *meaning*. When the second wave took hold, the nuances of that late sixties subculture were lost to the media anyway: the enduring popular image of the skinhead was of young, booted thugs, working-class, council estate, football hooligans who enjoyed 'Paki-bashing' and rape as codified by Richard Allen's popular *Skinhead* book, published in 1970. In essence, that potent caricature was what this second wave were playing with, using to 'shock', similar to how the Sex Pistols used the swastika.

It obviously means something to be a skinhead otherwise 'a way of life' wouldn't be their slogan. Weetabix wouldn't have spent most of the eighties with skinheads as a key tranche of their advertising, suggesting their breakfast cereal was tougher than the others. Blur wouldn't have co-opted the look in the nineties to emphasise their working-class cockney shtick. It's difficult to capture in a line or a paragraph, though.

The Last Resort, the quintessential Oi! band, have a song called 'Working Class Kids'. There's a telling line in it: 'Don't ask me what makes us tick.' I didn't ask. But I listened and I looked. And I hope this book resonates.

Tattoos are a good example of what I'm talking about. Oi! bands are probably the most tattooed in musical history. At gigs, tops were frequently off and entire torsos revealed, routinely fully inked. Tattoos were always on show: forearms, knuckles, Adam's apples, foreheads and skulls. This seemed to become more pronounced around the second wave of skinheads and grew into modern-day ubiquity. I never asked about spiderwebs on the elbows.

I did visit my first ever tattoo shop in Jarrow called Viking, owned by Chris Wright, the singer with Oi! rock band Crashed Out, and later briefly met the tattooist Lilly Moon at the Templars/Lion's Law gig she promoted at the 100 Club in London. I also noted that Darzo of Takers & Users was a tattoo artist and Lars Frederiksen, guitarist with Rancid, The Old Firm Casuals and The Last Resort, was a sometimes inker, closely associated with London's Skunx Tattoo shop. 'It's quite a small scene in the UK so everyone in the Oi! world knows each other,' Wright told me. 'I tattooed Lars in the shop when we supported Old Firm Casuals. And he tattooed me.'

I regret not bobbing along to Manchester to attend the tenth annual 'Tattoo Tea Party' in April, one of the biggest tattoo conventions in Europe, and where Wright was an artist. I'm sure it would have been an eye-opener, but the subject remains largely alien to me. However, I can point you towards a fifteen-minute short film called *Skindeep* that was produced while I was doing this book in the summer of 2022 by a female tattooist called Leanka Platt. She interviewed the celebrated London tattooist Lal Hardy who explained a little of the origins of the links between skinheads and tattoos. Also featured talking and showing off tattoos were several of the Oi! faces I interviewed for this book, such as Phil from The Templars, Wattie from Lion's Law, Trevor Taylor and Ralph Orton from Crown Court and music journalist Garry Bushell (who originally coined the term Oi! and championed the genre in music weekly *Sounds*).

In terms of skinhead fashion, I also steered clear. I noticed old-school Adidas trainers are acceptable as a footwear alternative to boots and this is a terrace influence. Football violence is ingrained in Oi!. Many Oi! band members were closely associated with hooligan 'firms', most notably Cockney Rejects, the first band to sing with real conviction about those experiences in the raw. The singer of The Last Resort, Roi Pearce, is also a well-known terrace face, and the Resort also have several songs, old and new, that anticipate or describe football match violence. In more recent times Crown Court sing of that same buzz.

There is, finally, a small but significant side of Oi!, sometimes called 'grey zone', that I could not give proper voice to. I had a long look (see chapter 12), considered approaching one or two bands, and even made plans to attend gigs, but I'm still not exactly sure what they mean when they refer to their music as 'the real Oi!'. It was intimated the 'grey zone' bands and fans might be a hangover from the eighties National Front-sponsored 'white noise' Oi! scene from which bands such as Skrewdriver emerged. Skrewdriver went on to lead a radical neo-Nazi lunatic fringe, first under the National front-funded Rock Against Communism (RAC)/White Noise banner and then with their own Blood & Honour (B&H) movement.

The 'grey zone' bands were not in that extreme category but have been ostracised in the modern world of Oi!. Paradoxically, when Oi! has occasionally featured in the mainstream media over the past decade, the focus has often been on this small rump, in a similar way as the 'white power' Oi! scene came to dominate headlines in the UK during the eighties and nineties. The neo-Nazi skinhead image still lingers. It's partly why contemporary music critics such as Stuart Maconie can get away unchallenged with describing Oi! as, 'Punk's stunted idiot half-brother, musically primitive and politically unsavoury, with its close links to far-right groups.' Exploding that myth is easy. Getting across the leitmotif of the 'grey zone' movement is far more complex, rooted in decades of working-class sociology and UK politics.

However, I *have* included an interview with the controversial Combat 84. In Derek Ridgers's highly regarded photo documentary book, *Skinheads 1979–1984*, there is a photo of an off-putting tattoo on the forearm of their singer that reads: 'Ein Volk, Ein Reich, Ein Fuehrer' (One People, One Realm, One Leader), a Nazi Party slogan. The band, however, have a pivotal role in the complicated Oi! story of the early eighties, the stars of a must-see 1982 BBC Two documentary called *Skinheads*. I understand there remains an element of unease about the band. I tended to use Spotify as arbitrator – the full Combat 84 discography is there.

The main reason for writing this book (as well as looking under stones and re-evaluating the Oi! pioneers) is to try and put the focus more on the incredible, current explosion of young, modern Oi! bands in the UK such as Crown Court. The best retain all the hallmarks of hard-hitting eighties Oi! with a style and attitude that feels fresh, vital and invigorating. Important. This is really a book for them and a new wave of bands like them around the world.

It is also a book for bands who kept the Oi! scene alive in the nineties and noughties, such as The Templars in New York, Lion's Law in Paris, Rotten Boys in São Paulo and Marching Orders in Melbourne. Perhaps the most remarkable aspect to this story is how the much-maligned UK Oi! scene inspired vibrant scenes around the world.

This was something else that needed acknowledging: the incredible esprit de corps of the Oi! community worldwide. The support networks are phenomenal: independent record labels, dedicated promoters, websites, graphic artists, specialist shops and loyal fans.

The modern Oi! world is completely different to the mainstream media's preconceptions about the genre. The music and narratives of the older faces is more nuanced, the new breed is the closest thing guitar music has to the raw power and potency of contemporary hip-hop, and the way the genre survived for over forty years is quite Shakespearean.

The scenery changes, but the steadfastnest of those involved remains a theme. Oi Oi The Shop in London is the thriving, positive UK hub for this modern world, in Camden Market. The Rebellion Festival in Blackpool is another. In truth, I had a blast: watching 3,000 people sing along with every word of every song by Cock Sparrer; Crown Court's cathartic thirty-minute outburst of new rock'n'roll in Bedford; rooted to the spot by an astoundingly vigorous Cockney Rejects in a tiny, grungy pub upstairs in Manchester; warmly welcomed by the Upstarts and their extended family in South Shields; allowed a glimpse into the strange world of Sham in Nottingham; given access to a world hitherto underreported.

Why? I am attempting a paradigm shift. 'I appreciate not all Oi! was racist but . . .' began one rejection letter to this book's proposal. I have already tested the waters and they are decidedly icy. Writing a three-page feature about the 'new wave of Oi!' for the *Guardian's Saturday* magazine published in late November 2022, the commission was clear enough: a little of the history of the genre, including what was politely referred to as 'the more problematic element', and a focus on what this current wave was doing differently while upholding Oi!'s heritage.

As the editing process came down to the nitty gritty, they wanted me to make UNAMBIGUOUSLY CLEAR that Crown Court and the other new breed of world Oi! bands had no far-right sympathies. There was also concern about *that* gig: the one that effectively finished Oi! first time round, tabloid front page, *NME* front-cover story, 'The Gig That Sparked A Race Riot'. Southall. 1981. 'Maybe we are underplaying it.' I'm not trying to knock the *Guardian*, particularly not the *Saturday* magazine culture editor, who encouraged me to expand on the initial successes of prominent Oi! bands (*Top of the Pops* appearances, John Peel sessions and Top 40 hits) and was fair-handed and open-minded. I just want to illustrate the mood in the mainstream circa 2022 towards Oi!, and show the hurdles and hostilities those in the scene continue to face.

'The media are fixated with one gig out of thousands,' Garry Bushell told me, exasperated. 'It's like mentioning Altamont in every Stones interview or Biggie and Tupac whenever hip-hop comes up. The real nature of Oi! is understood the whole world over. Only here is it wilfully misunderstood.'

'It is frustrating because they haven't got a clue,' said Bill Bennett, co-owner of Oi Oi The Shop. 'All they're thinking [of] is back in the eighties, they don't think about what is happening today. This is the whole problem – getting through to people.'

Nineteen eighty one? That's a long time for a news story to stick around. And for a new band to be forced to declare they are not neo-Nazis as an opener? That's quite something! But, as they say, if you want change to happen, start with yourself, a cliché worth repeating. 'We can't change the world unless we change ourselves,' said Biggie. So, if I'm being completely honest, this book is probably as much about me, the change in my own preconceptions about Oi! and the people who make it, as it is about the history of Oi!.

Some of the text and speech on the following pages comes from documents and interviews which use words and express views which are racist, sexist, homophobic or otherwise offensive. Neither myself nor the publisher endorse or support such terms or views. However, we recognise that these texts and interviews contain important historical information and context that scholars and the general public may wish to consult. As such, we present them in their original form without editing, redacting or deleting anything.

Chapter 1

The New Breed: Crown Court

'Now you know what we have had to put up with for forty years,' said Trevor Taylor, singer with Crown Court, when I explained to him how it stuck in my craw that the *Guardian* had needed to make it plain that he was not a neo-Nazi at the start of the article.

Nonetheless he wasn't pussyfooting around. He didn't have the time or inclination. The lockdown had robbed him of momentum and key years. He was 30, determined, at the peak of his powers. 'Did you think this is a nice genre? It's not,' he said.

I was talking to him after a show, discussing how some of the original early eighties Oi! bands may have ended abruptly when members were sent to prison. 'You grow up in the surroundings you grow up in, and these things are part of the picture whether you want it to be or not,' he shrugged. 'I'm not trying to justify armed robbery, but these things are part of the package growing up in this shit.'

It was Crown Court's debut album *Capital Offence*, released in 2016, that gave fresh life to the British Oi! scene, which, since the turn of the century, had been slowly regathering its sense of self-worth but lacking in any sort of genuine modern thrust. Taylor is a powerful London voice; the band's aggressive but playful music set flight to his raw lyrics that describe a particular slice of life, often unheard. Crown Court were also one of the only new UK bands to proudly declare they were Oi!. Even some of the older, reformed Oi! originals, are now calling themselves 'streetpunk'.

I saw Crown Court for the first time at the all-day Cream of the Crop Oi! fest at Bedford Esquires in early July 2022. It was £30 for a ticket but, as the date crept closer, I grew nervous about going, not knowing what to expect, full of my own preconceptions. It would be my first proper immersion. Bedford? Half an hour from Luton. Tommy Robinson's hometown. Someone had already mentioned to me there were a few bands on the bill who might not be welcome at more mainstream venues. Also, that the event might attract some right-wing skinheads wearing T-shirts of bands who I might not approve of.

Deptford John of Combat 84 had a word with the festival's promoter to vouch for me. I don't know how I would have been perceived when I turned up at the gates if he hadn't. The place was packed with hundreds and hundreds of skinheads, and many looked quite battle-hardened too – big lumps, a sea of boots, braces, jeans, flight jackets and tattoos. Everyone noted the food stand in the courtyard was uber-posh modern fusion cuisine and that Jo, the promoter, was a good sort. I noted the lad doing the sound in the main room, which held about 250, was Asian.

Crown Court came on at 4.30 p.m and, I don't know, maybe there was about a hundred of us in there. It was quite sparse, empty in the middle of the floor. 'Who wants to see me do something stupid,' Taylor said from the stage, towards the end of their short set. He lit a flare and waved it about during 'Sammy Skyves' a song all about a 'black lad' who was 'king of the skins' and his derring-do as a legendary seventies Spurs football hooligan. The flare shouldn't really have been allowed, looked dangerous for the band and crowd; carrying a flare into a football stadium was a criminal offence. It was very eye-catching, impressive.

I shouted for more when they'd finished, surprising myself because for the rest of the day was even dubious about getting my notebook out to check the list of bands I wanted to see, desperate not to draw any attention. The night before Taylor had sent me a long Word document answering questions I'd sent him. I was impressed at how articulate and thoughtful he'd been. In fact, I was the one who ended up looking a bit of an idiot. For instance, one of the best songs on *Capital Offence* is called 'Thames Sake' and I'd asked about the evocative line in it, 'red cross in grey sky', thinking this might be some kind of dog-whistle lyric. Turned out the red cross was on the Hammersmith church on the A4 and the song was 'an ode to an ever-changing London, a love song about the place.'

He wrote: 'This isn't the eighties. We don't tolerate dumb shit. Me and my mates are from north London and from very different ethnic backgrounds. We're not gonna wave no one's flag except our own. Point.'

As I was finishing writing this book, Crown Court released their second album, *Heavy Manners*. It begins with a minute of classical music before kicking into the best of the best of modern Oi! music: fast, intense, troubling. Reviews were all positive. There was one respite from the racket – a spoken-word poem protesting against the regeneration and 'gentrification' of Woodberry Down estate in Hackney by 'scum' developers.

'My grandad lived on Woodberry Down estate, and my old man just down the road from that, in Clapton, just next to Tottenham – they were all Hackney and before that they were Bethnal Green,' Taylor had told me. His mum, he added, was Greek and there were a mix of religions on his father's side.

Among other places, such as Southgate and Barnet, Taylor grew up on Green Lanes, an area of north London where he still lives. 'Real place full of Caribbean, Turkish, Greeks and cockney,' he said. 'Like a lot of places, now, yuppies are moving in and pricing us out. Most Tottenham and Hackney people are going to Enfield, Herts and Essex which is nice for the community but it isn't the same. I am overly stubborn and will absolutely not leave. They can take my council flat over my dead body.'

I'd missed out on talking to Taylor at Cream of the Crop. He got off back to London as soon as the Court's set finished. I did speak briefly to the band's bassist, a striking-looking young skinhead called Ralph Orton. He has a tiny tattoo of a cross on his forehead just above the hairline and a denim jacket decorated with patches and badges. I later learned he was an accomplished semi-pro boxer. I might not have been so bold to approach him if I'd known that. He surprised me by saying Babyshambles had been his favourite band as a kid. He also said he had another band going called Concrete Bollocks. I learned that Taylor was also dabbling in a side project, the cloak-and-dagger but highly rated Roughed Up.

I also spoke to Danny Swan, Crown Court's guitarist. It turned out he also had another band going called Half Charge. Danny was from Glasgow, Paisley, and happy to chat. We sat down for a while and I found out from him that Crown Court now was a completely new line-up, bar Taylor, from the one who had recorded *Capital Offence.* The band's original guitarist 'Chubby' or Charlie (Manning-Walker) had left a few years back to form Chubby & The Gang (he sings in the band) and The Chisel. Chubby & the Gang had signed to Partisan Records, the same label as Idles and Fontaines D.C, supported White Stripes, The Chats and Amyl and the Sniffers, and were making in-roads in that world.

Crown Court's new drummer is Jack Lewis, the band's only non-skin. Taylor told me he trusted Jack implicitly. Trust and loyalty seemed important in the line-up. Taylor had known Orton since they were teenagers and he'd known Jack, a one-time doorman on skinheads clubs, for well over a decade.

A month later I was stood watching Crown Court again. Another short, explosive thirty-minute set, this time at Rebellion Festival, the annual punk and Oi! gathering that everyone should visit at least once. They played on Friday, the second day of the four-day festival, at 2.45 p.m., on the third biggest stage, the Pavilion. Here, the band attracted a crowd of around three or four hundred, maybe more, a mix of skins, punks, herberts and sherbets like me. They soon had a small bunch of skins down the front doing the dangerous-looking dancing familiar to Oi! gigs worldwide, all arms and legs flailing, charged on adrenaline.

It was the band's first gig with a second guitarist, Ronny Hamersma, a Dutchman who, you guessed it, was also in another Oi! band, The Reapers (he played drums for them). I inched forward to get as close to the action down the front as I dared, carried away when they started up with 'Sect Fifty Nine'. I was in love with this 2021 single – blistering, shocking and very sassy. Lovely sleeve, too. It had put to bed for me any suggestion that the real talent in Crown Court had gone with Chubby.

''Sect Fifty Nine' is the end of an old thing and the beginning of a new one symbolically,' Taylor had written in our first exchange. 'The song itself [Section 59 is part of a law that allows police to stop a vehicle on grounds of suspicion] is about me liberating motors and going for joyrides knowing that the cameras would be picking up the reg plate.'

After the Blackpool gig I said hello again to the upbeat Danny, and to Ralph who was with Jenn, his black punk girlfriend. And I finally met Taylor for a chinwag. He had an hour or two before he was due to head back to the smoke, so we found a pub on the strip, close to the huge Winter Gardens complex that hosts Rebellion, and I bought him a pint. He was an intimidating, burly presence but still boyish about the face; like Ralph, who I now know is the same age, he could have been early/mid-20s. I noticed he was wearing a gold ring shaped into the initials THFC and had a large Spurs crest tattoo on his bicep.

A stream of punters approached to congratulate him on the band's gig. He was courteous, a ready smile. Later I read many posts on social media saying Crown Court were the best band of Rebellion, and I wouldn't disagree. There had been no flare lit (at this more regulated gig), although Trev told me the band was looking into making more 'tifo' statements, a reference to how football supporters make a visual display of choreographed flags, signs or banners. Later in the year, when the band played the outdoor Revolution Calling Festival in Eindhoven, Holland, Taylor again set off a flare, and amid the smoke and mist a couple of the band's entourage walked onto the stage waving huge Crown Court flags on 10-ft poles. It was a sight.

I learned a little more about Taylor that day in Blackpool, not just that he was a face. Both his parents had been social workers, which, given his lyrics, made sense. However, I was surprised to hear he was born in America – Boston, Massachusetts – after his parents emigrated there from north London. He said he spent much of his childhood 'ping-ponging' between Massachusetts and north London, listening to rock'n'roll. 'Bowie, Lizzy, Pistols, Kinks, seventies trash from my old man,' he said. He mentioned a series of compilations called *Boot Power*, downloads rather than actual releases, of glam/punk stompers from 1970–79, proto-Oi! 'Fucking crack to the teenage me,' he said.

He'd formed his first Oi! band in America aged 15 called Stomping Ground, in thrall to The Templars from New York, an Oi! band who he rated highly. 'To this day, the USA's greatest Oi! band,' he said. 'It was their sound that was so important – talk about putting the rock'n'roll and the grit and grime back into it . . . they are a huge influence on us.' Taylor said he moved permanently back to north London in his late teens and spent his time 'milling about, being a little shit'. Briefly he brought the lads from Stomping Ground over to London for a few gigs. He was 19. It was 2013. He put together a new band. 'When we started Crown Court, the Oi! scene in London was moribund,' he said. 'We came in at a really mundane part of Oi!, and we tried to put that rock'n'roll bollocks back on it.'

'I don't want to speak ill of anyone on the scene in London at that time because they were nothing but bloody supportive of our band,' he was quick to clarify. 'But it was too polished for what we wanted. We really wanted to focus in on why we loved skinhead music: we liked the eighties lot, the Rejects, Business and Last Resort, we liked '77 punk, we liked the dirty, the grimy, the ugly; we wanted to spit that back. Nobody was doing that, so we wanted to try.'

After a series of explosive early gigs at the Fiddler's Elbow in Camden, a venue he referred to as the band's CBGB, Taylor put the band on hold and joined the British Army. His experiences in Belfast added extra grist to new Crown Court songs such as 'The Province', another standout on *Capital Offence*. 'I missed a shotgun blast,' he told me. 'Through a window of my girlfriend's at the time. That was just the start.'

After four and a half years in the army he was posted back to England. 'It was a good move because at the time I really wanted to chase Crown Court among other things,' he said. A single, 'No Paradise' (lead track from a 2015 EP called *The English Disease*) raised awareness of the band and was effectively a state-of-the-nation address. 'An anthem for growing up on the estate and going to school in a nice area and seeing how that shit follows you around and how certain doors remain closed no matter,' he said. It was a theme he returned to on the 2022 Roughed Up demo EP, on the exquisite 'King and Council', a song simmering with hints of early Oasis and barely controlled aggression: 'When you left school, you left your class – mine followed me around and caught up with me fast.'

The Covid pandemic arrived at the wrong time for the band. Chubby quit and took the bassist. The drummer started a family. Taylor was suddenly without a band, with no chance of putting a new one together. 'When the first album dropped, we started getting attention,' he said. 'I left the army to pursue a real chance with the band but it seems that some people had other plans. I had to rebuild, and here we are. I now have the most loyal, most talented gentlemen around me I could have asked for. For that I am truly gifted.' He said he didn't really want to comment on his former bandmates or their new bands, but he didn't really consider them as playing Oi! any more. 'They came from the hardcore scene and were desperate to have an attachment to the London Oi! scene, and at the time I happily facilitated that,' he said.

Taylor, who is responsible for all the artwork associated with the band as well as managing their affairs, was a walking oracle of Oi!; steeped in it, knew most of the old faces and all the best bands around the world. He offered to introduce me to some of the key new faces such as Lion's Law and The Templars. I mentioned other young, new-wave UK Oi! bands: Grade 2 from the Isle of Wight; and Rise Up from Stoke-on-Trent, and he knew them too. 'I've known Grade 2 since the conception of their band,' he said. 'They do more of a softer approach but I think their heart is in the right place.' He called Rise Up, who had also played at Cream of the Crop, 'the teenage youth'. He added that he hoped they 'make the right moves because if they do, they will be something special'.

The right moves? I presumed he was talking about successfully navigating themselves in the thorny and often inward-looking world of the ageing UK Oi! scene while maintaining a modern sensibility and outlook, something Crown Court had achieved.

'You've got it,' he said.

Quite tricky, I imagine?

Taylor touched his head. 'You've got to use your canister. Focus on the good parts of the scene 'cos there's some shit, man, there's some shit,' he said.

Earlier, Taylor had intimated Oi! could be a clandestine world, was certainly tightknit, steadfast and suspicious of outsiders. He mentioned he had already heard from a few of the older Oi! faces, how they wondered what my intentions were, was I out to skewer them – an approach they had grown accustomed to over the years from the mainstream media. I found out when we met up again in London that Taylor had recently been guest vocalist for one of the most respected eighties UK Oi! bands, The Business, at a remembrance show at the 100 Club (the band's singer Micky Fitz died in 2016). Trev admitted he was cautious too – asking initially to see what I would write about the band.

I told him I felt some of the Oi! elders were particularly avoiding discussing the uglier side of Oi!. I said I hadn't meant to, but I'd already ruffled Garry Bushell's feathers in a lengthy email exchange. 'Please be careful,' Trev said. 'Come across with respect and I'm sure you'll get respect back. People get touchy about things and that's not your fault, but I think some people, especially in the eighties, the older faces, have been burned dirty.'

In Blackpool, we talked a little about being a skinhead. Ralph had mentioned to me how quite recently he'd been verbally assaulted by a random passer-by in the street who assumed he was some sort of neo-Nazi. Taylor was more understated in his appearance than Ralph, but still clearly a skinhead, cherry-red Dr. Martens on his feet. 'You're demonised just like that,' he said, clicking his fingers. 'Quickly assumptions are made, you'll be played down as a dumb cunt who hates so and so, demonised in the media for being young, working class and a skinhead, but Crown Court are unapologetically exactly that.'

Then he said the line the *Guardian* picked up on, about Crown Court, used as the headline for the piece: 'In a very politically charged moment in history we are probably everything that scares a curtain-twitching middle-class family.'

This was what had struck me most clearly when I first heard and saw Crown Court. They were a talismanic band. The hunt for a genuinely incendiary working-class guitar band is an evergreen topic, from Noel Gallagher's 'rock's gone middle-class' tirades, through Sleaford Mods spat with Idles about class appropriation, to the *Telegraph*'s 'The return of the great working-class rock band' feature that focused on Australian punkers The Chats and Amyl and the Sniffers.

I couldn't draw Taylor into making any bold claims for Crown Court, but he was aware the climate was perhaps shifting in their direction. 'I love The Chats and Amyl,' he said. 'I like that they are pushing the pendulum towards us but they ain't yob music. They ain't followed by Kev from the pub who wants a lager and a laugh after a week of painting and decorating. I think to be truly a working-class rock'n'roll band or movement there's got to be that link.' As an example, he pointed to the recent Liam Gallagher Knebworth gig he attended. 'The majority of the crowd were young football lads absolutely going off their heads,' he said.

Taylor is relatable in a way Oi! maybe hasn't been for a generation: an Oasis fan and a longstanding face among the modern-day Tottenham hardcore following. 'It's a family there for me and I'd trade it in for absolutely nothing,' he says about Spurs. 'It's my life.' And like some of the Oi! originals, Crown Court have a smattering of songs detailing a bristling sense of violence at matches among rival fans. The fury Taylor summons in these songs serves as something of a liberating howl.

On *Heavy Manners*, there is a song called 'Striped Up, Sent Down' ('Are you from north London? Are you here for fun then? The chairs ain't for sitting. Glass rain drops, it's pouring'). Striped up, Taylor said, meant being cut by a Stanley knife; the song being about a football hooligan incident.

I told him that lyrics which appear to almost celebrate fighting at football could, to an outsider, appear OTT?

'It's mad, I know,' he said.

It's a key element of the culture of Oi!, though, right?

'Of, course,' he said. 'That's it. The Rejects. Last Resort. The Business as well.' He turned back to what we'd talked about initially. 'Do you really think that when you grow up in the kind of shit we did that violence and fighting is not part of it? One of the most important men in history, Joe Strummer, said "sing about what you know". You listen to a Crown Court lyric or boil it down and pick apart words, that's all something that's happened in my life, every single one of those, from start to finish there's not a single one I didn't write without a nod or a wink or a complete explanation as to what I was doing at that time.'

It was cheeky but I wanted to know what kind of commercial life a modern Oi! band might have. Taylor had already told me about his work as a private contractor, a bodyguard, then, he said, doing close protection for a family in London. I had also totted up the copies *Capital Offence* and the band's singles had sold to date, chiefly on limited edition vinyl runs, and been impressed. Close to 10,000 sold for a band with no real mainstream exposure, certainly no BBC radio play, without an agent, plugger or PR.

'I don't wanna talk about money,' Taylor said. 'Nobody's making it rich off Oi! music and those who try to can fuck off – you're not cut from the same cloth as me. I will say I try to shoestring our finances together, and I've succeeded to an extent. We're Oi! music at the end of the day, not the Stones.'

Heavy Manners, he said, was being released by German Oi! specialist record label, Randale, one of the biggest labels on the scene, but no Universal. They had, however, afforded the band a small budget to make a video for 'Striped Up, Sent Down', with Roger Sargent, who has worked with bands such as The Libertines, Fat White Family and Sleaford Mods, directing. Taylor told me James Sherry at Division PR who handles The Chats among others loved *Heavy Manners* and had agreed to do PR for the album. There was a short American tour in the summer of 2023 and much demand for the band across Europe.

'My dream is to get on the BBC or something,' he said. 'These punk surges come in waves and I'd love to be part of the next boot up the arse. But we won't change, we won't beg for it. I'll never grow my hair or hang up these boots.'

In the *Guardian*, I'd written that Crown Court were the band most likely to break out of the underground scene, the ones to prove Oi! is nothing to be scared of. Although, I added, maybe it's best not to get too comfortable. 'Everyone wants a rebel but no one wants a rebellion,' Taylor had said. 'England doesn't like to empower the working classes. We are a smear on their society. If nice, prawn-sandwich families saw me singing about getting kicked to fuck on a night bus they'd hide their children.

'Think about everything at the moment,' he'd added. 'All the politics is about acceptance and everyone accepting everyone for who they are, and that's right. Good. I agree. But what about the Oi! scene too? What about putting the guitars, inspiration and focus on the working-class yobbos like when Oasis were doing their thing. Even if you hate that band, think about how many youngsters picked up a £20 guitar to try and be rock stars. Without that we are nothing.'

In Blackpool, although thrilled by the band, I was still as suspicious of Taylor as he was of me. I'd hesitantly asked him about the infamous Football Lads Alliance, which had been started by a Spurs fan and had attracted footy lads from across the country. The FLA had hit the headlines with a march in London in 2018 that resulted in violent clashes with police and anti-fascists. They had subsequently been linked to the far right and criticised for having an anti-Muslim agenda. I felt some involvement would not reflect well on Crown Court. The FLA had more recently been linked to violent scenes at the 2020 Black Lives Matter demonstrations in London from which had emerged a notorious photo of a 'footy lad' urinating at the foot of the memorial to PC Keith Palmer, murdered in the 2017 Westminster Bridge terror attack.

'FLA?' Taylor said without flinching. 'That was started with good intentions. I never attended [the 2018 march]. That was started after the two kick-offs [the Westminster Bridge attack and the bombing of Manchester Arena]. I was in the military at the time and I was very close to the shit that happened. I never attended the march because . . .'

He stopped himself. 'Listen,' he said. 'I do not have any political leaning in that way, in any shape or form. I'm not interested in dabbling in that shit and I won't have myself painted with that brush. I will say that the parties involved, and I can only speak for the gentlemen I know, were attending [the 2018 march] with the best intentions because they were wounded and hurt by what was going on at the time. I think that, again, what we talked about earlier, being from a certain background, being from a certain fabric of society, when you go to vocalise things, they don't always come out the way you want . . . and I think it [the movement] was tainted in a big way.'

He drew an analogy with some of the Oi! bands from the eighties. 'I know some really good geezers from that era,' he said.

'We're talking about growing up in the shit in the eighties, or you can backtrack it further to the seventies: You grow up working class with values that aren't maybe as modern, polished, as everybody else and when you try and vocalise them . . .' He trailed off. 'I think that's what happened in the eighties,' he continued. 'People weren't as savvy as they are today. Things have changed, we're very accepting of everybody in this day and age, but not the eighties – that was a different time, different society. It's really only more modern times that people started opening their eyes and society started changing a bit.'

He looked at me. Time up, ready to go. 'Listen, just as in any walk of life, you've got your cunts and you've got your good people – stay away from the cunts. That's the truth. If people are good people be good to them and that's the best way. If you choose to see things in tunnel vision then you're probably one of the cunts. Does that make sense?'

Chapter 2

If the Kids Are United: Sham

Sham 69 is where the Oi! story begins. The band's first release, 'Song of the Streets', a ltd edition 1977 one-sided 7-inch promo, was recorded live and had the foghorn call and response refrain: 'What have we got? Fuck all.' Again and again. 'What have we got? Fuck all.' It was almost a duet between band and crowd.

The Pistols and The Clash had never been as succinct or as brutal. The song was just short of two minutes. It remains one of the defining Oi! anthems. A memorable moment for me was seeing the band play it live in Nottingham in May 2022. It's still their set opener, and forty-five years later just as exhilarating, uplifting to be a part of.

It's difficult not to love Sham's later big singles, they were maybe the most successful band of the punk era with a remarkable five Top 20 hits in just over twelve months during 1978–79, sing-along stuff like 'Hurry Up Harry', 'If the Kids Are United' and their biggest hit 'Hersham Boys'. But it was when they first emerged that they were at their most inspirational, most potent – a new voice.

October 1977: their debut single proper, 'I Don't Wanna'. One minute forty-five seconds. Produced by The Velvet Underground's John Cale. In the song, singer Jimmy Pursey says fuck everything: factory job, dole, pension, drugs. The vocals and music are unapologetically roughshod and bludgeoning – barbaric. Jon Savage, in his Pistols book, described Jimmy as 'ur-Punk', which in the dictionary means 'primitive: denoting someone or something regarded as embodying the basic of intrinsic qualities of a particular class or type.'

They had other early songs that were just as raw and direct as 'I Don't Wanna' and 'Song of the Streets': 'Rip Off', 'Ulster', 'Borstal Breakout' and 'George Davis Is Innocent'. They dressed uncouth: cheap big black boots and worn ankle boot plimsoles, crappy shirts, market jeans and jackets, and they had real square haircuts. All in all they made the first-wave punk bands sound and look like Roxy Music – a bit put-on. And adding to the assault on the senses was, of course, the 'Sham Army', this hardcore fanbase, skinheads mainly. Oi! started somewhere between Jimmy's straining larynx and this mob down the front – there was the alchemy. There's a picture of a clump of the army, taken at Sham's infamous 1978 appearance at Reading Festival, in Nick Knight's 1982 book, *Skinheads*. Not a pretty sight: one young skinhead pulling back his Harrington jacket to reveal a Young National Front T-shirt.

You can hear the 'army' on the band's debut album, released in February 1978. The first half of the album was live. 'Jimmy is our leader' one screams out early on. They entertain themselves between songs, singing 'Knees Up Mother Brown', chanting, 'If you're proud to be a cockney clap your hands.' Often, they were affiliated with West Ham ('Knees Up Mother Brown' was also sung at Upton Park). Some of the more fevered among them came from backgrounds where the NF was ingrained in their lives, with maybe a dad working or standing for the party, their east London estates a hotbed of NF activity. Others were from the more sinister British Movement.

One of the Sham Army was Johnny Butler, interviewed by Garry Bushell for a 1978 feature in *Sounds*, 'A Day in the Life of a Skinhead'. He was a 'tall, tattooed West Ham supporter' in steel-toe cap brogues, a road digger, pals with some of Sham's earliest skinhead followers. 'When skinheads first started out, it was all "hate the wogs, kill the Pakis",' he was quoted as saying. 'I don't like 'em but I wouldn't go out of my way to have a go at them.' He added: 'I'm not interested in politics. All my mates said vote NF so I did but it ain't nothing to me. NF might say now we're going to do this and that but if they got into power it'd be terrible. My old man's Labour but to me whether Labour get in or the Tories they'll do something for you for the first few months but after that they shit on you. If the Conservatives got in it'd be terrible.'

I wanted to talk to Jimmy about his army. That's why I was in Nottingham at the Rescue Rooms on a Saturday night. The gig was sold out. Capacity 450. It's where and when I began to realise it might not be all that simple to get a straight answer out of Jimmy. He doesn't do soundchecks, or indeed travel with the band, two of whom, guitarist Dave Parsons and bassist Dave Tregunna, are original members from the band's pomp. They both went back to their hotel after soundcheck, so it was just Paul Sham, who'd been looking after Jimmy since the nineties and now tour-manages the band, and me on a backstage balcony overlooking a cobbled court, an hour or so until showtime.

There were quite a few meaty-looking old skinheads – green flight jackets, tattoos, cherry-red Dr. Martens – in the courtyard, pints of lager in hand. I wondered if maybe some of them had been part of the army. I'd read how, even in 1988, when Sham attempted a comeback of sorts, there'd been a big gang of skinheads who'd disrupted a gig in Manchester. Paul saw me looking at them. 'They're too old now to be causing trouble,' he said. 'They just want a night out.'

Paul wasn't his real name he said. I'd already surmised Sham wasn't his given surname. He said he'd changed his name after a stretch inside which had something to do with his long career working in the family business, which was Soho porn shops. I'm fairly certain when he wasn't looking after Jimmy's career he was behind a business called 'We Buy Any Porn'; there's a lucrative market in vintage porn. There was a song about him on one of the four albums Sham had recorded in the nineties, all actually pretty good, called 'Spunky Candy'.

I asked Paul if he could get me an invite down to Hersham, Jimmy's home village in Surrey, which in my imagination was a sort of Oi! Jerusalem. He said Jimmy didn't live there any more. He was in Addlestone, a few miles away, and lived on a farm with the ex-manager of Blancmange. Paul had a place close by. Jimmy, he said, had eight greyhounds.

The 'dogs' were a life-long passion. I'd picked up a story about how when he left school at 15, in 1970, Jimmy had run away from home to work on Wimbledon greyhound track before he worked the barrows on some east-end market. Later, when Sham were first being photographed by the music press, he'd posed 'down the dogs', the bona fide working-class lad pose that was his main calling card. He was vocal back then about how he wanted Sham to speak to and for dead-end, no future, council estate kids. 'The kids that this [punk] was supposed to get over to,' he said, but had been ignored in a blizzard of expensive bondage trousers and talk of situationism. Jimmy would be their voice.

There was some debate straight off about how genuine Jimmy was. He might just have fetched up working in a Hersham curtain shop or washing dishes in the local Wimpy. Hersham was about half an hour from London on the train, leafy, relatively gentile. I read his dad was ex-army, a plumber or a brickie. Mum a cinema usherette. Paul Sham said Jimmy had started to write a book about his life but it had all somehow gone wrong, as had much in Jimmy's later years. Anyway, he said he didn't think Jimmy was quite ready to talk about his life yet. Not honestly anyway.

I nodded. It was sort of unspoken but plain that there was an issue regarding the scene he'd been involved with as a teenager, when he was a leading face at the Walton Hop club, in Walton-on-Thames, a town near Hersham. There was a music biz paedophile circle in operation at the club and they'd prey on kids who wanted to be stars, the sort who'd volunteer for the competitions to see who was the best at miming to records. Jimmy was said to often be a winning mimic. The judges were people such as Bay City Rollers manager Tam Paton, producer Jonathan King, Radio 1's Chris Denning, *NME*'s Rob Randall. All convicted of child abuse. The guy who ran the show was Deniz Corday. He died while on bail not too long back aged 87. He'd been arrested over historic child sex abuse allegations.

Jimmy had thanked Corday on the back of the first two Sham albums and his first band, Jimmy & The Ferrets, was briefly managed by Jonathan King. I don't want to labour the point but ferrets are best known for going down trousers in a practice known as 'ferret-legging'.

I could only hypothesise what impact this might have had on Jimmy. He'd lost his way after Sham split in 1980 and a solo career failed to ignite. I got the impression he'd been a drug addict – the rumour was he'd sold the rights to all his big hits for peanuts and had been forced to live destitute in a caravan. If this was true it may have been particularly galling when McDonald's used 'If the Kids Are United' in a 2000 TV ad. I'd read about bizarre incidents in the noughties, a hissy-fit at an exhibition of his art, a punch-up with John Lydon at the United States Embassy in London, and, worst of all, what happened in 2002 when he was 47: the incident that put him on the Sex Offenders Register. The press reported he received a caution for indecent assault after admitting forcibly kissing a 16-year-old girl working in a newsagent, an incident which left her so traumatised she left her job. Sham had surprisingly briefly rallied: in 2006 Tony Blair used 'If the Kids Are United' as walk-on music for his Labour Party Conference speech, and Graham Coxon played guitar on their band's 2006 World Cup song, 'Hurry Up England', a Top 10 single. More recently figures as diverse as Chris Packham and Tim Burgess came out as fans. 'He's a real unsung hero of punk,' Burgess had tweeted.

Paul got a call. Jimmy was nearby. Paul huddled with the other member of the road crew to discuss about how best to get Jim inside the venue, to the dressing room. He couldn't go in the front entrance – too many fans. He'd have to come up back, up the stairs, on to this balcony and in through this back door. I felt it rather weird, unnecessary. This wasn't Shea Stadium.

Paul shrugged. While we'd been waiting, I'd asked him how Jimmy kept so thin – like, rake thin. He'd said Jimmy didn't eat. In the weeks that followed this gig, having seen him perform and considering this pre-gig palaver, I wondered if something else was playing a role.

Anyhow, this tall, elegant figure came trotting onto the courtyard, hood up, disguising his face, sort of jogging, a couple of others following, slalomed through the skinheads and up the stairs. He stopped on the balcony, looked right at me and paused a moment. 'Aright,' he said. That was as close as I'd get.

The gig was truly amazing. Jimmy came on, dressed in what looked like some sort of music-hall chimney sweep get-up, braces hanging loose, doing a frenetic crab dance, a bit like David Brent in *The Office*, and the band went bang. 'What have we got?' All 450 of us, the place was packed with essentially late middle-aged men, screaming back, fists in the air, 'Fuck all'. I was a bit nervy – there were old skins galore in there – but not as nervy as when I went to Cream of the Crop. There was no real let-up in the set that lasted about forty-five minutes, which I felt was perfect. All the classics smashed out of the park. No trouble, just a blast.

I didn't leave empty-handed, either. I'd spoken with Dave Parsons briefly on the balcony before the gig after Paul sent him over and we spoke again over the phone in late May. We talked for an hour or more. Dave was four years younger than Jimmy. He said when they first met, in 1975, they discovered they had both spent a large part of their childhood at the same farm in Hersham but at different times and never met. This farm – it was quite a weird story – belonged to a farmer who'd had a tractor accident which had somehow mangled his gymnastics so he couldn't have kids. So, this farmer adopted three sets of kids. 'Two really young kids, two middle kids and two older kids,' Dave said. 'Jimmy was playing with one of the older kids and I was playing with one of the middle kids.' Later Dave wrote a song, 'Simon', about one of these older kids. It was a song from the band's last album in their pomp, 1980's *The Game*, and had stuck in my head for obvious reasons. 'Simon was one of the older two kids at the farm who Jimmy used to play with, him and his brother Miles,' said Dave. 'They were both a little bit backward. [The song was about when] Miles went out into a field and blew his brains out with his dad's [the farmer's] shotgun.'

Dave said he had a school band who played a local gig with Jimmy's band circa '75/6, now calling themselves Sham 69, and he hit it off with Jimmy and Albert 'Albie' Maskell, Sham's original bass player. 'Jimmy was one of those characters that had a reputation around Hersham and Walton,' he said. 'Basically, everybody knew who Jimmy Pursey was.' Jimmy took over as a sort of manager of Dave's band, changed their name and put a mod image on them. Dave said Albie and Jimmy had a lot of attitude but not much talent. 'They had a couple of their own numbers but nobody in the band could really write,' he said. 'Albert used to sing '[A] Teenager in Love' and they'd do Shadows numbers.' It wasn't long after this that Jimmy, Albie and Dave decided to form a new version of Sham 69, one that Jimmy said was inspired by the Ramones.

I'd read they rehearsed on a pig farm, which I thought was cool. 'Albie had a pig barn and we did use to rehearse in there sometimes, not all the time,' Dave laughed. He recalled this being late '76 and the band being under the influence of pub-rock bands, chiefly Eddie & the Hot Rods and Dr. Feelgood, and the game-changer being when the Pistols appeared playing live on TV on *So It Goes* in September of that year.

By mid-'77 the band were regulars at the Roxy punk club in Covent Garden. 'Jimmy had quite a few lyrics and I had odd riffs and we just stuck stuff together and went out,' said Dave. 'I was still very much learning the guitar.'

Julie Burchill was an early fan. Her then-boyfriend Tony Parsons reviewed Sham at the Roxy, bottom of the bill, for the *NME* in August '77. He described Jimmy as a 'lanky, crop-haired big mouth yob howling in the face of King's Road chic' and wrote that Sham 69 were all ex-skinheads and 'a band who do everything except lie'.

It was a review that seemed to stick. 'People kept saying Sham were a skinhead band,' Dave said. 'We kept trying to say we're not a skinhead band, we're a punk band. Even when Oi! started, always the influence would go back to Sham – that we were one of the main influences for Oi!. I'm constantly saying to people now, Sham are not an Oi! band.'

Jimmy was 22, old enough to recall skinheads first time round in the early seventies and to have been one himself. He wasn't one now. He didn't drink, didn't follow football, didn't dress like one. But nonetheless, by late 1977, the Sham Army had started to congeal and trouble was brewing.

The second-wave skinheads didn't have much to go at early on. There weren't that many but they stood out. Most were football hooligans from the east end, and before the NF began to court them the British Movement had been something of a haven. They were banned often from discos or pubs, but punk clubs were more laissez-faire. Sham were one of the first bands they latched on to. Dave's guitar was dirty, raw and caveman crude. The songs' choruses often sounded like terrace chants. The subject matter was relatable: George Davis was an east-end bank robber and cause célèbre. Plenty of the early Sham Army had been to borstal – they had fuck all. They were teenagers mainly, lost and searching for anything to give life some meaning.

I asked Dave if he felt Jimmy or Sham had encouraged them (when other bands were quicker to control the 'exuberances', Sham had several key second-wave skinhead faces on their informal roadcrew). The sleeve of 'I Don't Wanna' for instance was an image of the infamous August 1977 National Front march in Lewisham, the so-called 'Battle of Lewisham' – 200 arrests, a hundred injured, over half of them cops. 'I don't know whose choice it was [to use that photograph],' Dave said. 'I can't tell you how that came about.' Both B-sides, 'Ulster' and 'Red London', could also be misinterpreted, I said. Later they would both be picked up and played by NF/RAC/B&H bands. "Ulster' is not really taking any sides for anything,' Dave said. 'It's really an anti-war song, anti-division. It was our 'If the Kids Are United' before 'If the Kids Are United' was written. It's a cry for hope. However naive, that's what was in our hearts. I think Jimmy later said it should have been called 'Belfast', and looking back we should have done a bit more research on it.'

And 'Red London'? 'Yes, looking back, I think, Bloody hell,' Dave said. 'I wrote that myself, the whole song, lyrics, everything. It was naivety again; the whole idea of communism for me was something taking away your freedom. It was really about wanting to be free, wanting to do what I want, not wanting to be boxed in or told what to do. I certainly wasn't making any political allegiances or anything like that.'

I persisted. There was another song on the band's debut album, *Tell Us the Truth*, where I thought the lyrics might be a bit ambiguous: 'Rip Off'.

'All the foreign feet down Oxford Street,' Dave asked?

You've obviously been here before, I said.

'Yeah. Faces from places I've never been.'

Yes, I said. That's the couplet.

'First of all, the words are not mine,' Dave said. 'But I co-wrote the song with Jimmy. Maybe I was just dumb or stupid but it didn't actually occur to me that it might be a red rag to a bull or offensive. At that point I couldn't even imagine why anybody would be BM or NF, or even what the fuck was going on with racism or any of that kind of stuff. But we can't really complain looking back [at] how some people read things differently.'

And so it goes. The early Sham Army, all skinheads, only about fifteen of them, if that, mob up at the Roxy and start giving it to the punks. When the bouncers pile in, Dave wields his guitar at them and Jimmy gets the skinheads on stage. It's a victory: arms round Jimmy, chanting, fist-pumping, fired up. It's publicised and more lads become skinheads, wanna be in the gang. A pattern emerges: kick-offs at Sham gigs all over the place, increasingly violent: the Vortex, the Roundhouse, London School of Economics, Harlesden and Kingston. As the 'army' grows, so too does the noticeable rise in the Sieg Heil salutes at Sham gigs.

'It took a while for me to make the connection,' Dave said. 'To connect the coterie of people on the side of the stage with the people out in the audience, the BM and NF, who were causing all that trouble. It took a while before it clicked. In retrospect it should have clicked a lot quicker.'

The core group travel out of London with the band for gigs.

'Standard practice,' Dave said. 'This was when we unknowingly allowed the infiltration to begin. It was almost like a Mafia-type thing. They had a big foot in the door and they were there. How the hell do you get rid of these people? When they were around us initially, they were your mates, being all nice to you . . .' he trailed off.

'Jimmy told me this story,' he started up again. 'We were on tour, and he was doing this interview with a local radio station. There was two of these lads who came on the road with us with Jimmy and when the interviewer came in, he was of Indian or Pakistani origin. These two took offence and they started saying to Pursey, what are you doing talking to this, whatever derogatory term they used for this person, and one of them got up and punched the guy.'

There was another incident he said Dave Tregunna had parlayed to him about a rape occurring in the back of the van as they travelled between gigs.

I asked Dave about some of the road crew in those early days, named on the back of early Sham albums. Jimmy seems to have enjoyed hanging out with them, got a kick out of being with the tough guys, and he and Dave appropriated aspects of their image. Sham would even use the patriotic 'Land of Hope and Glory' as their intro music.

Dave suddenly got quite angry.

'I look at all those cunts now and think what the fuck were we doing? Why did we tolerate them for so long?'

We talked about a couple of names, who would gravitate towards the Rejects once Sham split. I also asked about Gary Hodges, future lead singer of the 4-Skins, who I didn't think was that big a face with the Sham Army. Dave contradicted me. 'Hodges was,' he said. 'Gary fucking Hodges.'

Vince? I ventured. Vince Riordan? He would later join the Rejects as bass player. 'Vince was around but he was never a problem,' Dave said. 'I always got on OK with Vince.'

Jimmy told *Sounds* in June '78, when the problem was clearly out of control: 'I thought I could get them thinking the same way I was thinking. When they started those Nazi salutes I thought I could bicker them down. They know exactly what I'm about. In the early days the NF sent someone to see whether I'd work for them. I said you must be fucking joking, no way. So, when the skins start all that, I say what are you doing? Why come here and do that? You know I don't believe, so why do it? I don't beat about the bush. I'm a figurehead and they know I'm having a go at them . . . I think I'm winning if I can get someone aged 16 just thinking about politics so they're not going down the road and voting for the NF. It's hard when you're on stage to put it across like that.'

'It was one of the things I was kind of proud of,' Dave told me. 'It was such a small thing but you would have people coming backstage who were hanging out with these hardcore arseholes and for a lot of these kids it was peer pressure. There were quite a lot of kids I talked to and got them to see the other side of the coin and see what they were doing, and for a handful of those kids a light went on.'

He got angry again: 'If you look at the Reading Festival footage you can see half of them that caused all the trouble on the side of the stage. I look back and think, what the fuck? What are these people doing standing on our bloody stage? This happened so many times.'

August '78. Reading Festival. Friday night. The festival's 'punk' night. A big moment for Sham. In less than a year they'd gone from playing to five people at the Roxy to 15,000. 'If the Kids Are United' was in the charts, their first Top 10. Unfortunately, the violent fringe that followed Sham were out in force.

'It was like a war,' Dave said. 'When you see pictures of Reading and Jimmy breaks down at the end and he's in tears, it's like, what's that all about? It was the accumulative effect of all that had happened and seeing some of that shit still going on . . . it was like what can you do, where can you go? We were up against a brick wall and there was nowhere to run . . . it was so sad.'

I've looked at footage of Sham at Reading, the moment Jimmy breaks down during 'If the Kids Are United' (which is also the title of the obscure forty-five-minute punk doc the footage comes from). There's an incident at the back end of the song. An oldish, long-haired festival roadie comes onto the stage and pushes one of the young skinheads gathered at the side off the lip. You immediately see three or four skinheads start forward to retaliate. Jimmy lunges for the festival roadie, who falls over a monitor. Jimmy pulls him up, clings to him tight and has him up to the mic to sing the song with him, averting what surely would have been some heavy violence up on stage in front of everyone. The song finishes moments later, Jimmy collapses.

'It was endemic,' said Dave. 'It came to the point where almost every gig we were playing we were having to, at best, just stop for ten minutes while Jimmy lectured the audience saying, what the fuck's going on, stop. If it was a good gig they would quieten down and we could get on with the gig but there were plenty of gigs where we couldn't finish. And this started to happen to everyone, wherever these gangs of skinheads went, there was trouble at gigs for bands like The Specials . . . it was all over the place. But because the main guys were side-stage with us, we were the main band accused or associated.

'Several times the band stopped playing live to try and lose those arseholes,' Dave said, sounding exasperated even now. 'You're responsible, you're playing gigs, and you're seeing people get harmed at your gigs and it's going on and on, it's not just a one-off event. You have to ask yourself, can I live with this? Can I take the responsibility for this? There's only so much you can do when you keep asking people to stop and they don't stop. My memory of it is, most of the people at the gigs were cool and it was this small little element of people who caused us a shitload of hell basically. Once you've got a few people rucking and the whole crowd is erupting, it's easy for someone to look in from the outside and give it the headline next day, "Right-wing chaos at Sham 69 gig", which happened in the tabloids several times. People were starting to think Sham were a right-wing fascist band and that couldn't have been further from the truth.'

'It was why we wrote, 'If the Kids Are United',' Dave added. 'And these people didn't like it. It's only amazing, looking back, that we weren't the ones that got the shit kicked out of us, we can't have been that far away from it for some of the actions we were taking.'

Chief among them was the band's attachment to Rock Against Racism, a major aggravation to the hardcore Sham Army. There have been several books and documentaries about Rock Against Racism over the years, such as Daniel Rachel's *Walls Come Tumbling Down* in 2016 and Rubika Shah's award-winning *White Riot* film in 2019. Jimmy and Sham always feature prominently. I'm going to reference the 2009 book by Andy Beckett *When The Lights Went Out: What Really Happened to Britain in the Seventies*.

Beckett interviewed Roger Huddle, founder of Rock Against Racism and a graphic designer for the Socialist Workers Party.

Huddle told Beckett he started RAR in 1976 because he was deeply worried about the surge of the far right in Britain. The NF were calling for the end of, in their words, 'coloured immigration', and the repatriation of all immigrants already in the UK, the withdrawal from the European community and the return of capital punishment. There were said to be in excess of 15,000 paid-up members, with strong support for the party in the Midlands and London. In local elections held in 1977, the party beat the Liberals into third place in over a third of the London constituencies, polling especially strongly in east London, an area where racial attacks were on the rise, often carried out by young NF-supporting skinheads. One first-hand report described 150 white youths running down Brick Lane, an area with many Bangladeshi residents and businesses, shouting 'kill the black bastards' and smashing shop windows and car windscreens.

In pop culture, Huddle told Beckett he had noted Bowie's 'flirtation with fascism' (in 1976 Bowie had been quoted as saying: 'I believe Britain could benefit from a fascist leader') but it was an Eric Clapton onstage anti-immigration rant in 1976, including lines such as 'Get the wogs out. Get the coons out. Keep Britain white', that had first sparked him into action.

Huddle gave Beckett an astonishing quote about RAR: 'The battle for Jimmy Pursey became critical.' It was delivered, said Beckett, 'quite deadpan'. Huddle sounded out Sham in late '77. He took a gang of docker mates to a gig and said he had to hold them back from attacking some of the skinheads there. When he finally met Jimmy, Huddle said he found him to be a 'weird lad' but 'a good lad' and Sham agreed to play for RAR.

As far as I can tell, Sham played their first RAR gig at Central London Polytechnic in March '78 alongside Misty in Roots, a reggae band from Southall. Jimmy told the crowd: 'We believe that black and white should live together. We are making this stand at this gig to say that.' He added: 'Any trouble and we'll never play London again.' The *NME* covered the gig, noting 'the Front' (the paper was always unaware of what the BM was) were there but caused few problems. 'What have we got? National Front!' was a chant that went up briefly.

The *NME* did not report that RAR had organised a posse of some of Huddle's docker mates, heavily tooled-up anti-fascists, to protect the stage and that they had used pickaxe handles to beat and eject a hardcore group of the Sham Army, the main troublemakers.

From here on, Sham's gigs were bloodbaths and Jimmy got death threats over his involvement with RAR. There was a riot in Leeds in August '78 when forty NF skinheads fought with Anti-Nazi League members leaving twenty-nine injured. But before that was the big one. April 1978. Victoria Park, open-air RAR concert, 80,000 people present.

'I think it was deemed wise that we would no longer be advertised to actually play the gig so it didn't break down into chaos,' said Dave. 'That's how dangerous certain elements of our following were or how dangerous people thought it could get. Yeah, there was all sorts of shit going on which is why we marched there and hung out with The Clash and Jimmy got up and sang a number with them . . . we did 'White Riot' at the end of it.' There was another major RAR London carnival at Brockwell Park in September, Sham again advised to stay away. Jimmy showed up unexpectedly and gave a speech against racism – full of emotion.

In terms of record sales, the band were on the up. Sham went back in the Top 10 in late '78 with their 'Hurry Up Harry' single and 1979 would see even greater chart success. The BBC even aired a forty-minute documentary about them in April '79, *Tell Us the Truth*. It was made by their upmarket and influential *Arena* strand and was essentially a long dramatic skit based on the second Sham 69 album, *That's Life*, a concept piece which Jimmy said was 'about a day in the life of a kind of Asbo kid. They go to the pub, they meet some girls, they nick a car . . .' The documentary was intercut with an interview and live footage taken at Middlesex Polytechnic, Hendon, which showed violence erupting among the crowd, forcing the band off stage.

A critical backlash was inevitable. In the *NME*, Nick Kent described the band's audience as 'a sight to curdle the soul – skinhead behemoths with prison tattoos and someone else's blood on their Dr. Martens.' Julie Burchill sniped about Jimmy's cockney credentials: 'It must have been a bloody strong wind the day the sound of Bow Bells reached Hersham.' Other bands were emboldened to call Jimmy out. In November 1978, during a Joy Division interview in *Sounds*, Bernard Sumner called Jimmy a racist. It came when the band were being pressed on their own overt referencing of Nazi history. Sumner deflects: '. . . compared to Jimmy Pursey who was an out-and-out racist . . . nobody can remember the beginning of Sham 69 and the things he said then. Now he tries to disconnect himself from his past.'

Jimmy was looking for an exit from Sham by 1979. He had all sorts going on behind the scenes: his own record imprint/ production company, producing records for the Rejects, the Upstarts and mod-revival bands such as The Chords, and was trying out acting and radio presenting. There were also rumours he was being lined up to be the singer in a new version of the Sex Pistols, maybe under the name The Sham Pistols.

Sham started to do 'farewell shows' in June '79. The band's final concert, their most famous, their 'Last Stand', took place in July at the Rainbow in London. They managed twenty minutes before the gig descended into chaos, skinheads chanting 'Sieg Heil' storming the stage, causing mass panic, crowd fighting. The bouncers hid, the bar was wrecked, people were glassed, police with dogs called to clear the venue, police on horseback outside.

The *Guardian* review mentioned an 'army of thuggish youths, tattooed with swastikas, chanting "There's only one Hitler".' It was, the reviewer explained, the 'British Movement mob' and 'they'd had it in for Jimmy ever since he joined Rock Against Racism.'

Maybe there was about forty hardcore faces, the so-called British Movement's 'Leader Guard', but once the gig started that had built into a small army of about 200 skinheads running amok. 'God save the Queen' and 'Rule Britannia' being chanted.

Sham split soon after. Dave formed a new band that went nowhere. The Sham Pistols never happened. People still recall that odd avant-garde dance performance Jimmy did on BBC Two arts show *Riverside* in 1980, before a quick succession of solo albums stiffed. I read for a little while he worked in a children's home. Sometime in the noughties Dave allowed another band called Sham 69 into existence and they still play, which does little for the credibility of the original Sham. Bit of a mess, that.

The skinhead subculture continued to prosper, gaining momentum. Like Dave said, other gigs and bands were being disrupted by their presence. There was a much publicised gathering and some trouble over August bank holiday in Southend 1979. Strong mod vs skinhead vibe. Bank holidays would become a highly visible, en masse, skinhead day out into the early eighties.

Sham were unquestionably the most important proto-Oi! band, but there were four other '77 punk bands the first era Oi! groups often referenced. Slaughter & the Dogs were from dirt-poor beginnings, emerging from one of Europe's biggest council estates in Wythenshawe, Manchester, stealing drain covers and lead off roofs to fund their first demo. But it was mostly all about the one song of theirs, 'Where Have All the Bootboys Gone?' A classic, no doubt, but by the time they made London they were a glammy, hammy lot. Skrewdriver and Cock Sparrer were two of the lesser-known names (dealt with in later chapters). The most crucial other band of the period, by a distance, were Menace, evidenced by the fact two of their road crew, Hoxton Tom and Roi Pearce, went on to start the two most important early eighties UK Oi! bands: the 4-Skins and The Last Resort, respectively. Tom and Roi are both now Oi! icons, and by virtue Menace too. Everyone I spoke to had a soft spot for them. 'I love Menace,' Trevor Taylor said.

There isn't much to go at from their heyday: five singles, no album, no hits. The songs that really jump out are 'Screwed Up' (from August '77 and produced by John Cale) and 'I'm Civilised' (1978).

I saw them play those songs plus their other big ones, 'G.L.C.' ('You're full of shit') and the Sham-a-like 'Carry No Banners' at Cream of the Crop as the evening got going when the main room was full. The singer came across warm, level-headed, almost gentle, and although carrying a belly, looked great too.

I only realised later that quite a few of the other catchy songs in their set, which I presumed must also be from their punk era, such as 'One Two One Two', 'So Fuck You' and 'C&A', were from a long streak of six albums they'd cut after they reformed in 2000. If I was to pick one to recommend, it'd be 2014's *London Stories.*

What also stuck with me was this little spiel the singer did towards the end of their set. 'Right, you want to know who the real enemy is?' he said. 'It's the 1 per cent of people who have got all the money. And they're setting us all against each other. Don't listen to anybody's crap. Investigate. Forget Facebook. Investigate.' A call for unity among a crowd where some might have been looking for easy scapegoats.

I saw Menace again at Rebellion where they were playing the same Pavilion stage the Court played. By then I'd found out the singer was called Noel Martin, the only original member left in Menace, and he'd been their drummer. The band's original singer, Morgan Webster, had died in 1991. Menace had broken up in 1978, when he'd decided to quit. I'd asked various people at Rebellion how Morgan died and got different answers. Someone suggested he had choked on his own vomit. 'Nobody knows exactly,' Noel told me. 'His mother wrote to us and said he died from a methadone overdose, which is quite likely because he was a heroin addict. And another story was while he was cycling home from a gig he had an accident on his bike and hit his head and died from that.'

Noel was manning the band's merch stall. He was approachable, and asked if I knew that Menace were the first band to have 'Oi! Oi! Oi!' in one of their songs. I said I didn't. 'I believe we are,' he said. 'When we recorded 'Tomorrow's World' in

1978–79 that has got the line "Tomorrow's world is just around the Oi! Oi! Oi!".' True: last line of the song. 'I have nothing against us being classed as an Oi! band but wer'e not strictly Oi!,' he smiled. 'But us, Slaughter & the Dogs and Sham are probably the pre-runners of Oi!.'

We spoke again over the phone one early morning a couple of weeks later. Noel was on holiday in Ireland, where he was originally from. He was born in Galway, said he'd come over to London when he was 14 in the early seventies. Settled in Crouch End. He and two school pals, Steve (Tannett, now music director at Marshall Amplification) and Charlie, formed a pub-rock band called Stonehenge, and in July '76 recruited Morgan, a Canadian, then living in Islington.

When the Pistols hit the headlines, the band's interest was piqued because John Lydon had been at the same Roman Catholic school in Islington as them. 'Steve was in the same year as him, and Charlie and I were in the year above,' said Noel. Stonehenge decided to go punk, became Menace. They were 20 or 21, Morgan was 19. 'It only took us a week or two to write some songs,' Noel said. 'We had 13 songs: it was all we ever had.'

Almost immediately they started playing gigs down the Roxy, often with Sham. 'We were their main support band for a long time,' Noel said. They shared a booking agent and for a while a record label boss, Miles Copeland. His Step-Forward Records, also home to Chelsea and The Fall, had released Sham's 'I Don't Wanna' and Copeland's other label, Illegal Records, put out the Menace debut single as well as The Police.

I asked Noel what those gigs with Sham were like? 'Sham had the skinhead following and Jimmy tried to calm them down but he made it worse,' he said. 'I chatted with Jimmy and he said, we're middle class, our families are middle class, living out in the suburbs, out in Hersham, we feel like we shouldn't really be playing this kind of music, 'Song of the Streets', stuff like that. I said, mate, you can't look at it like that. You look at it like it's what's in your heart and soul; don't worry about where you come from, just go out and do it.'

Menace's own skinhead following was kept in check. 'We had one particular guy,' Noel said. 'I don't know where he is now, he was just "Big Steve" – he was huge. I'm fairly sure he was a West Ham chap. He was what was known as a "face". When he was there the skinheads all respected him. He'd say, no, don't go there, and the trouble would stop. He helped us out in a big way to stop all that escalating violence that Sham had; he didn't allow that type of aggro to start with us. We also had Steve English, he would come to the odd show. He was a good friend of ours from before punk. This was before he was Johnny Rotten's bodyguard.'

What about Hoxton Tom? 'Tom was a big friend of ours from Islington and he used to come to gigs. Very educated man – he's got ten O levels, something like that,' Noel said. 'It was after one of our shows on his way home he got stabbed seriously – he nearly died. We used to go visit him in the hospital, and then after that he joined the 4-Skins and became a full-on . . . he was always a skinhead but he started to do that.'

I got the impression Noel wasn't really a 4-Skins fan. Menace were hard-hitting but had a melody and a sense of musicianship at their core. He added: 'Suggs used to come and see us, before Madness – Dixie, Suggs and Toks – the three names in Islington who were the skinhead guys.'

And Roi? 'Roi Pearce was a roadie for a little while,' Noel said and sort of chuckled to himself. 'People said they were Menace roadies but we didn't officially have Menace roadies – people used to come and help us in with the gear. Roi was a face, same as Big Steve. But Roi was quite a small chap back in the day, slight build, but a reputation comes from the people you're with, and he was with the Millwall crew.

'Roi had some doors opened for him by saying he was Menace's roadie,' Noel added. 'We still chat and I'm not averse to doing a gig on a mixed bill [with The Last Resort, as he had at Cream of the Crop] but I don't want to do a gig where it's completely skinhead bands or can be completely misunderstood. We generally avoid gigs that have got very Oi! kind of patriotic-type bands. I'm not an out-an-out Antifa preacher but I am completely left wing – I am about equal rights for everybody from gays, lesbian, trans.'

Noel explained how he'd been a skinhead in 1969, but by 1977 the band 'weren't skinheads any more.' He said he liked football, supported Arsenal, but wasn't a hooligan. He felt what the skinheads the band attracted had identified with was that Menace were quite obviously, in Noel's words, 'very working-class punk'.

The Menace look was very down-at-heel, boot-boyish. 'I used to wear the tank top,' Noel said. 'Dr. Martens were standards, and in the very early photographs we had done I think Steve was wearing a Ben Sherman shirt, so there was still a bit of the skinhead iconography. People thought we looked hard, had an aggressive image.

'We didn't go to art college like all the rest of them,' he added. 'We left school and went to work. Johnny Rotten left school and went to art college, same as Siouxsie, same as Sid. Me, Steve and Charlie worked right through the band. When you talk about working class, if you don't work for three months you just starve, right?'

Chapter 3

Never 'ad Nothin': Upstarts

After Jimmy Pursey, Thomas 'Mensi' Mensforth was the second great voice of Oi!. He died in December 2021, aged 65. The *Guardian* obituary headline read: 'Charismatic, outspoken frontman of the punk band Angelic Upstarts, pioneers of raw and raucous Oi! music'. The obit ended with him being survived by 'at least sixteen children from various relationships'. That caused quite a stir online.

Jimmy produced their records. You can hear him all over their first two magnificent hit singles in 1979, 'I'm An Upstart' and 'Teenage Warning', especially on the terrace-chant choruses. The Upstarts were also managed by Sham's manager and Sham's skinhead fanbase followed them, but they had their own identity, shaped by Mensi, a strapping 6 ft-tall former apprentice miner, from the arse end of South Shields. He left school at 16, formed the band after almost four years down the pit at a time when communities across South Tyneside were being destroyed by the decline of heavy industry, the area known for having the highest unemployment rate in the country. Mensi was disgruntled, a hardcase, a Sunderland football hooligan. He was angry and he was righteous, 21 in 1977, switched on by The Clash.

I interviewed him before he died for my Stone Roses book around 2011. John Squire and Ian Brown were big Oi! fans in the early eighties, and Brown had briefly been a roadie for the Upstarts. I was trying at the time to put to bed these whispers about teenage Brown and his politics. He'd had a Union Jack tattooed on his upper arm and the word 'England' written beneath it, the same tattoo, I notice now, as Jeff, teen singer in the Rejects. At the time I imagined Brown had been influenced by the Upstarts' controversial 1981 song, 'England', hijacked by the NF and covered by many RAC Oi! bands subsequently.

Mensi was on great form that day. Discussing Brown, he said he was glad to have him as a roadie because back then the gigs were always full of NF or BM skinheads causing problems, and Ian was 'a little bit skinny but a game fucker'.

'I wasn't interested in whether my roadies could string a guitar, I wanted to know they could hold their hands up in a row,' he'd said. Then he gave me a great line, typical, I guess, of his eye for the dramatic. 'I remember someone interviewing Liam Gallagher and saying, you think you're a bad boy? You want to get along with Mensi and the Upstarts and you'll find out what a bad boy is. The violence was very, very heavy.'

It was the first day of April 2022. Friday. My first ever Oi! gig. South Shields. A memorial for Mensi featuring current and former members of the Upstarts and guests. I had no idea what to expect but I had a contact, bought my ticket direct from Chris Wright, singer with Crashed Out. His band were playing the gig and he was also going to be fronting the Upstarts. I got there around soundcheck time. The venue, Hedworth Hall, was an impressive, old art-deco building. There were two young lads smoking outside. It didn't cross my mind they might be in the Upstarts. But they were: Mick Robson on guitar, who also had another band, Bastard Face, and Andy Wilkinson on drums who said he also played in Red Alert, a revered early eighties Oi! act from the north-east. They went off for chips. Then two more fellas rolled up, much more likely candidates, late 40s, 50s.

One was John Woodward, a jobbing cockney bassist who had played in Garry Bushell's band The Gonads (twice) and in the reunion version of Long Tall Shorty who were originally discovered (produced and renamed) by Jimmy in 1978, one of the first mod revival acts; their singer Tony Perfect changed his name to Tony Feedback and joined the Upstarts circa 1982. There were many such band member switches to the Upstarts story.

'Newts' was the other fella. Neil Newton. He was from South Shields and had played guitar with the Upstarts for sixteen years, since 2005, leaving the band briefly to complete a PhD in sonification. Newts came from an estate close to Brockley Whins, the estate Mensi grew up on, said he'd been 9 or 10 when the Upstart's released their incendiary self-produced debut single 'The Murder of Liddle Towers' in 1978, the one that brought them to the attention of Jimmy. Even as a kid Newts said he knew the story of the local fella Mensi was singing about, who'd died after a beating in police custody. At first his death was ruled as justifiable homicide. At an appeal in '78 that ruling had been changed to death by misadventure.

The single, backed by another belter called 'Police Oppression', made the band notorious locally and saw them heavily harassed by the Northumbria police force, even more so when they began to routinely take a pig's head complete with bobby helmet on stage with them (which would invariably be booted around during the gig).

The Upstarts were hot property after the Liddle Towers single and Jimmy had helped get them signed, via his production company, to Sham's label, Polydor, for a £25k advance. They were, however, soon sacked from the label: Mensi gave a member of the Polydor staff a headbutt during a skirmish. Jimmy and his manager, Tony Gordon, took them to Warner, picking up another £25k. A few months later, the Upstarts were on *Top of the Pops* doing 'Teenage Warning'. Mensi had a skinhead and Jimmy had the sleeve of their Top 30 debut album decorated with a 'Clockwork Orange' theme, a key skinhead reference. Jimmy suggested Mensi might actually front Sham 69, but as much as Mensi liked Jimmy, it was a no.

Wright showed up. Another teen fan of the Upstarts. 'Knew all their stuff from an early age,' he told me. He said Mensi had done much to support Crashed Out; the two bands even released a split album together, *The Dirty Dozen*, in 2011. Wright had also become Mensi's tattooist. 'He went from having nothing to being quite heavily tattooed at the finish,' he said. 'He was a big lump in his later years but he was a larger-than-life character, very outspoken, highly intelligent, stood by what he believed in.'

Wright seemed to be in charge of organising things. He was 50, but looked younger, fit and healthy, shaved head, tattoos. Crashed Out were about to release a new album, *Against All Odds*, on Demons Run Amok, a German metal/hardcore label that also released Grade 2 records (*Against All Odds* would be voted an album of the year by the influential *Vive Le Rock* magazine, one of the few UK outlets fully supportive of Oi! and streetpunk).

Wright said Crashed Out had been included on *Oi! 40 Years Untamed*, a 2020 Oi! compilation put together by Garry Bushell which featured new songs from many of the scene's big hitters such as Cock Sparrer, Lion's Law, Last Resort and the Rejects. Wright supplied the photograph that featured on the album sleeve, an image of his young nephew, fist raised. 'Garry Bushell said he was looking for an image of a tough-looking young street kid,' Wright said. 'Watford Jon, the singer in Argy Bargy, told him I coached kids at a boxing gym. Garry didn't want old and fat on the cover.' He smiled. 'At the end of the day the scene's quite old with a lot of middle-aged fellas.'

After they had soundchecked, Newts offered to take me to Mensi's old Brockley Whins estate. We drove via the tarted-up South Shields seafront. It was only when we headed out of town, past the former shipyards and docks on the River Tyne, things began to look bleaker. Brockley Whins was a sprawling council estate, and felt hollowed-out and feral. Newts showed me the estate's pub, The Jester, where the Upstarts were formed – a frightening-looking box.

It was a good gig that evening, one I was glad to have been at. The place packed with about 300 skins and punks, mostly in their 50s and 60s, in tartan, denim, leather, liberty spikes and studs, braces and boots. On stage Wright, with a flat cap, capped-T and Brian Johnson vocal power, was convincing and the band sharp and tight. They played all the group's best-known numbers, and various Upstarts who I didn't recognise came on to compliment the line-up. Some of Mensi's family were there. It got quite emotional when they all got on stage and at the end, Wright told the crowd we'd help raise £6,892 which was being donated to the ward and unit at South Tyneside Hospital that'd cared for Mensi before he died.

Afterwards I met Spin, the long-time Crashed Out bassist who in the eighties played bass for infamous RAC band Skullhead, based in Newcastle. He was heavily tattooed, some of them he said he regretted. He had long detached himself from any white power associations and seemed embarrassed by his involvement in Skullhead. His favourite band was Oasis and I noticed he had my Stone Roses book, that I'd brought up as a gift for the band, in his bag. Wright explained Spin was the band's 'reader'. Newts also introduced me to Gaz Douglass, a towering, burly skinhead, also heavily tattooed. Newts said he was the Upstarts' number-one fan. We had a quick chat and he invited me to his house in South Shields the next day.

Douglass had grown up on the Brockley Whins estate too. He said Mensi, Decca and Mond (the three original Upstarts) *all* came from the estate. As a kid he would knock on Mensi's door to ask for band badges. 'All us kids did it,' he said. He recalled Mensi's dad handing them out. 'He was called Tommy as well, big man, a miner, dry as sticks, hands like shovels, same as Mensi,' he said. 'He used to come to the door and we'd say, mister have you got any badges? And he'd grab a handful and throw them on the lawn and all us kids used to be fighting just to get a badge. I've still got mine.'

He said he also saw one of the earliest Upstarts gigs. It took place on Brockley Whins. 'They did the park behind the shops,' Douglass smiled. 'Everybody says it was on the garage roofs but they couldn't get the gear up so they just played in the park. It was the kids' playground but the council had taken all the equipment away, so it was an empty park. They plugged all the wires into the house of a lad called Dave Coleman. The women who owned the fish shop phoned the police but the

Upstarts did a good few songs; all the kids jumping about and everything. It was brilliant. The police tried to get into Dave's house to unplug them but he barricaded himself in. He was in there for about an hour before they broke the door down and unplugged everything.'

I asked Douglass if he knew the original, infamous Upstarts manager, Keith Bell. 'An arsehole and a bully; his dog lost a fight one time so he dropped it off the cliff, cunt,' Newts had said. I'd read Bell was a former boxing champ, fancied himself as a gangster, masterminded the band's infamous prison break-in, when the Upstarts played a short set at HMP Acklington in 1979 in front of 150 prisoners. 'You're better off in [the] nick if Thatcher gets elected,' Mensi told the inmates. It was a situationist romp covered by Garry Bushell for *Sounds* that generated much publicity for the band.

'Keith sort of made himself the manager,' Douglass said. 'Mensi and his mates used to go into the pubs down South Shields and Keith asked, do you need a manager? – I'll get you gigs. He was a big man but he also had a lot of people looking after him, so he could go anywhere and say my band's playing here tonight or next week. He was a horrible man in later life, did some terrible things, especially to their families. He burned down Mensi's sister's stables, she bred horses.' I must have looked shocked. 'Aye, killed a few horses,' Douglass said. 'He tried to say he was on holiday at the time of the fire but it was proven it was him.'

'People were scared of him,' added Douglass. 'He called himself "The Sherriff", used to walk his white English bull terrier up and down King Street, the main street in South Shields. He just thought he was the hardest man ever. In the early days of the band [drummer] Decca was drinking and hardly turning up for rehearsals, so Keith and his mates took him to the beach and beat him up, nearly killed him, stripped him naked and threw him in the water.'

Douglass had a clippings file he'd kept on the Bell saga, headlines such as 'My Life of Fear by Mother of Punk Star', 'Shotgun Buried', 'Popstar Beaten on Beach'. There was retribution for Bell's actions. 'Some of them [named in court as Decca's dad and Mensi's brother-in-law] said they didn't know Kenny Pearce [who recently died; his family lived in the house behind Mensi's mum and dad] had a gun in his coat, a sawn-off shotgun,' Douglass said. 'They [those three] got there and knocked on Keith's door and Kenny pulled the gun out. Keith grabbed hold of one of his muppets and pulled him in front of him so this fella got shot in the legs, in the knees. It all came out in court, they all got jailed. That feud lasted until Keith did the stables [and was jailed for four years] and then one of the conditions of his bail was he had to move out of the area. And that was the last thing.' Keith Bell died in 2017.

Mensi had written a great song about all this, 'Shotgun Solution', for the band's second album, *We Gotta Get Out of this Place*, released in early 1980. This album included 'Never 'ad Nothin'' which was an update of Sham's 'Song of the Streets' and another working-class skinhead anthem, but it (and the album) failed to chart. EMI picked them up for two more studio albums and they scored a Top 30 live album for the label in 1981. The band also had two tracks on the first Oi! compilation, sponsored by *Sounds* and released by EMI in November 1980. 'We got lumped in with the Oi! scene but that wasn't by choice,' Mensi had said to me. 'I always protested that we were a punk band.

When we first went to London we used to fight with the British Movement and the National Front.'

'Mensi always said he didn't start out to be political but when the neo-Nazi skinheads started turning up at the gigs saluting, he just started fighting against that,' Douglass said. He added that (guitarist) Mond got stabbed in the back at a gig in Glasgow. 'Mensi told me there was a scuffle in one of the bars between the band and a few other people when that happened. He said some people from the bar came and helped them beat the lads up and one of those who helped was Dennis Waterman, and he punched a few of the lads too.'

There was lot of skinhead-related violence at the Upstarts gigs. In the next chapter, the Rejects describe a strong BM skinhead presence at a gig they did with the Upstarts at the Electric Ballroom in 1979. I also read how a NF skinhead gang turned an Upstarts' Wolverhampton gig into a riot with seventeen injured, five of them stabbed, and a fruit machine thrown off a balcony. A gig in Nottingham was also stopped after Mensi denounced the NF from the stage and it all kicked off.

Mensi became an outspoken anti-fascist campaigner with the scars to prove it, but he didn't join Anti-Fascist Action until *after* the band's infamous Main Event gig at the Astoria in London in 1988. Here, the Upstarts were showered with Sieg Heil chants from a Blood & Honour skinhead gang led by Skrewdriver's singer Ian Stuart who claimed Mensi had sold out his nationalist beliefs to make more money being left wing. I had heard this whisper too and was keen to put it to bed.

Mensi had always made political points in his music (for example, 'Two Million Voices' about unemployment on their third album) but became significantly more upfront about it in the mid-eighties: playing a benefit for striking miners alongside Red Alert, starring in a *Play at Home* Channel 4 TV documentary about the decline in north-east shipyards, and, in 1985, releasing the *Brighton Bomb* EP shortly after the 1984 IRA assassination attempt at the Tory party conference in the city. They'd been called 'the sickest band in Britain' for that.

Their popularity dwindled during that period to the extent that they were largely forgotten and the Main Event gig was their biggest headline show in years. What was behind their booking or why they were targeted for such a high-profile assault seemed oddly personal. The trouble escalated quickly, and Mensi was attacked on stage with two huge planks of wood, clobbered with a mic stand, and forced to retreat. The police were called to break up the violence in the venue.

'Yeah, that's when he got involved with AFA,' Newts said. 'Someone took him aside in a pub and said, look you're having bother with the right wing and we want to chase them out of London. Mensi said, how you going to manage that, we're outnumbered? The fella said, watch this, made some signal and everybody in the pub stood up and they were all AFA. Mensi was well impressed. AFA would go and confront the NF, take it to the streets – they'd come and protect the Upstarts from the boneheads.'

I read a classic example of this in a book called *No Retreat: The Secret War Between Britain's Anti-Fascists and the Far Right*, a vivid and very violent account of anti-fascist street politics from 1977 to 1997. An Upstarts gig in Sunderland in 1990 was believed to be under threat from Blood & Honour, who were holding a gig on the same night in Newcastle featuring Skrewdriver and Skullhead. 'Stewards' from Red Action, the infamously hard-line

AFA affiliate, travelled to the north-east to act as security and the gig went ahead untroubled. The book describes how afterwards a dozen Red Action stewards piled into Mensi's van and headed to Newcastle. They were tooled up with hammers, bats and bottles. They soon spotted a big gang of 'boneheads' in a chippy and piled in, Mensi in the thick of it. When the cops arrived, he and a few of the others were arrested.

Mensi's later persona was built on such incidents. What was confusing to me was the mixed messages the Upstarts sent out during their early years when Mensi seems to have, perhaps, got himself caught up in the same sort of situation as Jimmy Pursey. For instance, in the band's first major feature in *Sounds* in early '78, the Upstarts were pictured wearing swastika armbands (they also posed in front of a sign that read 'Fascism kills' and 'Smash the Front'). 'Mensi said it was just a fashion thing then, it wasn't to say anything, no meaning in it,' Douglass said. While it was true there was nothing new to Nazi insignia (sort of straight-baiting) in rock, from The Who to Sweet, Stooges to Motörhead, even the Ramones, and then most infamously with the Pistols and Sid Vicious, there was also a growing number of young NF and BM skins for whom the swastika, alongside the sun wheel, eagle/phoenix and Union Jack, was now a badge of pride. The BM logo was a blatant homage to the Nazi Reichsadler.

The Upstarts did feature on the bill of the Rock Against Racism Militant Entertainment Tour in '79 at Alexandra Palace when Jimmy joined them on stage but soon Mensi was attacking RAR in print. Also among their songs on the first album were antagonist, sneering lyrics about leftist student politics and the Socialist Workers Party. On the band's second album, the track 'Capital City', derided 'queers' *and* foreigners. Most startling on this album, however, was a song called 'Lonely Man of Spandau' about Rudolf Hess (a neo-Nazi cause célèbre). 'England' had been on the third album, their first released by EMI in 1981, a track praised in *Bulldog*, the Young National Front magazine, as 'a classic patriotic song'. It was also said to be one of the most popular records to be played a YNF discos.

Then there was the Enoch Powell quote. It was from an interview Mensi did with the then-popular fanzine *Rising Free* around 1980–81. Straight off he dismisses the SWP, RAR and the associated Anti-Nazi League. He also calls NF skinheads 'thick', just 'followers of fashion'.

'The pub where we drink has some NF/BM people but some of their mates are darkies,' he said. 'People are entitled to their own views, whether I think they're right or wrong. It's a free country.'

He added: 'You shouldn't be ashamed to be English and white, which is another thing the SWP put over. It's as if it's our fault we were born white, we should all have been born niggers. I've got nothing against niggers but I'm proud to be white. But the way things are in this country, if you're proud to be English and white you're branded as a Nazi, and it's time it's stopped.'

And finally: 'I'll tell you who I thought was a really good politician who got slagged down, and that was Enoch Powell. I don't think he was a racialist at all, he just predicted things that *did* happen. He was probably the most under-estimated politician of all time . . . The papers branded him as a racist. If the *NME* get hold of this fanzine and read this interview, they'll brand me as a racist. I think he should have been prime minister, there you are.'

I read somewhere he was drunk when he did the interview. I think he took a lot of speed. I know he wrote a lot of songs in a short space of time, coming up with lyrics spontaneously in the studio, and much of it was essentially filler. Nonetheless, some of these early Upstarts songs and such unvarnished proclamations in print, plus the Sham associations, led to NF and BM skinheads attaching themselves to the band, an attachment strengthened by 'England'.

Here's what he told me in 2011, when we were talking about the song and I'd asked if patriotism was something the Upstarts stood for?

'Absolutely,' he said. 'At the end of the day there's nothing wrong with having pride in your country. This is what I tried to put forward with 'England', which was a celebration of the working classes who fought the two [world] wars. It's always us working-class kids who have to do the fighting. The only thing I used to say was you've got to have respect for everybody else and them having pride in their country. I used to lecture everybody.

'In the early days I used to encourage right-wing skinheads to come, and I was of the idea then that I could berate them, cajole them, anything to get them round to my way of thinking. My idea was to convert them through the music. It was intentional. When you're young and in a band you think you're famous, all-powerful, all-conquering but it actually means very little, to be honest. It was only later I became disillusioned with talking with them, especially when they started getting violent towards what I consider to be innocent people. That's when my doctrine changed slightly.'

He added: 'I was a bit of a skinhead thug but a left-wing one not a right-wing one. There was a famous quote from a Nazi skinhead, when they asked him, what are you doing at an

Upstarts' gig? He said, we love the music but we hate him, talking about me. I'd be upset if they liked us. I revelled in their hatred. We wore the Green MA1 jackets and they wore the black ones. So I started wearing the black one with a red star on it to confuse them. I loved aggravating them. I used to wear a Harrington jacket and I put an England badge on it. Then I'd have a little red star on the lapel and fuck their heads up – which wasn't a difficult thing to do at the time. They tried to hijack aspects of patriotism. The song 'England' was about taking the flag back from them.'

I'd also asked him about the band being featured on the cover of *Rebel*, the Socialist Workers Party youth magazine. 'I was totally against the Socialist Workers Party,' Mensi told me. 'I never got on with them. At the time our politics were very similar but they had no idea about physical confrontation. It's no good standing with a banner and chanting, we want the Nazis out. I wanted to smash the banner over their heads and smash it down their throats. The SWP said my real indulgence was gratuitous violence. I said, what do you want us to do, wait until they attack me? If the boneheads were coming to my shows they weren't coming to sing along to the words of 'Kids on the Street' [from the Upstarts' third album: "All you kids, black and white, together we are dynamite"]. I became pro-active defensive. It was like turning up for a fight and an Upstarts gig breaking out sometimes. In the end you had to actually win – that was the idea – it was no good them turning you over.'

The second great voice of Oi!, as confusing and contradictory as the first? He'd adopted the skinhead look, there's photographs of him in Lonsdale and the Last Resort crucified skin T-shirt, and he seemed to have sympathised to some extent with the BM/NF skinheads before turning vehemently against them. He was certainly a complicated man.

Gaz Douglass didn't live far from Brockley Whins. At the entrance to his council estate was a cluster of historic miner's cottages. He lived on a long terrace row; his house inside spick and span, and his wife made us coffee and brought biscuits. Douglass explained that the cats belonged to his daughter, Angel, who was a recent university graduate and a graphic designer. He said she'd helped design the flag he'd had made to go on top of Mensi's coffin at the funeral. Wright had sorted the wake.

Douglass said he had got to know Mensi, the man, when he started helping him do up properties in the mid-eighties. This surprised me. I'd heard Mensi dealt second-hand cars but didn't know he also flipped houses. 'I was 17, 18, ten years younger than him; he saw me in The Jester, someone must have told him I was serving my time as a joiner,' Douglass said. 'I worked for him for twenty-five years plus, on and off, doing up houses in London, Kent, all over. He would do them up, sell them on or rent them out. With the cars, he used to buy them up here, do them up a bit, and take them down to London and sell them for a lot more money. Mensi always had his fingers in a lot of pies, an Arthur Daley type and good at it. He was a really brainy man. He went to grammar school but I think he got expelled.'

I said I'd read Mensi describing himself as a very lonely man, in fact the loneliest bloke in the world. 'I'm covered in Angelic Upstarts tattoos,' Douglass said. 'Mensi said to me, I've been in the band all these years and I haven't even got an Upstarts tattoo. He didn't even have a record, didn't own anything to do with the band. He used to tell me he'd never get married but he was married three or four times, later two or three times to Thai women. I think the last one he got married to, he got divorced straight away. She was much younger than him, looked about 19, 20. To Mensi I think it was a bit of an image thing. I know loads of his ex-partners and they were always getting a house and car and then he started to see other girls. Then when they found out he'd say, if you don't like it, go, and loads of them just put up with it. He'd have three or four girlfriends going at the same time. Decca said he had about 18 or 19 kids. When I finished working for Mensi I could have counted 21 or 22 but he obviously had kids in Thailand that I don't know about. I was still doing houses for him when he started going out to Thailand. He'd jump on a plane and go whenever he wanted.'

Mensi was part of a biker gang in Thailand, a chapter of the Philippines Mad Dog Motorcycle Club. 'They reckon he got made up to top bloke,' Douglass said. I asked if he knew anything about the terrible bike accident that Newts told me about, happened sometime in the nineties. Newts said Mensi had lost his spleen and from then on walked with a slight limp. He'd explained how the band had planned to tour South America in 2018, Colombia and other countries, and been really looking forward to it but Mensi couldn't have the required yellow fever shot, something to do with the spleen and medical issues, and so the tour had to be cancelled.

'Mensi had a Triumph Bonneville,' Douglass said. 'He was coming to a roundabout, there was an articulated lorry and Mensi had the right of way but he got halfway round and the lorry went over him. Mensi went under the back wheels. He was pretty badly crushed. The spleen is like your immune system.

All the years I knew Tommy, the slightest cold, he would catch it bad. I think it's why he lost his life because his body wasn't strong enough to fight it.' Mensi died after catching Covid.

But he was also massively obese in his later years too, right? He was sometimes referred to as 'Mensi Marx', but 'Fester' was another nickname, and if you look at pictures from the period you can see why. 'He did put a hell of a lot of weight on, but sometimes he could lose it pretty quick,' Douglass said. 'I used to see him big and then a few months later slim again, a lot of people said he was taking slimming tablets.'

I asked Douglass to tell me more about Mensi from the time when he came back to live in South Shields in the nineties after the Upstarts split in '92. 'Tommy still had family, children and that, down in Kent,' Douglass said. 'He started living in a house around Sunderland but then the girl from Kent came to live up here and Mensi bought a pub in Bishop Auckland, so they were living together on a farm not far from the pub. Me and my mates were doing the pub up, The Sly Fox. This was late nineties.' Mensi, he said, had another pub in Jarrow for a while. 'Tommy always moved around, didn't seem to stay in one place very long. That house he had in Simonside [where he was living when he died] is the longest he'd stayed in one place.'

I heard about a couple of unreported incidents while in the north-east that portrayed Mensi as a vicious, almost psychotic, street brawler? 'I've only seen him fight two or three times and he was an animal,' Douglass confirmed. 'He was [a] really hard man but only when he was provoked. There used to be a video on YouTube of a gig in Leeds. He'd only done two or three songs, must have been skinheads saluting, and they stopped playing and Mensi said something to them and then he dove off stage into them, fighting into the skinheads . . . so he wasn't scared.'

Had Douglass seen right-wing skins at Upstarts gigs in person? 'At a punk festival in Morecambe, Holidays in the Sun, when they reformed,' he said. 'There was me, Mensi, Max Splodge [who became the Upstarts drummer for a period, but before that had featured on the first two Oi! comps with his own band, Splodgenessabounds, who had a hit in 1980 called 'Two Pints of Lager and a Packet of Crisps Please'] and my mate – four of us. We were in the bar before the gig and there were these five big skinheads staring at us. At the gig, the Upstarts played two songs and these skinheads, seven or eight of them now, started saluting and shouting stuff. They were big lads. Mensi stopped the song and said, why do you do it now? I've just been in the bar and you could have had it out there and then, you had your chance. Why do it now and spoil the gig? And they walked out.'

Mensi was attacked on stage again by right-wing skins around 2005–06, was quite seriously injured, and became unsure about performing live afterwards. This was when Wright had first sung with the Upstarts, at Rebellion, asked to step in at the last minute. 'Mensi got hit with the bottle' Douglass said. 'He could have lost his eye, his sight.'

'He told me he had loads of death threats, prices on his head,' Douglass added. 'He said to me, people know where I live. If they're that bothered, why don't they come and look for us. I didn't see it but people said it was shocking what right-wing groups were putting on Facebook when he died.'

I asked Douglass if he knew Crashed Out bassist Spin? 'Mensi said to me, do you think I should take Crashed Out on the road to Germany with the Upstarts, get their name known? He said he wasn't so sure with Spin, having been in Skullhead. I said, I don't know but everybody can change. Mensi started taking Crashed Out on tour and got them to where they are, gigs all around the world. He realised with Spin that [it] was just a phase of his early life. That could have damaged the Upstarts name but that proved right.'

Before I left South Shields, we talked, a little sadly, about Mensi's death. Douglass and Mensi had fallen out a few years before, although they did make up when Mensi fell seriously ill. 'I think he had an idea something was going on health-wise,' Douglass said. 'My mate saw him in Asda in Boldon and asked him when his next gig was and he said, oh I'm too old now, I'm knackered. My mate said he wasn't walking very well. I said he's always had a limp since his bike crash, bit of a swagger. My mate said, no, he looked as if he was walking canny bad. His family were saying they thought he had the beginnings of dementia. He did a gig in Sunderland where they were gonna do the full *Teenage Warning* album and Mensi couldn't remember half the words. He got tested and they said he was alright. The last ten years of his life he changed, spent a lot of it in Thailand.'

The same day I spoke to Douglass, I went to visit another Gaz, Gaz Stoker, at his Sunderland terrace house quite close to the bracing seafront. He had played with the Upstarts for eighteen years after they reformed and been one of the guests on stage at the gig the previous night. I'd met him backstage afterwards. Stoker was also a member of Red London, a much-loved north-east Oi! band from 1981 until they split in 2002.

Aged just 16, in 1977, the Upstarts, he said, had inspired him to form Sunderland's first punk band The Rebels. The band's drummer Wora (aka Sticks) soon joined the Upstarts when Keith Bell kicked Decca out of the band. 'Gave him a right old hiding and took him to the pier in South Shields and he flung him off,' said Gaz. 'That was the end of Decca in the band until years later when he re-joined on a few occasions.

'The Rebels rehearsed in an old community centre in Sunderland,' Stoker added. 'Keith Bell got my phone number from someone and rang me to ask if the Upstarts could share the practice room with us. At the time people wouldn't even let the Upstarts rehearse they were that notorious. They couldn't play many gigs, trouble followed them. The police would pull Mensi in and try to charge him with all sorts. They would go to venues the band were booked to be playing and threaten to close them down or make their lives a misery if they put the gig on.'

The Rebels also came to the attention of Jimmy Pursey and he agreed to put them on a tour he was organising, featuring up-and-coming punk bands, under the banner of 'Pursey's Package'. 'The plan was there'd be three or four bands playing each gig, but all hell broke loose at one of the first ones and they scrapped the idea.' Stoker said. 'I was gutted. I went to see Sham at Sunderland Poly and there was loads of trouble; loads of "dodgepots" [as they refer to the far-right skinheads in this part of the country].'

Red London took their name from the Sham 69 song. 'Originally it just sounded like a good name for a band but because the band members were all working-class socialists the "Red" in the name grew in significance,' Stoker said. Attila the Stockbroker (a poet who featured on the fourth Oi! comp in 1982) was chief cheerleader for the band and was instrumental in getting them a deal with Razor Records [home at the time to Splodge and Cock Sparrer] and they made an EP, *Sten Guns in Sunderland*, and the album *This is England* in 1984.

Stoker explained he was also in another north-east Oi! band, Red Alert, for twelve years, from about 1983. They were a sort-of sister band to Red London with many familial and friendship ties. 'Red Alert formed in 1979 and they got a load of publicity through being on the [third] Oi! compilation album, and they were doing gigs with Blitz and other bands who were on the same label as them [No Future].' Stoker's brother, 'Kid' Stoker, was in Red Alert (and Red London) and the band's singer, Steve Smith (who sadly died in December 2022) was the brother of Red London's singer Patty Smith. Guitarist Tony Van Frater seems to have beaten Stoker in this game of north-east Oi! Top Trumps: he was in The Rebels, Red Alert, Red London, the Upstarts *and* the Rejects (Wora/Sticks also went from the Upstarts to the Rejects in the early eighties!). 'We were all mates,' Stoker laughed. 'There was friendly rivalry between the bands, trying to write better songs and outdo each other but we were all mates at the end of the day.'

Stoker fanned the flames on the Upstarts reunion, putting together a tribute album to the Upstarts in 1998, featured left-leaning Oi! bands such as Klasse Kriminale from Italy, The Oppressed, Red London and Red Alert. At the same time, Van Frater put together similar tribute albums to the Cockney Rejects and Blitz. Van Frater then teamed up with Mensi for an Upstarts comeback album and when it came time to tour, asked Stoker to join the band.

Gaz Douglass had earlier told me he'd seen this line-up of the Upstarts at a 'comeback' gig in 2002 in a pub called The Office in South Shields. He said it was the only time he ever saw the pig's head getting booted about. 'Mensi didn't want to but the lad who owned the pub bought a pig's head and had it in a carrier bag,' Gaz said. 'Mensi put it on top of a speaker and said, we'll leave him there. But soon as the Upstarts started playing someone got on stage, grabbed the bag, and chucked it and everyone was stamping on it, people were covered in blood, a lad broke his leg, there were people with black eyes. It was a wild night.'

The new Upstarts began to tour consistently, popular on the growing punk/Oi! festival circuit in the UK and Europe. Mensi's newer songs were often crude with titles such as 'Nazi B.N.P', 'Red Flag' and 'Tories, Tories, Tories (Out, Out, Out)'. The band's final album was called *Bullingdon Bastards*. He also grew cantankerous, calling out the politics of Oi! bands from the eighties who were increasingly back on the punk festival circuit, such as Condemned 84. He even fell out with a member of Infa Riot, an Oi! band he had originally championed in the early eighties, because he was playing with a 'grey zone' band Mensi did not approve of.

'A lot of trouble came Mensi's way because he called others out for flip-flopping,' Newts had told me. 'He called those bands "fence-sitters", the sort who would say, "we're not political".'

In 2009 Jamie T briefly shone a spotlight on the Upstarts when he sampled a short Mensi speech from the band's 1981 live album. It was included on the hit album *Kings and Queens*. A few years later, Mensi was in the news again when he was one of the anti-fascist protestors arrested for 'breach of the peace' at an English Defence League march held in South Shields.

Derek Ridgers

Trouble from London: the best new Oi! band in a generation, Crown Court (Danny Swan, Jack Lewis, Trevor Taylor and Ralph Orton).

Martin Andersen

Crown Court's Trevor Taylor in action (in sheepskin jacket). An outtake from *Can't Smile Without You*, a book of photojournalism which documented Spurs fans home and away – Oi! is indelibly linked to football hooliganism.

'I'm Civilised': Oi! favourites Menace, a series of unseen photographs from the collection of drummer Noel Martin (top left, tank top). The death of Martin Webster (top right), the band's original singer, remains something of a mystery.

The band were followed by a coterie of clued-up skinheads, including future members of Madness, 4-Skins and The Last Resort.

All photos on this page: Noel Martin

Denis O'Regan/Getty Images

Classic Rock Magazine

Erica Echenberg

Hersham Boys: Sham 69 (above) became figureheads for the growing late-seventies skinhead revival. Singer Jimmy Pursey (top left) was left in tears after skinheads marred the band's headline slot at Reading Festival in 1978.

Pursey's songwriting partner, Sham guitarist Dave Parsons (top right, leather jacket), told me the band were 'infiltrated' by right-wing skins. 'It was almost like a Mafia-thing,' he said.

Pursey was the centre of a whirlwind of controversy, arrested (right) after a Sham gig on the rooftop of new Soho punk club, Vortex (note Menace's Noel Martin on the far left).

Avalon/Topfoto

Chris Wright

Gaz Douglass

Northeast Connection: Angelic Upstarts (top). Singer Mensi (Thomas Mensforth, RIP) raising a fist, Steve Forsten (with cigarette), Mond (Raymond Cowrie, leather jacket) and, on the right, Sticks (Keith Warrington).

Top Fellas: (above, from left of table), Gaz Stoker (Red London, Red Alert and Angelic Upstarts), Jonnie Halling (Crashed Out, Angelic Upstarts), Chris Wright (Crashed Out), Wright's pal George, Spin Brown (Crashed Out), Mensi, Steve Straughn (U.K. Subs) and Neil 'Newts' Newton (Angelic Upstarts).

Gaz Douglass (right), life-long friend of the Angelic Upstarts and a close associate of Mensi.

East End: The Cockney Rejects became the most successful of the first wave of post-punk Oi! bands (middle right, performing on *TOTP*). Singer Jeff Geggus was only 15 when he was first featured on the cover of *Sounds* (top left).

The 4-Skins founder, Tom McCourt, with brothers Mick and Jeff of the Rejects (bottom left, middle, Tom on the right) was a prominent Oi! figure.

A febrile atmosphere characterised the 4-Skins live gigs, culminating in the infamous Southall riot (top right).

Avalon/Topfoto

Tom McCourt

Graham Saxby

The Full Monty: Iconic Oi! band, The Last Resort. Teenage skin Mick Furbank deigned a series of graphics (top left) for the Last Resort shop (from which the band took their name) and designed the cover of the band's debut album (middle right).

Original singer Graham Saxby (middle left, yellow shirt) was superseded on vocals by bassist Roi Pearce (bottom left, in glasses) and with the addition of the older Arthur Kay (bottom left, right) the band began to fulfil their potential until violence at gigs closed them down in 1982.

Martin Dean

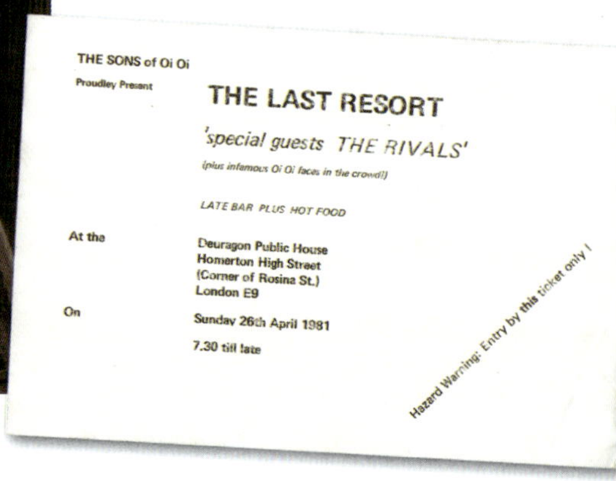

Graham Saxby

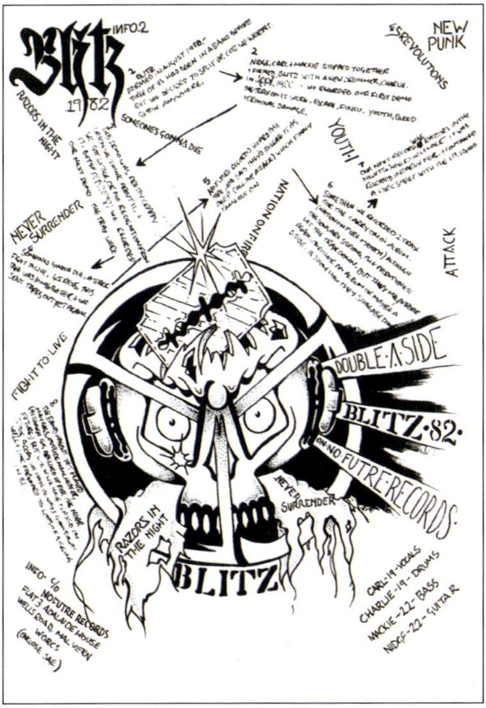

The Mancs: Blitz (bottom image, L-R) Neil McLennan, Carl Fisher, Charlie Howe and Nidge Miller RIP. Their debut 1981 EP, *All Out Attack*, was the beginning of a new, ferocious Oi! sound dubbed 'brick wall rock and roll'. Their graphics (top), created by bassist McLennan, were also popular. McLennan's designs can still be seen on tattoos, T-shirts and various merchandise today.

Blacklisted by the press: Combat 84 were the culmination of the first wave of British Oi!. (Middle right, L-R) Jim 'Gibson' Moncur, Brownie, Chris 'Chubby' Henderson (RIP), John 'Deptford' Armitage. The band only played live a handful of times before disbanding (top).

Armitage (centre left), is now one of the UK's most highly-regarded guitar technicians.

'The EDL tactics were similar to the NF,' Newts said to me when I'd mentioned the incident. 'I'm a Newcastle fan and St James's Park was infested with NF in that late seventies/early eighties period. More so than Sunderland. With the EDL, a load of the young 'uns at the matches got hooked in. It's the influence of older people and they will be flag shaggers [saying], we need to control immigration, same old story.'

I left the north-east with the impression that working with Mensi, in a band or otherwise, might not have been the easiest thing in the world. He had a temper, a nasty streak, mood swings, could turn violent. Someone even compared him to Ronnie Kray! There were hints that some of his behaviour: towards women but more frequently regarding money, did not chime with his left-wing persona.

In regard to his early-eighties experiences in London there was still some mystery attached. 'He told me he used to go to this pub in London and watch the football, and there used to be NF skinheads in there but he kind of tolerated them,' Wright told me. 'He said, I wasn't that outspoken then, I wasn't really that bothered because they were just idiots.'

As for his private life – all those children! More than the *Guardian* had reported. There were also whispers online that some of his Thai brides and girlfriends were underage but that was flatly denied by all those who knew him. He seemed to have a sense of humour about his promiscuity. 'Can't Help Falling In Love' by Elvis was one of the three songs played at his funeral.

There was one other final bit of north-east inter-band stuff to clear up with Stoker. Red London also shared a member with Skullhead, Raish Carter? 'He was the drummer when we first got the band together,' Stoker said. 'But he mugged somebody and got jailed and we kicked him out the band. In jail he met [Skullhead singer] Kev Turner and when he got out he joined Skullhead. Raish didn't understand the politics or what he was getting himself into. He was saying it was brilliant and he'd done this gig down in London and they were coming from all over Europe to watch them, but they didn't tell you where the venue was, you got directed, and they had these skinheads called "the security". I was horrified. I tried to tell him but he just looked puzzled . . . he wasn't really racist he just wanted to be in a band, and like I say he was easily led and very, very naive.'

There was a bit more to it. 'On one of Skullhead's albums we found out that they had recorded two Red London songs that Raish told them he'd written,' Gaz said. 'He'd heard a demo tape we recorded in 1985. One song was 'Wish the Lads Were Here'. There's still confusion online over that. We eventually got sick of people thinking they had written it so we re-recorded it for the *Symphony for the Skins* album to set the record straight.' It was the new Red London album. The band had reformed in 2018 at the request of Attila to support him at a one-off gig in Sunderland and decided to stick together, gigging regularly since, rediscovering the strong skinhead following they'd picked up in the mid-eighties.

I'd met Red London singer Patty Smith and drummer John Foster alongside Stoker. Foster laughed when he introduced himself and said he had also played drums in Red Alert and that his brother, Matty, had also drummed for both bands (good luck Pete Frame with this one). Patty was 60, a striking-looking skinhead, immaculately turned out. He talked a little about the method he had for bleaching his jeans back in the day and the skinhead crossover with mod revival bands in the late seventies. 'Secret

Affair, Purple Hearts, The Chords – those bands were also singing about the British way of life,' he said. I asked him what it felt like to be a skinhead in those times. 'People would look at us back then and think we were hooligans but Red London were always an anti-fascist band and always will be,' he said. 'But I can recall in Sunderland a black person taking one look at me and crossing the road, made me feel really uncomfortable – that's how bad it was, the perception. Skinheads got bad press and a minority of skins deserved it, but a lot of people tarred all skinheads with the same brush. Most skins were sound, just working-class lads.'

He knew Mensi back then, too. 'We all used to drink in a pub on the seafront in Sunderland called The Roker Hotel, and Mensi used to drink in there from time to time,' Patty said. 'One time we hadn't seen him for ages and he came in, a sheepskin coat on, and he said, come and have a look at my car. It was a big Rolls-Royce. It was one of the cars he was going to sell in London and he had borrowed it for the weekend to drive up to watch Sunderland play.'

Patty had written a poetry book, *Gutter Rhymes* (published in 2013) but I wasn't sure how to get something more poetic out of him. I mentioned to Patty the raw anger Mensi had in his voice as a young man and whether that was something he'd also felt at the time. 'Mensi was a miner at Westoe pit in South Shields,' he said. 'So I should imagine a lot of his aggression was coming through that lifestyle at the time – Thatcher's government in the north-east brought a lot of hatred out of a lot of people. We all felt it, all the early north-east punk bands. It was difficult circumstances we were living in at the time, mass unemployment, shipyards closing down, families on the breadline. Music was our escape.'

Chapter 4

I'm Not a Fool: Rejects

The explosion. Big bang. Fireworks. Crash! Crunch! Bang! Wallop! Bosh! The Cockney Rejects. The band who put the Oi!, Oi!, Oi! in Oi!

The teenage Geggus brothers from the east end. Both have written illuminating books. Jeff's *Cockney Reject* (2010) and Mick's *Life After Lloyd* [2019]. Together they've also produced a superb documentary about the band, *East End Babylon* (2012).

I saw them play the small upstairs room of the Star & Garter pub in Manchester. It was a Friday night, 25 November, 2022. Same night England played the USA in the World Cup. The place was packed with a couple of hundred old faces, punks and skins mainly, with a little firm of teen/early twenties skins going crazy down the front. The band ripped into the set like they were teenagers again. People said they'd never seen Vince Riordan so animated in years. Mick's guitar sounded astonishing.

Jeff was electric: grabbed the room straight off and never let the energy drop. When he wasn't singing, he was shadow-boxing. 'To me it's just about giving a show, whether you've got 150 people, or in the summer at some of the festivals with 15,000 people,' he'd told me when we finally sat down for a chat in the pub back room a couple of hours before the gig.

I'd been circling him since we first met at Rebellion in the summer. The band were great there, playing to 3,000 people on the main stage, but to see them up close in a small, dark, grimy pub, a shithole essentially, was something else. Somehow perfect. And they won't be playing such places again. The band had announced they were quitting after a final world tour in 2023.

Everyone said it: the Rejects were the real deal. Where everything culminated; a band who everyone else took a piece of afterwards. And it was all over in twelve months. They, like the Upstarts, hobbled on for a bit into the mid-eighties once the initial blaze burned itself out, and similarly came back for a long second act after their song 'I'm Not a Fool' was featured in a Levi's ad in 1999. But it was in that year, 1980, their pomp, when no one could touch them.

They released two albums, *Greatest Hits Vol. 1* and *Greatest Hits Vol. II* (both EMI) and both were great, but the debut was essential. Remains so. An Oi! cornerstone. They were the closest Britain ever got to having a band as superlative, devastating, brash, bratty, as the New York Dolls – a real them vs. everyone else gang, utterly alien and self-contained in their own little world. It is no surprise that one of their biggest cheerleaders is long-time Dolls obsessive Morrissey. He wrote the foreword to Jeff's book (more on this later).

Who was in their little gang? Who wasn't? It reads like a proper list of the good, the bad and the ugly of Oi!. Mostly they were West Ham hooligans, from the infamous Inner City Firm. All in their mid-to-late teens, early twenties tops. Some were Rejects road crew, others were there for the laugh, and a few would be called on whenever they were needed as 'unpaid security'. Many of them gravitated over from the Sham Army and Sham's road crew following Vince who joined the Rejects shortly after they released their first single, an EP, in August 1979. They were quite a rum bunch. Notorious. Some went on to critical acclaim, like young teen stalwart Grant Fleming, who became the official Primal Scream photographer. Others such as Carlton Leach became infamous (the film *Rise of The Footsoldier* was based on his memoir, *Muscle*). One or two ended up in prison. A few even formed their own Oi! bands.

Bizarre to think that the lad at the centre of all this was, in 1980, just 16. Jeff Geggus. Took the stage name Jeff 'Stinky' Turner. His right-hand man and sort of leader of the band was his older brother Mick, or Micky, who was just 19. Vince was 21. Vince's uncle was Krays associate Jack 'The Hat' McVitie, murdered by Reggie Kray in 1967.

Jeff and Mick were top amateur boxers. But they were something other than hard as nails: they were barmy. They came from, in Jeff's words, 'the arsehole of the east end', Custom House, but they still seemed to see everything in technicolour. They would make up superhero characters for themselves as per the Marvel comics they devoured, imagined Ilford as New York. Jeff was the fifth of seven, all in a tiny terrace house. Their dad was from Greek stock, hence Geggus, a dog trainer over at Walthamstow, then a dock worker, like his own dad. He was a Labour man but became disillusioned with the party when the docks began to close in '77, ripping the heart out of the east end, putting thousands on the scrap-heap.

At 13, Jeff had won the Essex Schoolboy Boxing Championship

and got to the British Schoolboy Finals, went on to represent England. He was no good at school, though, and hostile to teachers who he saw selling the SWP newspaper up Stratford market. In the late seventies one suspects, what with the NF having a strong foothold in east London, there was an atmosphere in Custom House. In his book, Jeff says he was nicked and found guilty, aged 14, for harassing an already harassed Asian man on the estate (the man regularly had his windows put through). Jeff was also done for threatening behaviour at a West Ham match but found not guilty. He'd been going to West Ham since he was 6 and one or two of his elder brothers were hooligans. Jeff always had tinpot bands on the go (The Postmen, The Shitters). Mick was more the go-getter type. He was the one who blagged Garry Bushell at *Sounds*, who blagged Jimmy to give them a break. From the get-go everyone who met Jeff and Mick couldn't help but be charmed; their cheek and front and perfect look, small and aggressive but somehow a bit cute. They didn't have a band or really any songs, had never played a gig, but that didn't stop them. Jimmy took them into the studio. Sham producer Pete Wilson played drums (they didn't have a drummer). Then Mick blagged Small Wonder Records in Walthamstow, who had signed The Cure and Menace, to put out the Rejects' debut EP. On the cover there was a picture of Jeff, Mick, Bushell and Jimmy in the studio. The standout track was 'Police Car'. One minute twenty-six seconds. At the start Jeff shouts, 'Freedom, there ain't no fucking freedom', and then the band shoulder-barge in. 'I like punk and I like Sham. I got nicked over West Ham,' shouts Jeff, introducing himself to the world.

What was immediately apparent was Jeff's voice was special in a way that put him above Jimmy and Mensi. Morrissey wrote that he sounded as if he was singing 'in order to avoid murdering someone'. It was a bionic voice, thick with cockney and a hint of lisp, so full and furious but clear as a bell. It was quite insane. Absolute cartoon.

The EP sold 30,000 copies and was an indie number one. *Sounds*, Bushell particularly, went to town on them. He called them 'the real Sham', the 'new punk', 'harder than the rest'. They never really got much praise from the *NME* but by then *Sounds* had started to outsell all its weekly music press rivals anyway.

Jimmy got stuck in: he and manager Tony Gordon. They got the Rejects a deal with EMI (a massive £140,000 four-album deal) and Jimmy (and Pete Wilson) set to producing their debut album. Like the first Upstarts record you can hear Jimmy all over it, especially the first EMI single 'I'm Not A Fool/East End' (with its massive terrace-chant chorus). Mick was said to be playing through Steve Jones's Pistols guitar/amp set-up. It sounded that way. 'Bad Man', the second EMI single, was a beaten dog howl, quite revealing. 'Fighting in the Street' was all front, about aggro at footy, anthemic, threatening, slightly daft, right in your face. They even had a song about their own gang on the album: 'Join the Rejects' ('and get yourself killed'). 'Here comes the new punk,' Jeff started this one with. The only whiff of politics was a line about 'wankers hand out leaflets, better not come near me'. Jeff said they hated 'the hippy Left'.

'We stand for punk as bootboy music,' Jeff told *Sounds*. 'Harringtons, boots, straights [straight-leg jeans], that's what we're all about.'

On stage they were shaky. Raw. Off colour. Off key. Their first drummer ran a fruit-and-veg stall. They were careless with their image, forever flashing the Vs in photos or gurning ugly faces (an everlasting Oi! image is Jeff doing both on the cover of the first Oi! compilation album). Jeff was photographed wearing a Union Jack T and a Sex Pistols T with a swastika on it. He also wore pyjamas on stage. They used a Union Jack flag that had the West Ham crossed hammer logo across it as a backdrop. Mick had an armful of tattoos. They never did cash in on Jeff and Mick's puppy-dog pin-up pop-star appeal. Instead, they always looked ugly. Volatile.

Incidents piled up. Mick gave a journalist a couple of backhanders in the *Sounds* office. They ransacked the recording studio, nicked loads of gear. Early on there was an infamous kick-off at a 'Pursey's Package' night at the Moonlight Club, Hampstead. Then Jimmy and Tony Gordon sorted it for them to support the Upstarts at the Electric Ballroom. July 1979.

They did their spot, a bit underwhelming, the album wasn't out yet. It was what happened when the Upstarts were on that really opened eyes. The Rejects gang saw there was a mob of about forty skinheads, a BM/NF mob, causing problems at the front, lots of Sieg Heil-ing. The Rejects gang were no angels. And many of them would have known some BM/NF skins, especially the West Ham ones.

In fact, at the first or second Rejects gig, at the Bridgehouse in Canning Town in September '79, some of the most notorious BM faces – the ones who had caused Sham problems – were there. It was the same gang of West Ham skins who'd turned a small corner of Upton Park during the 1978–79 season into a pit of racial hatred, 'Sieg Heil' and 'Ain't no black in the Union Jack' chants, bananas thrown at black players.

'We were prepared to tolerate them as long as they didn't cause us any grief,' said Jeff. 'Our firm was heavier, but they were older and we were a bit wary. They had a reputation.' Among them were two notorious brothers. 'They were out-and-out Hitler-ites, Himmler-ites, they could have been Goebbels' God kids,' Jeff said. 'I was a kid then, they came to the Bridgehouse a couple of times, but we were ready to front them, they never ever came near us.'

Jeff even belittled the BM in *Sounds*, called them 'the German Movement'. There were no skinheads among the Inner City Firm by this time, most were now casuals. And the BM skinheads were unpopular with the ICF because they never appeared to travel to away games. 'Me and Micky would go into pubs and people would look at you and go, well you're supposed to be on our side,' Jeff wrote in his book. 'I'd reply, no we just go to football.'

The lot causing trouble for the Upstarts at the Ballroom were said to be mostly north London, some associated with the Madness crew, with maybe a few Chelsea FC skinheads in the mix. Mick had had a recent run-in with Brendan Smyth, Madness co-founder Chas Smash's brother, at a party in Islington. Mensi up on stage was concerned but doing nothing about some punks getting bashed about by the skinheads, Jeff said. Vince said, 'Fuck it,' and him and H – former Sham roadie Steve Harmer – led the charge, with Hoxton Tom (£150 mohair suit, light blue Perry and Hush Puppies) right behind. It was quite brutal.

Jeff, only just turned 16, said in his book he had mixed feelings about this vicious fight. He was worried his band would never be booked for another gig, sorry for Mensi, but they *had* saved the punks a serious beating. Anyway, he wrote in his book: 'It was out of my hands.' This was his gang. 'That's how they operate,' he wrote. 'Unfortunately, from that day on I was in.'

It's difficult to be precise on the dates, Bushell says February 1980, but there was another infamous run-in between the Rejects and the BM skinheads, this time the east London/West Ham contingent, said to have been sparked by the BM beating up a black skinhead from Becontree. Jeff said there was 'twenty of us and twenty-five of them'. H, he said, smashed their leader. 'We decimated them.'

This period just after the first album came out (and made number twenty-two in the UK), 'March and May 1980' said Jeff in his book, was 'the best it ever got for me'. Their breakthrough single, 'The Greatest Cockney Rip-off', a Jimmy co-write, went to number twenty-one in the charts: Jeff was actually 15 when he mimed to the song for his *Top of the Pops* debut. It was swiftly followed in the charts by a new single, 'I'm Forever Blowing Bubbles', a tie-in with West Ham's appearance in the FA Cup final. In the space of six weeks they were on *Top of the Pops* three times. Predictably their entourage had caused chaos at the BBC. H threatened to kill Steve Wright; Jeff had tried to strangle someone; Mick punched someone else.

From 'Bubbles' on it was downhill, swift and cruel. First, they fell out with Jimmy. Many reasons. He was wearing a poncho and a beret. 'Lost the plot . . . thought he was Clint Eastwood and a Messiah for the kids,' said Jeff. He reckoned he'd made the Rejects but now they wouldn't listen to him. They thought the lyrics he wanted them to sing were naff. Then the Rejects and a few road crew barged in on him recording a solo album and there was a big punch-up with some locals in a boozer nearby during which Jimmy got sparked. There were also issues with Jimmy's younger brother, Robbie, whose band with Grant Fleming often supported the Rejects.

They also found that having aligned themselves so openly to West Ham and the ICF, their gigs became sort of football match extensions and rival firms sought them out. The most famous one was in Birmingham. Ended in mass violence. Some of the Rejects road crew were glassed and stabbed. Mick was hospitalised after being hit with a glass ashtray. Jeff said it was very 'traumatic'. The next day some of the Rejects gang went looking for revenge. Mick was among them. He was charged with GBH, malicious wounding and affray – the police said he was looking at a five-year stretch.

Liverpool went off too. In other places the problems of footy-related violence and far-right skinhead violence conflated. Huddersfield. Leeds. It was a mess. The media grew increasingly wary. In London, the ICF went at it with Arsenal outside a gig at the Electric Ballroom. It was the same in Europe: a brawl with far-right skins in West Ham shirts in Berlin, a riot in Paris after three songs. 'I now understood why Pursey just quit,' Vince said.

And just like Sham, as live shows turned to bloodbaths, they continued to sell records. *Greatest Hits Vol. II* made number twenty-three in October 1980, and in November they were all over Bushell's first Oi! compilation. Their track 'Oi!, Oi!, Oi!' opened the compilation and they also had another track, 'Here We Go Again', included on it. There were also two tracks by Jeff's revived schoolboy band, The Postmen, and Mick teamed up with Grant Fleming as Terrible Twins for 'Generation of Scars'. That's five of the seventeen tracks. Jeff gave his everlasting quote about Oi! to *Sounds*: 'Oi! is bootboy music for the working class and if you ain't working class you'll get a kick in the bollocks.'

Problems mounted for the band: Jeff got done for GBH after a fight outside EMI. Both he and Mick were involved in a family-related street fight 'beef' that saw Jeff charged with another GBH and Mick with another GBH and wounding.

Then in December 1980 ITV ran the documentary that finished them. It was part of the channel's *TV Eye* current affairs strand, about the 'alarming growth' of the right-wing British Movement. The show began with a segment showing a BM march. Although membership of the BM was said to be 4,000 in 1980, police outnumbered the 600 turn-out, the bulk of which were skinheads, teenagers. Then in a sit-down interview one BM member, disguised, talked about being asked to beat people up: 'Jews, Catholics, Protestants, coloureds,' he said. He himself specifically hated blacks. Said the BM organised attacks on blacks. He'd been away on a BM training camp, Bradley Moor, some of the instructors were in the army. The main BM political thrust, he explained, was towards devotion to Nazi Germany and Hitler and the leaders had forged links with the KKK and fascist/terrorist organisations in Ireland, Germany, Holland, France, Belgium.

Next, the documentary showed a speech being made on the march by the BM's then-leader Michael McLaughlin, aged 40, a survivalist, ran army surplus stores. There were more young skinheads watching, some of these likely to be 'Leader Guard', supposedly McLaughlin's personal bodyguards. The narrator said this lot liked their music 'loud and violent'. The documentary segued straight into the Rejects, who had agreed to be filmed live at the Bridgehouse playing 'War on the Terraces' from the second album. The narrator said: 'They have a strong BM following and some of their audience was on the march. It is at rock concerts like these and football matches in the east end where BM recruiters are active.' There were only one or two skins in the Bridgehouse footage, most were casuals (and it's disputable how many had been on the BM march).

Jeff said the band agreed to appear because they'd thought the documentary was going to be about football violence. When they saw it, they asked their manager Tony Gordon to sue. It was too late to rescue their reputation, though. Even when Jeff and Mick somehow avoided jail for the various bits of violence (both got suspended sentences), they were doomed. In the short term they had to soldier on, planning another EMI album and a new half-cocked new wave rock direction, Jeff's voice smoothed out to sound like Billy Idol. A live album *Greatest Hits Vol. 3 Live & Loud* (recorded at Abbey Road studios) made number twenty-seven in April 1981, but by then the band was a husk.

When Southall happened in July 1981 and Oi! was also linked to far-right skinheads, it was game over. They weren't at the gig. 'We weren't even on [second Oi! comp] *Strength Thru Oi!*,' Jeff protested. In fact, he publicly declared the band were disassociating themselves from the Oi! movement completely. Didn't matter. Their reputation was mud. Venues refused to book them and record stores refused to stock them. The new album bombed. EMI dropped them. Jeff had just turned 17. He was soon signing on the dole.

I met him at Rebellion. I'd been told, despite their reputations, both he and his brother were the sweetest of guys. He was stood by an impressive Rejects merch stall, chatting amiably to fans as a couple of women flogged the gear. He looked healthy. Flat cap. Capped T. I told him he looked 'fighting fit'. He said he was still doing his boxing training. He also did a lot of running and tennis. Didn't drink. He seemed full of life and good cheer.

Jeff said he didn't like Oi! music, never had, preferred ZZ Top and Led Zeppelin, The Doors, Hendrix.

'I'll be brutally honest with you, Si,' he said. 'See this Oi! thing? What the fuck is it? I didn't want to be part of no movement. We were our own gang. I did love seventies punk, The Stranglers, Clash, early Damned, Ramones, Gen X, Skids, that was my punk but what it morphed into is not me.'

He was interested in the book I'd done on Steve Marriott, said he liked the Small Faces and in the mid-eighties, after two heavy metal/rock Rejects albums on independent labels had flopped and an American tour bombed, explained how Mick had talked Marriott into trying to produce the band. 'It was a disaster,' laughed Jeff. 'He was in a terrible state.' After that, Jeff took up painting and decorating. A few years later, in 1989, he allowed Mick to talk him into doing a few gigs in Europe and recording one more album, in a studio that was 'above [a] hairdressers in Hastings'. Then they'd knocked it on the head for ten years.

He told me the story I knew already. It was his stock go-to when talk turned to Oi!. How the Oi! genre got its name. The Rejects were reviewed at a gig in Leeds in February/March 1980 by a short-lived music paper *New Music News*, 'not the *NME*,' Jeff stressed. The gig was panned and the reviewer had said Jeff 'could only muster three words between songs, Oi!, Oi!, Oi!'. The band found that funny and wrote a song with that title for their second album. 'All of a sudden, God bless Garry, I love him, he's a good mate, it was Oi! the Album and Oi! this and that,' Jeff said. 'I never wanted to be a part of that.'

I told him I'd read his and Mick's books and one Bushell had recommended to me called *Legacy: Gangsters, Corruption and the*

London Olympics (Bloomsbury, 2019). It was about the turf wars in east London that had erupted after the deprived borough of Newham became the location for the Olympic Park and land prices went through the roof. It centred on 'the Long Fella', Canning Town's David Hunt, but there were a few of the old Rejects firm mentioned, quite a lot of action going on around the Peacock pub and gym which Jeff had a long association with, gone now. He looked impressed and I later found out he loved crime books, Mafia stuff especially.

I said I didn't want to ask about the band, I knew most of the story, but I did have a few questions and maybe we could do an interview later in the year at the gig in Manchester. He thought I was still talking about the crime families of east London and said, 'You ask away, Si, but I've got a good reputation so whether I answer or not is another thing.'

More fans were waiting. The Rejects were playing later that day, Saturday, in the main room, 8 p.m. just before headliners Cock Sparrer. 'Make sure you come to the talk, Si,' Jeff said. Sunday, early afternoon, he was due to speak at the literary stage. I'd seen a few interview/Q&As in this room over the four days (including a rather stilted one with Roi of the Resort) but nothing compared to what Jeff summoned. The room was packed, all the chairs taken and many more stood in the space at the back and sides. And this was no Q&A. Once he was introduced Jeff talked, and talked, and talked, non-stop for almost eighty minutes. I've transcribed it. There was endless laughs but at about the sixty-minute mark you sensed Jeff was getting overwhelmed, by the story, but also by how warmly he was being received in the room. I started to well up too. He eventually cracked and let out a few sobs, tears. The crowd stood and applauded. For a long time. Jeff recovered, continued. It was just incredible.

He told us the story of his childhood. His parents were quiet people, never argued or fought in front of the kids, no swearing. 'I think they had seven bunk-ups and seven kids,' Jeff said. He talked about school ('It was like Colditz for me, school: any lesson they put me in, I was like an officer, it was my mission to escape'), about discovering boxing, West Ham and punk music. 'Me and Mick wouldn't discuss the music,' he said. 'I'd look at the bass players and say, who do you think would win a straight-up out of Jean-Jacques Burnel out of The Stranglers and Paul Simonon out of The Clash?'

Jeff said that regarding music he 'always believed there was a lot of theatre in it' – which I thought was quite telling. He talked about how the band developed, from him bashing away on a couple of Quality Street tins with a spoon to Mick getting Vince Riordan to join. 'I went, oh not that cunt.' Cue laughter. 'Vince had a fearful reputation, he was a few years older, been in borstal, this and that, ICF, and all that game. He was a good thief, too. He turned up at rehearsals and he'd just nicked a Fender bass.' More laughter.

Jeff said he was still at school when they got the EMI deal. 'We got 500 quid each,' he said. 'I've got it all in pound notes, made a rare appearance at school, straight up to the tuck shop and went, who wants what? I didn't touch drugs or alcohol so I bought an Atari Space Invaders, about 120 quid, pair of Dr. Martens [with steel toe-caps] and took my young brother Trevor, with an old dolls pram from the shed, and cleared this shop out of 200 quid of fireworks.' He galloped right on through the fight with BM at the Upstarts gig. 'We lost our cherry there,' he said.

'We made a stand, that we were not gonna have this 'cos the BM skinheads ruined Sham, they ruined the Upstarts. God bless Mensi but he was crying on stage. I thought, that will never happen to me and my firm.'

He talked a little about the road crew, the fighting at gigs, described a vicious fight he had with Mick at a gig in Sheffield from which he still carried a scar, and the fall-out with Jimmy, how Jimmy's little brother Robbie didn't help Mick when he was arrested after the Birmingham fight. But he said what had really done the band in was cocaine, which he said he was deadly set against for about ten minutes. More laughter.

He was painfully honest about life once EMI dropped them. 'I was quite embarrassed,' he said. 'I'd made a go of it and it flopped. Fifty per cent was our own fault, we were divs, we went about things the wrong way.' He described the 'heavy metal thing' as a 'pipe dream'. He said when he was doing that he had 'grand delusions that somehow we'd break through and I'd be able to get back to what I was doing'.

He talked about the Rejects comeback. How it started. 'I got a call from my brother about 3 a.m., he was pissed. I said, fuck off I've got to be up for work at five. He said, there's a Levi's ad featuring 'I'm Not a Fool''. Jeff said he got paid about £600 for the ad and 'had a holiday in Butlin's with my ex-wife and kids'.

After the Levi's ad, people wanted to book the band again, offering decent money. They got Tony Van Frater on board. 'I was very worried, very scared about getting on stage again but then things started snowballing,' he said. They played all over Europe, Japan and America to big crowds, especially at festivals – Rebellion, Punk Rock Bowling, Punk & Disorderly – and then they did it again, more territories, never stopped.

'The West Ham thing all those years ago worked against us,' Jeff said. 'But now I'm going across the planet, places like Argentina, Mexico, Chile, even El Salvador, and there's people decked out in West Ham stuff but we're getting no stick.'

Then, he said, the call came, 'the crowning glory'. 2016. West Ham played their last game at Upton Park and the Rejects were asked to play. Vince was back following the death of Van Frater.

'We turned up and they had the little stage in the middle of the pitch,' Jeff said. 'We could tell we was outcasts but I couldn't give a fuck. Pissing down with rain and all the players had to stand there and watch the four men they couldn't hang doing 'Bubbles'. They probably hated every minute and I thought, good, have that you cunts. All the years I've paid to see you and all the disappointment you've given us, have some of me.

'That might have been a good time to go out but you always want more,' he said. 'It was very bitter-sweet and I'm proud of that moment because we were the last people to walk off of that ground. It was bitter-sweet knowing I'd never go over there again and that was the greatest upbringing in life you could probably have going over them terraces.'

This was when the tears fell. Everyone stood. Clapped. 'I've never been like this,' he said composing himself. 'It makes me very humble. I've been a lucky, lucky, lucky fucker in my life. Someone comes up to me and asks for a photograph – I'm honoured they want that. No one's pestering me because it's you, you are the people who make it. If other bands haven't got time to answer a text or stop for a photo or sign this and that, that makes 'em wankers. The bands would be fuck all without you.'

The floor was briefly opened up. Someone asked about the fall-out with Jimmy, which seemed to have grown bitter. 'Stems from a lot of things,' he said. He told a story about the Rejects being booked to do Sham's 40th anniversary show at Norwich Waterfront in 2017 but Jimmy 'got on his high horse and said, I don't want them, I don't want an Oi! band [the Upstarts supported Sham that night instead]. I could go into deeper things with him as well . . . what people don't know, maybe they do know, he's on the Sex Offenders Register.'

When asked, he said he didn't live in London any more but his mum, who was 90, still lived in the same house he'd grown up in. She'd been there since 1932, had been born in that house herself. He said he didn't like London any more. 'There's all high-rise penthouse apartments on one side of Custom House, but you come over the other side, just across the bridge, and it's the second most deprived borough in London and one of the most deprived in the country.'

The next time I saw him was in Manchester. The Rejects had released their new album, *Power Grab*, in the interim and announced a swathe of farewell tour dates around the world. I started out asking him about Morrissey.

'In 2003/4 somebody told me he came on stage and said, tonight – y'know like [TV show] *Stars in Their Eyes* – I'm gonna be Stinky Turner. I thought it was a wind-up but they were saying, no he's a massive fan. And then it come round to doing my book and Blake Publishing had an email from Morrissey, he wants to do the foreword. So I went, right, let Morrissey do it, then. I thought what he wrote was really funny.

'I didn't really get to meet him, though,' Jeff admitted. 'He asked us to do Morrissey's Meltdown at the big venue on the South Bank [the Royal Festival Hall, 2004], it was quite a weird line-up: he had what was left of the New York Dolls,

The Ordinary Boys, Nancy Sinatra. I went to the gig thinking we'd meet but his band said he was having a "no talk" day. When we went on stage, I looked up and, having a laugh, I said something to the effect of, you ignorant cunt, if you don't come down and say hello, after you've invited us here, when I see you I'll cut your fucking quiff off, and the crowd started laughing.

'After we played the gig, he used to send these mad emails to Micky – all in the space of about two weeks, constant. He'd ask things like, you train at the Peacock Gym, do you think that's doing a disservice to peacocks? And, if they do a film of your life am I alright to play your Uncle Bert? Mental stuff but nice mental, I suppose. Then the emails just stopped. I admire that, if someone's off the wall like that – a bit of mystery about someone.'

He said he thought he knew why Morrissey had such an affinity with the band. 'Somebody said to me that in 1980, in Manchester, he ran into these skinheads who were going to beat him up because he looked a bit weird or something and he said, don't do that, I'm into what you're into – my favourite band are the Cockney Rejects. Apparently they said, sing the lyrics of one of the songs, and he sang 'Subculture', one of the songs on *Greatest Hits Vol. II*. And they went, you're cushty mate, you're with us. I don't know if that's true. I'm grateful he wrote the foreword for the book. For someone mainstream – in a way – to be in your corner was good: we never had no fucker in our corner so fair play to him.'

He was far less benevolent about Jimmy, brought out a bit of a nasty side. He still seemed put out about being 'fucked over' by Sham in 2017. 'I always said, he helped us a lot on that first album and I'll always be thankful for that,' he said. 'That's why I can't see why there was a rift. He's an arrogant cunt, horrible.'

It was what he said about Jimmy being a sex offender at his Rebellion talk that I was most interested in. I said, I felt maybe it was a bit harsh. Could he not contextualise the offence?

'Listen, I could see he was fucked up when I was [a] 15-year-old kid and he produced our album when he'd have been 24, 25. Being streetwise, you could see somebody who was falling apart,' he said. 'And I definitely do think there are connotations from that Walton Hop but you got to say these things. I'm a grandfather and father and it's just not right in my book. He's a sex offender. I don't give a fuck, he can't sue me, can he? I won't take that back. He's a sex offender. That's it. A paedo is a paedo in my book. There's a few of them about.'

It was getting closer to the gig. The doors were open. There was one last thing I wanted to ask, something which always baffled me. I'd read or been told some quite problematic things about a few of the skinhead faces around Sham who had subsequently followed the Rejects. I mentioned a few names, one who road-managed the Rejects for a short period. 'They were a lot older than me but they never had any right-wing affiliations when they were with us,' Jeff said. 'I suppose you can get tainted. When Sham come about in 1977 and then 'Borstal Breakout' in 1978, all of a sudden you started noticing the rebirth of skinheads and you heard these horror stories about the National Front thing – but we were never skinheads and as for them neo-Nazi skinheads, we were their nemesis, mate.'

I asked Jeff about Gary Hodges, the 4-Skins singer (see next chapter)?

'Hodges and H, they were more Poplar boys, Canning Town,' he said. 'I remember Gary [Hodges] coming into a rehearsal room near Poplar, in 1979, just before we signed to EMI. He come in there. Hello Gal. Hello Jeff. And that was it. When we come with the band, we had the Sham following and we had a lot of "Glory Boys", who'd been following [mod revival band] Secret Affair.'

Grant Fleming was one of the Glory Boys, a mob of about 100 east end mods and skins, mostly West Ham. Hoxton Tom, although he supported Tottenham, was probably the most infamous.

'I knew Tom well,' Jeff said. 'Tom was [a] good man.'

He mentioned some of the names I'd first brought up, a little agitated. 'Because it was an east London thing and West Ham, there was all sorts who came to follow the Rejects,' he said. 'For me, going over West Ham was with my mates, my own little mob from Custom House. I knew people who followed Secret Affair, suedeheads and this and that, but I wasn't knocking about with no skinheads. Yes, I used to love a fight over the football but only when I was 15/16. I never hurt anyone. I was just wrapped up in it.' He pointed to a prominent scar on his brow. 'Look at the Mars Bar down my face, I got another one there. They were naughty times, mate, you were fighting for your life. That's what it was. It wasn't the politics for me it was the football. We was West Ham. I enjoyed a punch-up until it got too much and when I got to the age of 17, I walked away; thought, fuck this.

'Let me tell you this: nobody ever showed that [right-wing side] in front of us, and if they did, they would have been gone, they would have been fucked off. We were boxing boys, me and my brother, we were Custom House, different mentality to a lot of them, we're not even Canning Town, we're Custom House, there was a divide there. And most of the hangers-on, where do they go? They all fuck off, most of your entourage, when your money is gone anyway. They come and stay at a nice Holiday Inn with you, when you're doing well, all jibbing in, then you don't see 'em when things start to go badly.'

Then he surprised me.

'At that time there was a lot of heavy, heavy British Movement and right-wing people saying what they were going to do to us,' Jeff said. 'My mum used to get phone calls: I'm so-and-so from the British Movement, tell your sons I'm going to shoot 'em. They would never leave a name. We used to drink in a pub called the Barge Aground in Barking and they started getting in there so I said, if you want to meet . . .'

He went on: 'I'm not a Nazi, fucking hell, I come from Greek immigrant stock, I boxed in boxing clubs all my life which was a mix of black and white kids. I wouldn't have personally known about any of our lot who had any links to that, but I do know when we went to fight them neo-Nazi cunts, at Barking station, H and Hoxton Tom and the crew who were with us absolutely battered the fuck out of them.'

Jeff seemed regretful about the 'politics bollocks' that had attached itself to the Rejects. 'I wouldn't say jealous but when I see, on the heavy metal scene, bands like Saxon, there's no politics,' he said. 'There's no cunt down the front going, fuck off you cunt, and giving it all that, you don't get that – they are there for the music, they enjoy it. I'd have loved some of that instead of all the grief and aggravation. But it is what it is, you can't have it all.'

People now wanted to shake his hand, have their photo taken with him, sign some merch. I asked why, aged 58, with the Rejects seemingly more popular than ever he'd decided to quit.

'I've got no mates in the game,' he said. 'I don't knock about with anyone; all my mates are fucking worlds apart from this game.' And the game, he said, was 'on its knees, finished.'

'Geezers at Rebellion, no disrespect, God bless 'em but you've got 70-year-old punks in tartan trousers; the guts have gone out of this game,' he said. 'You've got to be true to yourself – I wouldn't write a song now about fighting and throwing bottles. If there's bands in their 50s, 60s, singing about how they wanna have a riot, then grow up . . . because you're not doing that.

'Never fake who you are, just be straight,' he said. 'I was living that life what I was screaming and shouting about it. I don't live that life no more. I'm one of the most boring geezers in the world. I don't do fuck all. All I do is train hard for my gigs so I can jump around at places like this.'

He suggested if festivals like Rebellion wanted to rejuvenate themselves, they should put young bands 'like Crown Court' on the main stage as headliners, not the same old acts like the 'Rejects, Sparrer, Sham . . .'

Two young skinheads wanted their T-shirts signing. I recognised them from Rebellion where, as Jeff said, youth did tend to catch the eye.

'I've fought all my battles,' Jeff said to me before he got up to go. 'I'm having one more year at it next year and that's my lot. I'm going to fuck off. I'll still play the odd festival here and there but all the touring, going out seven or eight dates on the trot, I don't want to do that any more. Sometimes it's best to try and grow old a little bit gracefully.'

Chapter 5

Chaos: 4-Skins/Last Resort/Business

'A violent culture, a violent time, that's the way it used to be. Everybody needed money, everyone was pissed off.'

Roi Pearce, origin unknown

'The utter pits of rock'n'roll.'

Ian Penman, *NME*, review of *Oi! The Album*

Garry Bushell put the 4-Skins on the cover of *Sounds* straight off before they had a single out. 1 November. 1980. A picture of Gary Hodges aggressively pointing straight down the lens, skinhead with parting shaved in, shirt, braces, slacks. Cover headline: 'Your Country Doesn't Need You: New Punk'. Inside, across the spread (Hodges pictured in a green flight jacket) was the headline, 'The New Breed: A Teenage Warning' and a subdeck that just quoted Hodges' lyrics from their song 'Chaos', one of two tracks the 4-Skins had on *Oi! The Album*. It called for 'civil war now' with 'skinheads taking over'.

'Chaos' was produced by Mick from the Rejects. The music

throbbed and it had a lovely simple guitar hook. What stood out, marked the band, was Hodges' voice. It was astonishingly violent and threatening. This was next level, more crazed than Jeff. It sounded as if Hodges was beating someone up, putting the boot in as he sang. And the 'Chaos' lyrics *Sounds* didn't print were even more brutal. 'People we don't beat up, we're going to fucking shoot,' Hodges threatened.

Bushell wrote that the 4-Skins had been a band for around a year, part of the Rejects-led 'east end punk revival'. They had started playing as more of a laugh, similar to another Canning Town/Poplar band, Barney & The Rubbles (who were also on the first Oi! comp and who Hoxton Tom also played with). Now, wrote Bushell, they 'have seriously reformed' and were at 'the vanguard of an exciting and dynamic, but often disturbing, new breed of punk bands.

'Born from the Pistols via Menace, Sham and Skrewdriver, and in the pioneering wake of the Rejects and the Upstarts, this new breed are blowing up in your face,' Bushell continued.

H, from the Rejects road crew, played guitar and Skully, also of the Rejects road crew, was supposedly the 4-Skins manager. Skully also played in a few bands himself: Barney & The Rubbles, East End Badoes and East End Loonies. His music career was short-lived, however. He was sent down on murder charges relating to football violence, and when found not guilty after serving twenty-one months on remand, fetched up with a twenty-year sentence relating to armed robbery and an audacious helicopter rescue of two prisoners from Gartree Prison.

Even before he was on the cover of *Sounds*, unemployed bricklayer Hodges, 21, was already notorious. He was known to be one of the earliest second-generation skinheads and got his mug on telly in '79, the main voice in a short feature on ITV's *The London Weekend Show* presented by Janet Street-Porter, which explored the skinhead revival, and the Sham Army, as skinheads became a much more visible cult in London.

Hodges was interviewed alongside three other well-known Sham Army faces, in a Canning Town boozer; the area, said Street-Porter, where the revival started eighteen months ago. He explained the appeal the look had for him back in '77: 'You're different ain't you? You're jack the lad, you're walking along the road and you get people looking at you and they sort of stand back, they don't want to come too close.'

Hodges and his mates had the boots but weren't skinheads any more. They had short hair, wore shirts, V-necks, jeans, slacks. Hodges did have a Crombie but they all looked more like casuals than skins. Street-Porter said none of the current skinheads she'd spoken to were members of the BM or the NF, though some had been last year. Hodges said: 'A lot of them are in the NF, I reckon. They started off earlier in the year, jumped on the bandwagon, followed along with all the BM skinheads 'cos they started getting a bit of publicity in the press going to Sham concerts.'

He added: 'A few skinheads were in it [the BM]. I was in it and a couple of other blokes was in it [nodding at the other three lads] but we've left it now. There's still a few in there and they carry on with it 'cos they're anti-black, anti-this, anti-Communist and all this.' His words picked up pace. 'I mean they've got to live with the people. Most of them in the Socialist Workers Party who's against the NF, talking about living together and all that jazz, they're all living out in the sticks. They don't have to live with the people. When you don't have to live with the blacks or the communists that's when you say, oh everyone live together, because they got the money to move out the place, the money to move out the area.'

The 'seriously reformed' 4-Skins had only a tiny repertoire of songs, all seemingly specifically tailored towards a skinhead audience, and they hadn't really done any proper gigs per se, just fucked about on stage for a few minutes at various places (Mick had briefly played drums). The other song they had on the Oi! comp was 'Wonderful World', a riff on the famous song but where things were less than wonderful – police harassment, unemployment, knife crime. Clocked in at 1 min 38 secs. They'd actually recorded three songs for the comp, but EMI had refused to include 'A.C.A.B.' (All Coppers Are Bastards, 1 min 29 secs).

Besides Hodges, there were two other crucial members of the 4-Skins. On bass was Hoxton Tom, 19, who put down as a job in *Sounds*: engineer. Tom had earned a reputation as a trendsetter: early punk, then one of the first of the second wave of skinheads, and latterly an early mod revivalist. He'd been a face around Menace, Sham, Secret Affair and the Rejects, big and game. Photographed for *Sounds*, he had a suedehead, wore a shirt and tank top, cravat and Crombie.

The other face was drummer Gary Hitchcock, 23 years old, a plasterer. He was also one of the first skinhead revivalists, said to have adopted the look as early as 1976, when there was only about thirty of them. Hitchcock told *Sounds*: 'When it started it was extreme to be NF. There was only a few of us who were BM. I used to think it was great but the BM hated us and slung us out. They thought we were degenerates for going to gigs. I'm not political any more.'

He added: 'Sham 69 were the first band we followed but Jimmy used us. He dressed like us and he encouraged us to come but as soon as he started getting famous, he didn't want to know. He started slagging us off in the music press.'

Like H (who told *Sounds*, 'We've got nothing to do with politics. There's nothing worth voting for. They're all the same'), Hitchcock wasn't in the 4-Skins for very long. He became their manager instead. What was troubling to discover was that his interest in the extreme did not seem to have ended as he claimed. I read, in a book called *White Nationalist Skinhead Movement: UK & USA, 1979-1993* by Eddie Stampton and Robert Forbes (2015), that he was a face at 'white power' gigs in the mid-eighties. The book portrayed him as being active in that scene. In another book, *White Riot: The Violent Story of Combat 18* by Nick Lowles (2001; Lowles is chief executive of HOPE Not Hate and former editor of anti-fascist magazine *Searchlight*), I read that Hitchcock was a member of, and had been active in the founding of, the notorious neo-Nazi terrorist group Combat 18 in 1992. Lowles wrote that Hitchcock, 'solidly built and short-tempered', joined the NF before switching to the BM, where he was one of the Leader Guard, and had drifted towards the BNP in the late eighties.

After the *Sounds* cover, the 4-Skins recorded two new tracks, '1984' [George Orwell's *Nineteen Eighty-Four* had become a key Oi!/skinhead-reference book alongside *Skinhead* and *A Clockwork Orange*] and 'Sorry', for the *Strength Thru Oi!* comp, released in May 1981. The album was another *Sounds*/Bushell effort but this time not on EMI but another major label, Decca. By now the 4-Skins had acquired a new drummer and guitarist and could actually play live as a proper band, and in June 1981 this new line-up cut a John Peel session (it never aired – ditched in the uproar after Southall).

Around this time Hodges told *Rising Free* fanzine he'd like to do the band full-time but had got 'a wife and kids to support'. He also talked more generally about the Oi! scene. He drew a direct lineage between his band and Menace 'because they were a working-class band'. Not Sham. 'I knew Sham personally 'cos I used to hang around with them,' he said. 'They weren't really a working-class band, it was all put on, really. The bands that are around now are the real thing.'

Who else was around? Hodges and Hoxton Tom both especially praised The Last Resort and The Business. They were the other two bands who played Southall alongside the 4-Skins. There had been a meeting of minds when the three bands (plus Max Splodge and Cock Sparrer) played at the Bridgehouse in May 1981, a birthday party bash/gig for Bushell who was turning 26.

There was talk of these bands sticking together and forming their own label, Clockwork Fun. The first single to emerge was the 4-Skins debut 7-inch, 'One Law for Them'. Bushell made it Single of the Week in *Sounds*. Hodges' lyrics, in hindsight and perhaps even at the time, were contentious. It was 'one law for them', and 'one for us' with a mention of 'rivers of blood', a clear reference to Enoch Powell's famously controversial 1968 speech. The song, essentially, was about the recent high-profile riot in Brixton (April 1981) associated with police discrimination (chiefly stop-and-search) and poverty: there was a recession, inflation had been running above 20 per cent, and unemployment was up to 2.5 million. The Brixton riot precipitated a wave of such protests in black communities across England.

The single's B-side was 'Brave New World' – named after another slice of dystopian fiction that caught the Oi! imagination. On the surface it seemed to be about Thatcher's ruining of 'our fair land', 'this land of hope and not a lot of glory'. Hodges coupled that line with 'Remember the future is going to be a completely different story.' In this future Hodges wanted people to go on the attack, throw off the 'leeches and parasites on their back'. He saw a 'phoenix in the sky', and the 'birth of the new breed'. To anyone with an interest in the NF/BM skinhead scene, the song had obvious connotations. The Nazi phoenix/eagle sat on top of a sun wheel; the emblem of the BM. The single came out in July, on the eve of Southall.

The Last Resort were something else. Again, on the surface this was mostly down to their singer: Roi Pearce. The music did what it had to do, basic and aggressive. Roi's voice was never as deranged as Hodges but as a package the Resort came across somehow more sinister than the 4-Skins. Roi was a Millwall face, aged 21, and he kind of looked odd. You can see him in that era on the cover of Derek Ridgers' book *Skinheads*. He's the one in the glasses, stood next to Chubby from Combat 84. He looks cheeky rather than threatening, bit podgy. Never really had a skinhead. Short, buzz cut, maybe a cow flick. Boots, jeans, T-shirt and Fred Perry jumper. Of course, he wasn't even the singer originally in The Last Resort. He played bass when the band started.

Graham Saxby was the original singer and he wrote the lyrics to many of the early and best Resort songs too. I saw him play with his current Oi! band The Warriors at Cream of the Crop. Not on the main stage either, the little one downstairs. I'd clocked him before he played. He was turned out. Suedehead. Loafers, red socks, slacks just so. Sherman shirt. Perry tank top. The Warriors dropped a few Resort songs into their set. They lacked the menace Roi put into them but they still sounded great.

I saw him and The Warriors again at Rebellion and asked if he might talk. He said he would but looked a bit wary. A few weeks later we spent an enjoyable, after initial cagey exchanges, couple of hours on the phone. Saxby was born in Peckham but his family had moved to Herne Bay, the Kent seaside town, when he was a kid. He was a junior railman, sweeping platforms and a regular at West Ham, when he met Roi in '74/'75. Roi had just moved to Herne Bay from south-east London, from a Bermondsey tenement block. He was working in a factory in Deptford as an apprentice engineer.

They started listening to punk in '76/'77 and by '78/'79 were dressing the part, taking the coach together to London to see gigs: U.K. Subs, The Stranglers, Adam and the Ants. It was actually Roi who suggested doing a band and for about a year they just messed around, roped in a couple of local lads, didn't do any gigs, just rehearsed at a local church hall. They did covers, including 'Insane Society' by Menace. 'Me and Roi liked what we called working-class punk bands – the Upstarts, Sham, the Rejects, Cock Sparrer, Slaughter & the Dogs, but we really liked Menace,' said Saxby.

Saxby and Roi morphed into skinheads about 1979. 'We started wearing boots and jeans again and then the next thing you know we got braces and that was it. It was a natural progression.' They were already regulars at the infamous The Last Resort skinhead shop in east London. 'It was a punk shop when we first went,' Saxby said. 'They never opened on Saturdays because the owner, Micky [French] used to go watch Millwall play. But a lot of shops in that area, Aldgate, because it was a Jewish area, didn't open on Saturdays. We'd go up there on Sundays and it'd be really busy, not just the shop but the whole area and it gradually switched to being a skinhead shop [it was close to Brick Lane where BM and NF skinhead gangs congregated to provocatively promote their politics].

'When we started going to the shop some of those younger London skinheads would have been 15, 16, so we were five or six years older and we didn't have any animosity towards punks whatsoever but they did,' Saxby said. 'A lot of them ended up being right wing because the bloke from Skrewdriver Ian Stuart started going in the shop. I met him one time in there. He was a year older than me and he was holding court with all these little young skinheads looking up to him. It's like when I was a teenager going to watch West Ham, there'd be guys selling *Bulldog* outside the ground because they were trying to get football hooligans to be National Front, they were recruiting. Same happened to some of these young Oi! skinheads. They were politically naive, and they looked up to people like Ian Stuart.

'How far Micky [French] was involved politically I don't know,' Saxby said. 'He was probably just trying to make a few quid knowing Micky, he was a bit of Del Boy-type character. At the Last Resort shop you also had left-wing skinheads, non-political skinheads, who were traditional skinheads back then, and there was glue-sniffing skinheads – that was because they were so young they couldn't afford beer and you could get glue for 10p or 20p. Some of those Oi! skinheads didn't realise there had been skinheads before; they were that young they didn't know they were actually the second wave. Some of them would sell their bums, male prostitutes. It was a weird scene.

The guy [Micky Furbank] who did the actual design [of the classic crucified skinhead, a graphic French exploited endlessly and is still hugely popular today in various forms, especially tattoos] was a gay skinhead [a former rent-boy and artist, 19 in 1981, from Leeds].

'So you had all that in the mix but people only remember the right-wing skinheads, the boneheads,' Saxby said. 'But there were lots of other types of skinheads that had nothing to do with that.'

French became a key figure for Saxby and Roi. 'I said to Roi, how about we call ourselves The Last Resort, Micky French can be our manager. I was thinking, like the Sex Pistols with McLaren and the shop Sex, bit like that. I also said, Herne Bay is also like "the last resort", it's the last place you'd go on a holiday at the time. At the time it was a really awful, sad, rundown seaside town. And also we weren't that great so The Last Resort was actually a really good name.'

French, sometimes referred to as 'Fagin', said he'd do it, manage the band. The Last Resort played their first proper gig in August 1980. 'We did seven or eight gigs with me singing and then after that I left and said, look what I'll do is I'll still carry on writing lyrics and give them to you and if I can go to gigs, I'll come along and maybe I can sing backing vocals,' Saxby said. He was having problems with his then girlfriend. 'I went to quite a few of the gigs as backing vocals, probably about another seven or eight, but then in the end every one of the gigs ended in a punch-up so I was glad not to go. It got a bit stupid.'

Sounds reviewed one Resort gig that ended in violence at Acklam Hall in Ladbroke Grove, London, March 1981. I asked Saxby why he thought the gigs were so violent? 'It was a few things,' he said. 'It was Thatcher's Britain, '81, the summer of riots . . . also looking back The Last Resort mostly had trouble when they went to west London. It was fine when they played in east London or south London, 'cos a lot their fans were West Ham and Millwall fans bizarrely (meaning there was no trouble between these two famous rival firms at gigs). It was when they went to places like Southall and Ladbroke Grove. That [the latter] gig was casuals, QPR fans someone said, trying to smash it up, different football factions. Obviously, Southall, it was an Asian community which was probably a bad idea to have one there in the first place. It was a mixture of things and in the end, it snowballs.'

Before he left the band, Saxby sang on a Last Resort demo, which French released himself as a three-track cassette single in 1981. Sold it out of the shop, £1.50. 'He sent one to Garry Bushell at *Sounds* and Bushell liked it,' Saxby said. 'He wrote about it. I don't know how many Micky sold but he did OK with that cassette.'

One track on the cassette single became a Last Resort anthem, called 'Violence in Our Minds'. It was about skinheads walking down the street 'looking for some aggro, just to pass the time'. In the song they punch a 'stupid hippy', beat a soul boy 'black and blue' and pile into someone mob-handed at football. French had passed the lyrics to Saxby, saying they were by a skinhead kid knocking about the shop known as Mirror Dean, so-called 'because something happened and his face was in the *Daily Mirror*,' Saxby explained. 'I changed a couple of the words,' he said. 'This kid had a line that went, "beat a Paki black and blue", so I said, nah, I'm not doing that, and changed it to "beat a soul boy black and blue".'

What Saxby didn't know at the time, and only discovered in 2010, was the lyrics were not really by this kid but an almost direct lift from a folk song from 1970 written as a satire on the thuggish reputation of the first wave of British skinheads. 'It turns out it was a song by Miles Wootton, some old folk bloke who wrote it as a piss-take,' Saxby said. 'It's pretty much the same, not exactly, [Resort guitarist] Charlie put a different tune to it, and the original didn't have the chorus, "we've got violence in our minds", but it's 90 per cent the same song.'

Saxby laughed. 'The song is, when you think about it, very tongue-in-cheek . . . you're boasting that there's twenty-five of you beating up one person. I don't know if people get that. You can take it literally or laugh at it. When we do it with The Warriors, I always say this is one I recorded when I was 22, you'll have to excuse the lyrics.'

The Resort, with Roi on vocals, had two tracks on *Strength Thru Oi!*, their first outing on vinyl. Saxby had written the words for both. "Working Class Kids' included a dig at Jimmy Pursey and the chant 'Oi! Oi! music for working class'. Otherwise, it was a song about going down the pub, getting pissed and having a tear-up. 'Johnny Barden' was more complex, about a kid who killed some fella who had sexually abused him. 'He still lives in Herne Bay,' Saxby said. 'It's a true story. He told us what had happened, and we went, what?! And then he went in the army. When he'd been in the army a few weeks he handed himself him. He just couldn't live with himself. The bill thought there was a gay ripper going about – someone else got killed at the same time. In the end he got eight years for manslaughter and he did five-and-a-bit.'

Saxby also wrote the words for other tracks that would feature on the 1982 Resort debut including the highly controversial

'Stormtroopers in Sta Press'. 'One of the gigs we did, Garry Bushell reviewed it and I'm sure he put Stormtroopers in Sta Press [in the review] and I thought, that's a good title for a song,' Saxby said. 'Then Micky [French] said you can't call it that because people will get the wrong end of the stick – stormtroopers – people will automatically think of Nazis. So, they changed it to 'Skinheads in Sta Press'. I wasn't thinking Nazis when I wrote it! It was storming government, like the working-class overthrowing Thatcher. The line, "Smash windows and burn beach huts" – West Ham had won the cup, 1980, and we'd had a beach party and the police came.'

Saxby was pally with Arthur Kay, also from Herne Bay, who replaced Roi on bass when Roi replaced Saxby as singer. Kay was an experienced musician, 30, another Millwall regular, had released a single 'Ska Wars' in '79 and was running his own band, Arthur Kay & The Originals. 'He wrote 'King of the Jungle' and 'Rebels with a Cause' [both Oi! classics from the Resort's debut album],' Saxby said. "King of the Jungle' was one of his ska songs and he adapted it to be an Oi! song. I always say the best thing that ever happened to The Last Resort was me leaving because when Arthur joined they went up a level.'

At the time of Southall, The Business were essentially unknowns. They weren't on either of the first two Oi! comps. Singer Micky Fitz [Fitzsimons] and guitarist Steve Kent were school pals from Lewisham, south-east London, and had attended the same grammar school that Garry Bushell went to. Kent, in fact, had played in a band with Bushell before he and Fitz started The Business. Bushell was also mates with Lol Pryor who managed the band. Pryor and Fitz were both West Ham fans. Skully and a few other West Ham faces were early Business supporters. Fitz looked good, had a grown-out skinhead, wore a green flight jacket, but as a band they were putty, still being shaped.

As the talk of the three bands, the 4-Skins, Resort and Business, collaborating on a record label went on, it made sense that they should play gigs together. Three were planned: Southall, Hastings and Crayford. The only gig that took place was Southall. Hambrough Tavern. Friday 3 July. 1981.

Southall, west London, had long been seen by the National Front as symbolic battleground. It was one of the most racially diverse areas in London. Almost 50 per cent of the population had been born in the Commonwealth, many were Sikhs from the Punjab, according to a 1976 survey. That year a local teenager was stabbed to death by a National Front-inspired gang. The NF chairman was quoted as saying: 'One down – a million to go.' The teen's killers were never convicted. In 1979 anti-racist protester Blair Peach was killed in a riot that ensued when the National Front decided to hold an election meeting in the area.

The Southall Youth Movement had been formed in response to the NF targeting the area. They had a deep-seated and not unfounded distrust of the police. Prior to the Oi! gig, representatives from the area's Asian community and the pub had met. Among the Asian community, skinheads meant only one thing – a declaration of your interest in the far right. There'd been more much publicised violence in Southend over the bank holiday weekend in April 1980. 'Beasts – boot gang savages a victim' was a *Daily Express* front cover, followed by 'Skinheads: The visitors no one wanted.' It was being predicted that up to 200 skinheads would attend the Oi! gig. The headline acts, 4-Skins and The Last Resort, were both seen as playing music that could incite violence. The pub held firm, suggested maybe the early closure of Asian shops.

There was a febrile atmosphere on the day of the gig, the recent explosion in Brixton only adding to the mood of determined discontent. French had organised two coaches to take fans from The Last Resort shop to the venue. I read an eyewitness report in the Stampton/Forbes book from one of skins onboard. He said soon after getting off the coach at the gig, a skin girl was attacked by 'Pakis' so he and a mob went off 'to do some Pakis'.

There were reports of skinheads acting up in local shops, rumours circulating of abuse aimed at women and elderly people, of windows smashed and racist slogans chanted. There was also talk of white power leaflets being passed to local residents.

The Business claimed their van was attacked by a gang of Asians as they approached the venue. They'd arrived late, at about 8 p.m., didn't soundcheck; the pub upstairs was already packed, and went on stage about half past.

Terry Hayes, who sang in Skully's band, the East End Badoes, knew the three bands well, either through a pub night he ran in Poplar/Canning Town, or the football; he was a hardcore Millwall supporter. He said online, 'It was a stupid place to hold a show like that in the first place. Provocative being an understatement – it was not an attack or invasion by the far right as reported by [the] press it was just a show in the wrong place. For days in advance the Southall Youth Movement had been stoked up by the SWP to demonstrate and come out in force . . .'

The Resort followed The Business, and by the time they had finished playing a crowd of protestors had gathered outside the pub, said to be 400 strong. The police had arrived by now, but only thirty initially, and they formed a cordon, trying to disperse the crowd. There was talk of stones being thrown at the pub, and abuse and Sieg Heils being hurled back from the upstairs windows of the pub. The 4-Skins were on stage when the police started to use truncheons on the increasingly aggressive crowd outside. Bricks and petrol bombs were now being thrown at the pub. By 10 p.m. a fire had started inside the pub. It spread alarmingly, curtains ablaze, lots of smoke. There was chaos.

By 11 p.m. there were 600 police present trying to control the scene. They shepherded the 200-strong Oi! crowd out, as the riot rained down. Cars were being overturned; a police coach was set on fire. Bricks flew through the air. In the end sixty-one policemen were injured and there were seventy arrests – sixty-eight of black or Asian people.

'Terror in Southall' was the *Daily Mail* headline. The police said they had no evidence that any of the Oi! crowd were members of the National Front. 'The coaches had an NF banner and they were all wearing National Front medallions,' one local was quoted as saying in a *Guardian* report on the riot the next day. A spokesman for the Southall Youth Movement told the press: 'The skinheads were wearing National Front gear, swastikas everywhere, and National Front written on their jackets. They sheltered behind the police barricades and threw stones at the crowd. Instead of arresting them, the police just pushed them back. It's not surprising people started to retaliate.'

The press coverage of the riot continued into the Sunday papers. The *Sunday Times* reported: 'Trouble started quickly. A group of skinheads attacked the wife of the owner of an Asian shop, the Maharajah general stores. Later, her husband,

Darshanlal Kalhan said: "Whatever our boys did was purely in self-defence. It was an unprovoked attack".' In the *News of the World* one of the injured Asians, 35-year-old Narotam Lal who had been knocked unconscious by police, said: 'One of the policemen told me, you will be another Blair Peach.'

On the streets in Southall, confrontations between Asians and the police continued throughout the weekend in scenes reminiscent of the Brixton riot. It triggered further unrest around the country: Liverpool erupted with four nights of rioting in Toxteth; Moss Side in Manchester also exploded. The following weekend the rioting intensified, with 2,000 on the street in Southall and riots in thirty towns and cities across the UK.

The *Daily Mail* would not let it go. On 9 July they attacked *Sounds*, 'The Skinhead Bible of Hate from an Establishment Stable', and the next day ran another feature: 'Exposed: The Racist Thug on the Cover of this Evil Record'.

This was the topless skinhead in violent pose on the cover of the *Strength Thru Oi!* comp. A striking image that had appeared across the advertising for the album, in print ads, on posters and T-shirts. Nicky Crane, 6 ft 2 ins, one of the most infamous BM skins, Leader Guard and Kent branch organiser. It was said he first gained a reputation for trouble at Sham gigs and had led skinhead gangs into violent attacks on Asians in Brick Lane. In May '78, following a BM meeting, he attacked a black family at a bus stop in east London with a bottle and was jailed for twelve months. The Old Bailey judge labelled him 'worse than an animal'. In March 1980, aged 22, he led a hundred-strong BM gang – armed with iron bars, knives, clubs – down Woolwich High Street and attacked black filmgoers outside the Odeon cinema. The same day the gang jumped some black kids at a train station and then fought arresting police. Crane was sent to jail for four years.

When the album cover photograph of him was taken was unclear. The photographer was Martin Dean, a *Sounds* contributor, chiefly associated with photographing Oi! bands, and a well-known face at the Last Resort shop. A tattoo Crane had on his arm that identified him as Leader Guard – and L and G either side of a Celtic cross/sun wheel had been airbrushed out.

A week after the gig on 10 July, the same day the *Mail* ran its Crane exposé, Margaret Thatcher met Southall community leaders. She blamed 'racists' for the riot. 'Thatcher attacks fascist groups over riots' was one tabloid headline. Ken Livingstone, newly elected leader of the GLC, made similar comments.

The *NME* then stuck the knife in with a cover story, dated 11 July. Under a black-and-white photograph of the burned-out skeleton of the Hambrough Tavern with a burned-out car in the foreground was the headline: 'The Gig that Sparked a Race Riot'. An editorial carried the headline: 'Oi – The Disgrace'. In it the *NME* claimed the skinhead on the cover of the *Strength Thru Oi!* compilation was a member of the 'NF Leader Guard', said to be 'loosely based on the Nazi SS'. *Sounds* editor, Alan Lewis, called on to comment, said they didn't know at the time the album went to press. 'It was just an aggressive image to go with the aggressive music.' Now he felt 'pretty sick'. Deram, the Decca subsidiary, responsible for the record, said they were taking immediate action to delete the album.

A reporter from the *NME* tried and failed to find out who booked the gig, only unearthing that Cock Sparrer had been the next band due to play the venue. The 4-Skins were lambasted in a full-page feature, headline: 'Playing with Fire'.

The *NME* claimed the feature had been written up and ready to go before Southall, having interviewed the band in mid-June. In it they were described as a 'down-at-heel punk group' who had adopted 'an odious image' to cash in and it had backfired. Oi!'s 'repulsive imagery' was mentioned throughout the feature. Gary Hodges said skinheads Sieg Heiling was just to shock, a joke, and paparazzi were paying young skins £5 to do it for staged photos. Hitchcock told the NME: 'All you're interested in is writing on your front page, This group's a Nazi band – the National Front's giving 'em money.' The feature declared Oi! dead and buried. At its best it was a 'sour tragi-comedy'. At its worst, 'well . . . we don't need that violent-racist-sexist-fascist groove thang!'

On the opposing page, the *NME* ran a separate full page article that saw them catch up with the 4-Skins the day after Southall, while they were recording in a studio on the Old Kent Road. Hodges said: 'The reporters have been going round getting quotes from the Asians who are making things up to justify their own aggressive behaviour. It was the blacks that made the first attack, but the press, as usual, believe it's the skinheads that caused all the trouble.' He said the two coachloads of skins arrived at 8 p.m. and went straight into the venue and the gig started at 8.30 p.m. There was no trouble during the night until right at the end when the 4-Skins were doing their encore. 'The windows of the pub at the back and sides went through,' Hodges said. 'The police were in the place straight away and they asked everyone to stay in the pub. We co-operated and tried to restrain everyone and most of the lads stayed there. When the police told us they'd cleared the way we went out and everyone made for home sharpish.'

What about the Fascist flyers? he was asked. 'We didn't know about the leaflets because that was going on outside the gig. The people involved with that have nothing whatsoever to do with the 4-Skins.'

He added: 'None of the things that happened was our fault. It was already in the air.' He said before the gig, before any crowd showed up, he and his wife were having a walk in the area and a car with 'two black youths in it' had tried to run them over.

The *NME* also gave a further half page to an interview with Micky French, blaming his organisation of 'the two coachloads of East End skinheads decked out in Union Jacks' for inflaming the situation. 'Why can't you wave your own country's flag in London?' French said. 'I'm a loyalist and proud to be British – I'm certainly no fascist.'

Many in the Oi! community reference a *Guardian* feature as being among the fairest articles written in the aftermath of Southall. The views of Bushell, Garry Johnson (who had three spoken word poems included on *Strength Thru Oi!*), and Max Splodge (who featured on both Oi! comps to date), were included. The main colour of the piece was provided by the reporter attending a Tuesday night gig by new skinhead Oi! band The Elite at the Walmer Castle in Peckham. Many of the same crowd who'd been at Southall were there. Gary Hitchcock was present, quoted as saying: 'We're finished. After everything that's been written, we'll never get another gig. We'll probably just have to fold up.'

The reporter also quoted a handful of un-named skins at the gig, had them saying stuff like: 'Posh people can fly a Union Jack and they are patriotic. If you're working class with the

Union Jack, you're just a Nazi.' Another said about Southall: 'The Pakis overreacted. They went berserk over nothing; it was probably only a few geezers asking how many rupees for fish and chips. If they'd been more tolerant there wouldn't have been no fucking aggro.' Asked about politics another said: 'I hate Mrs Thatcher but I hate the Labour party even more.' He explained it was a given that posh people hated you, but the Labour party was supposed to be on your side and now they were ignoring the working class, poor kids like them, and taking the immigrants' side. Lol Pryor, also at the gig, echoed what Hitchcock said: 'Where can we play now? Promoters are already backing out.'

The 4-Skins weren't quite finished though. In August, they organised a secret gig in a pub back room in south-east London, close to Kent, invite only. The BBC were one of those invited and ran a short thirteen-minute feature about the band fronted by *Nationwide* presenter Tony Wilkinson. He called them 'the lepers of the music business, banned by radio stations, boycotted by record shops, blacklisted by promoters'.

Wilkinson stood outside the smoke-charred husk of the Hambrough Tavern to recap what had happened there – hundreds of skinhead fans, 'many known NF supporters', some 'assaulted elderly Asians in the street and daubed shop windows with NF slogans'. The BBC showed a large 'NF Rules' spray-painted on a shop window. The 'Asians retaliated and what followed turned into a full-scale race battle'. An Asian lad told Wilkinson how the skinheads 'invaded' and 'our women [were] beaten up'. What made it even more shocking, he said, was the lack of response from the police. 'Large groups of fascists doing Nazi salutes, writing NF on the condensation of the windows.'

The band were also interviewed. Hodges, polo shirt, braces, slacks, cardigan, was the only one quoted. 'The Pakis just went a bit mad didn't they,' he said. 'They used that gig as an excuse . . . to riot.' Didn't he feel any guilt? 'I don't feel guilty about nothing,' he said.

Wilkinson said Oi! bands were 'pro violence, anti-black, anti-police'. He went to a record store and picked up a copy of *Strength Thru Oi!* from a stack of them on a rack, said the title was based on a Nazi slogan and the man on the cover was neo-Nazi now in prison. He said 'giants' Decca claimed to have banned the record but evidently not so and they continued to make money from it.

There was time for a Rock Against Racism spokesperson to speak about the NF and BM infiltration of rock, for John Peel to expound on punk's flirtation with Nazi imagery. There was footage of a far-right march, lots of young skinheads Sieg Heiling, some draped in Union Jack flags. The Union Jack was the adopted emblem of the NF, Wilkinson said. Although he refused to appear on camera, Joe Pearce, the editor of *Bulldog*, the YNF magazine, claimed 'all Oi! bands are NF bands, the musical wing of the NF'. He said if they denied it they faced consequences, mentioning the trouble that had ended the career of Sham. Pearce said at a recent Madness gig he had distributed 700 copies of *Bulldog*.

The short piece ended back at the gig, the one intended to clear the 4-Skins name, prove they were a band who just wanted to play music. 'The concert had been going half an hour when things started to go wrong,' Wilkinson said. A mysterious power cut and the fans took over. There was footage of the band doing 'Chaos', Hodges swamped by young skinheads on stage, crowded out, pawed, some throwing half-hearted Sieg Heils, some in Union Jack Ts. It ended with the young skinheads, led by older-looking skins, all up on stage singing 'Rule, Britannia!', followed by 'God Save the Queen'.

In October 1981, Secret Records, surprisingly, released a new 4-Skins single and a new Oi! comp, *Carry On Oi!!*, which featured a bullish 4-Skins track called 'Evil'. Hodges on the attack, breaking bones, knifing, booting and strangling. 'I'm Evil. Evil. Evil. Evil.' Bushell's name was attached to this third Oi! comp, on the front cover, but *Sounds* was no longer involved. Secret was a new London punk indie label, flush from their success with The Exploited whose debut album had gone Top 20; the band were currently in the Top 40 (and on *Top of the Pops*) with a single, 'Dead Cities'. *Carry On Oi!!* also featured another new Secret signing, the teenage Infa Riot, tipped for success by Bushell, and the album sold a healthy 20,000 copies despite zero radio support.

There was talk of Malcolm McLaren wanting to manage the 4-Skins but there wasn't much left to manage. The Secret single, 'Yesterdays Heroes', was the sound of Hodges leaving the group, his vocal half-hearted, and he hadn't even sung on either of the B-side tracks. Secret, Hitchcock and the rest of the 4-Skins persisted, roped in a new singer, Panther, who'd been a band roadie and was another former BM skinhead. Their debut album, released in 1982, actually sold well, made indie number one, peaking at UK number eighty. The following year they had a new singer, Roi from the Resort, a new label, Syndicate, run by Splodge manager Dave Long, and a dwindling fanbase. They finally broke up in 1984.

The Last Resort only managed about another six months after Southall. Secret was said to be interested and 'King of the Jungle' was another standout track on *Carry On Oi!!* but their gigs continued to be a magnet for violence. 'After Southall everybody thought we were Nazis,' Roi said in a 2003 interview. 'It's a horrible misconception to get rid of. Even today, I still have this reputation.'

'It got to the stage where they couldn't play any more,' Saxby said. 'It was like a riot coming to your doorstep, every other gig was a riot. Micky said, just go and record an album. They done a set of demos at the same place [we did the original cassette] in Folkestone. They went two or three times, just weekends. By the time Micky released it in 1982, The Last Resort wasn't going. They had got rid of Micky and . . . called themselves The Warriors. The album was a demo, that's why it's . . . I was going to say not that good but it *is* good, but it's sort of good because it's not good, it wasn't over-produced. They weren't very happy about it being released at the time.'

The album, *A Way of Life – Skinhead Anthems*, is better than good. It's iconic. The sleeve was designed by Micky Furbank; with a graphic of a skinhead who stands with a raised fist against a Union Jack background. French released it via the shop, put it out in red, white and blue vinyl. It was said to have sold maybe 15,000 in quick time. It was 'Dedicated to all true skinheads everywhere'.

Roi's new band The Warriors had a track called 'Horror Show' ('This is Clockwork Orange land') on the fourth Oi! comp *Oi! Oi! That's Yer Lot!* released in September 1982 by Secret, but soon split. 'The Warriors did two gigs and I went to both of those,' said Saxby. 'They did one at the 100 Club and one at Skunx [in Islington]. I probably got up and sang. A little bit after that, by the end of '82, they'd called it a day or I think it just died a death, there was no interest, no one could get any gigs. And then Roi joined the 4-Skins.'

'What happened was I used to be a doorman down the 100 Club,' Roi said when I saw him at the Rebellion Q&A. 'And Panther was leaving. Gary Hitchcock come and got hold of me and said, do you wanna come and have a look. It was only [Hoxton] Tom and Gary [Hitchcock] really from the original 4-Skins set-up. We did an album and then this soppy pair of fuckers got put in prison and it put paid to it. And we come out and Gary [Hitchcock] organised this live album basically and did it down Waterloo in the studio, we brought a little crowd in from where [new guitarist] Paul [Swain] and that come from [Hatfield] in north London. Then I left the scene. I wasn't around any more.'

The Business had two tracks on the *Carry On Oi!!* comp (the lyrics for one, 'Suburban Rebels', were by Garry Johnson) and Secret Records released the band's debut single in November 1981, 'Harry May', a Sham-esque chanter, about a gangster gone to seed. It was a minor indie hit.

Manager Pryor was desperate to clean up the name of the group. The perception of Oi! as a far-right vehicle had been strengthened by a Trevor Griffiths made-for-TV play *Oi For England* that was shown on a Saturday night on ITV in April 1982 (the play then toured the country). Written after the summer 1981 riots and set in Manchester, it centred on a skinhead Oi! band offered a gig at an NF rally. Pryor floated the idea of The Business playing for RAR. It had also been suggested to the 4-Skins too in the aftermath of Southall, but Hodges had refused to consider it, didn't want to be a poster boy for 'Trotskyism'. Fitz too baulked at the idea, calling RAR the 'Trot front'. Pauline Black of The Selecter also refused to play RAR for a similar reason, so it wasn't just an Oi! thing. In fact, in the *NME* Paul

Morley complained of the organisation being orchestrated by 'political extremists and crackpots'. The Business *were* photographed posing with Asian skins (around the same time the 4-Skins minus Hodges posed with a couple of black girls). Many saw such stunts as tokenistic.

Pryor and Bushell (and something called the 'Oi! organising committee' which Pryor was chairman of) put their heads together and came up with an Oi! tour featuring The Business, Infa Riot and Blitz under the unwieldy banner 'Oi Against Racism and Political Extremism But Still Against The System', and a few gigs did take place. Pryor also attempted to organise a benefit gig in support of militant trade union members blacklisted by bosses (the flipside to 'Harry May' had been about this) but singer Fitz pulled out at the last minute saying he was posing all along and that he voted Tory. The band then split.

Neil 'Mackie' McLennan, of Blitz (see next chapter) put me in touch with Chris Mundie who'd drummed with The Business for the final ten years of Fitz's life and had also spoken at his funeral. Mundie now ran the popular Salty Dog pub/venue in Northwich, was a staunch socialist and long-time Labour party member.

'Mick [Fitz] told me about it and I spoke to Steve Kent, and basically after Southall I think the rest of the band went, well, you know what? This isn't really for us, and Mick said, right, that's fine, I'm gonna carry on,' Mundie said.

I asked if Fitz had ever said anything about Southall? 'The only thing Mick told me was they had to hire a van from Enterprise or whatever the equivalent was and they were in the van when it kicked off, and the van was shaking and he said, we better get out of here, lads. He said they got out and just as they did a petrol bomb goes through the window, blows the van up, burns the van out completely. The next day it was on the front page of the *Mirror* and there's a picture of outside the venue and this burned-out shell of a van. So, what they did was just taped the keys to a cut-out picture of that and posted it back to the hire van company saying, really sorry, if you want to pick up your van it's here. I'd always wanted to ask him about it, what happened, did you know . . . blah blah blah . . . it was a sketchy situation, probably pretty terrifying at the time.'

Lol Pryor put a new line-up together around Fitz. This included, on bass, Mark Brennan who ran gigs in Deptford, just up the road from Lewisham, in the King's Head pub. There was a strong skinhead scene in Deptford, focused on the King's Head and another pub The Fountain. Fitz was said to be a fan of a band called the Afflicted, closely associated with this little scene. They featured an infamous BM Leader Guard, one of the West Ham skinheads who'd run up against the Rejects. Nicky Crane was also said to have played with the band at some point. Among their audience were some of BM's most feared faces, more Leader Guard, including West Ham skins and members of another notorious BM-affiliated band, the Ovaltinees.

The new Business line-up started strong with the standout track on *Oi! Oi! That's Yer Lot!* called 'Real Enemy' and a late '82 EP also released by Secret called *Smash the Disco's* reached indie number three. The main song on it was a reworking of 'Day-O (The Banana Boat Song)', the Jamaican folk tune. Seemed odd. Pryor was sacked and then the band fell apart. The drummer joined Deptford John in Combat 84. The Business debut album was released post-split, by Secret, in 1983.

In 1985, Fitz and Brennan and guitarist Steve Whale returned with a new album, *Saturdays Heroes*, on their own Harry May Records. Their big number was the jokey, Chas & Dave-esque sing-along 'Drinking and Driving'. They also covered Sham's 'Hurry Up Harry'. This was when Oi! was dominated by the NF/RAC scene (see chapter 8). The Business were said to be popular with an NF-affiliated gang of skins known as the 'Hounslow Mob' who also followed RAC's main band Skrewdriver. In this period The Business also played with bands who would be later described as 'grey zone', such as Indecent Exposure and Condemned 84 but eschewed approaches to become an RAC-affiliated band. It was said to be at a Business gig in 1985 that Nicky Crane, now out of prison and head of 'Skrewdriver Security', told support act Indecent Exposure, 'You're playing for us now.'

'I remember Mick telling me about one of the gigs in London getting smashed up by the British Movement,' Mundie said. 'They'd been approached to become one of their bands and Mick had the sense to say no. And one of the guys from a very prominent one of those bands said, "look you don't have to believe in it, you want to see how much money we're making selling these records, because it was a big thing at the time, especially in America." Mick didn't want to know and The Business had one of their gigs smashed up as a payback. "Look, if you're not with us we need to make a stand to show you're not with us, which means we're going to smash up one of your gigs. One gig gets ruined but everyone knows we're not with these guys, who are the baddies." I guess you'll take that.'

I had noted that a photograph of the band was online of them playing in front of a swastika flag in Holland in 1986. Mundie knew the photograph. 'I think it was right out in the middle of nowhere, some little town, just as part of a tour,' he said. 'Mick said, we're on stage playing and all of a sudden fifty big lads turn up with all this shit and walk on stage with it. It's obvious they've planned to do this. They wanted to get the photograph and he's like, what would you do? There's four of you, you're out in the middle of nowhere, you're surrounded by all these guys who will do you damage – it's all well and good being principled and going, we will not stand for this, but when it comes down to it, are you gonna try and fight fifty boneheads off? What do you do in that situation?'

The band split up again and Pryor and Brennan formed Link Records in 1987, which until it folded in the early nineties chiefly focused on repackaging the music of Oi!'s biggest name bands, while continually releasing Oi! compilations such as *Oi! The Resurrection*, *The Hills are Alive With The Sound of Oi!*, *Oi! Glorious Oi!,* and *Oi! That's What I Call Music*.

Fitz teamed up again with guitarist Steve Whale in 1992 and the band started to have success. They became favourites of Lars Frederiksen of Rancid, the first of several UK Oi! bands to benefit from his Oi! obsession. Rancid, alongside Green Day, Bad Religion and The Offspring, were reviving mainstream interest in punk rock in America and, as a follow-up to their platinum selling '95 album . . . *And Out Come the Wolves*, Frederiksen produced The Business album, *The Truth, the Whole Truth, and Nothing but the Truth*. It sold in the thousands. Fitz became a bit of a celeb, guested on stage with Rancid, and was feted by up-and-coming punk bands such as the Dropkick Murphys. He also became an alcoholic, and the band broke up again.

In 2006, after an almost five-year hiatus, Fitz put a new line-up together. 'I was 24 when Mick asked me to be in the band,' Mundie said. 'He was sort of rebuilding his band and reputation, some bridges had been burned. One of the big watershed moments for our line-up was playing the Rebellion Festival 2008. We played the Arena stage and filled it to capacity, the fire marshals had to close the doors. That was like Mick saying, right we're back now, as a force to be reckoned with.'

Mundie was a teenager when The Business had their nineties resurgence and like many others it was via Rancid, specifically the first and hugely popular Hellcat Records sampler, *Give 'Em The Boot* (Hellcat was an offshoot of Epitaph, home to Rancid and The Offspring, founded by members of Rancid and Bad Religion). "Spirit of the Street' by The Business was on that,' Mundie said. 'I was into all the American stuff and was like, what's this? I think that's what made it a bit easier for me joining – I knew there was that crossover to the thing I'd grown up with, the Rancid connection, the Hellcat stuff and they did the stuff with the Dropkick Murphys [a split single in 2000].

'Mick really enjoyed going to America and he really enjoyed the bond with the bands,' Chris said. 'And we couldn't go anywhere in America without people from bands on the NY hardcore scene like Agnostic Front turning up at gigs to pay their respects.' I asked what the big songs were in the set? "Drinking and Driving' was a big sing-along,' he said. 'Mick saw it as bit throwaway but it was a great thing to finish the set with, the entire crowd singing and bouncing about. 'Harry May', the first single, was the other big tune. 'Suburban Rebels' was always a big one. And 'Smash The Disco's'. 'Product' from *Carry on Oi!!* went down well with the older fans and you had the stuff off the *Truth* album that worked well.'

In the time Chris was in the band The Business toured the world: America several times; Europe, Chile, South Korea, Thailand. Trouble, he stressed, was rare. 'Maybe years back it was a different sort of thing but in my tenure in the band, Mick wanted people to have fun,' he said. 'He always wanted the gig to be a party. We used to come on to 'Happiness' by Ken Dodd. Mick was good at setting the tone, he had the knack of being able to defuse aggressive people. All these big tough skinheads in Germany would turn to little puppy dogs talking to Mick.'

Chapter 6

Someone's Gonna Die: Blitz/Bushell/Oi! – The Professor

On the strength of a demo they had sent him, Bushell mentioned Blitz, 'from Manchester', in the 4-Skins late-1980 *Sounds* front cover feature, one of the handful of younger bands he'd claimed were part of the burgeoning new punk/Oi! movement.

In a short time, the band signed to a newly formed indie label, based in Malvern, Worcestershire, called No Future, and recorded a batch of tracks that would make their name legend worldwide. No Future, whose mission statement read, 'dedicated to hardcore punk and skinhead bands only' also carved out a strong reputation for itself, signing up new Oi! bands The Partisans and Red Alert. Crown Court took their name from a song by a No Future band called On Parole.

In the months that followed Southall, and amid growing backlash, No Future supported Bushell and Oi!. The label supplied several songs to the *Carry On Oi!!* comp including the standout 'Nation on Fire' by Blitz, about the summer of '81 riots, a sort of early Clash-alike. However, it was the band's debut EP, called

All Out Attack, released towards the end of 1981, that cemented the Blitz name in Oi! history, especially the opening track 'Someone's Gonna Die'. It was a new level of onslaught, with an 'Oi! Oi! Oi!' chant to boot. The apogee of Oi!'s early 'brick-wall' sound, I wrote in the *Guardian*. It suggested there was life in the movement, a musical future. It also inspired many other bands, especially in America.

'*All Out Attack* was done in a little eight-track studio in Stockport,' the band's founder and bass player Neil McLennan told me. 'We were in the red [overloading the recording signal, creating ugly buzz], the engineer was saying, it's breaking up, it's breaking up! We said, fuck it, it sounds fantastic. People try to replicate that sound now. We just plugged in the shitty gear that was in there and cranked it all up. Although people love the [debut] album [*Voice of a Generation*, released June 1982] they say it was weak compared to the single, which it was.'

I met with McLennan in early June 2022. He still lived in the small semi-rural town Blitz originated from, New Mills, about thirty minutes from Manchester Piccadilly on a train. Smartly dressed, healthy, and switched on, in his late 50s with two grown-up daughters, he is known on the Oi!/punk/hardcore scene as Mackie. His well-regarded second band, Epic Problem, split in 2019 after ten years.

Mackie said it was actually him who had coined the term 'brickwall' to describe the sound on the band's debut EP. 'It said "pure brickwall punk" on the ad in *Sounds*,' he said. 'I meant like the punk version of the [Phil Spector] "wall of sound".'

He'd formed Blitz with his best pal, the band's guitarist, Nidge, when they were teenagers in the late seventies. They were both big Manchester Utd fans, regulars at the matches, been bootboys.

'We weren't hooligans,' smiled Mackie. 'We wanted to be.' They'd met Blitz singer, Carl Fisher, on the coach travelling down from Manchester to London, on their way to see The Clash at the Rock Against Racism gig in Victoria Park in 1978. Carl was 14, a couple of years younger than them and it was him that, after a leopard-skin hair and kilt phase, first turned skinhead. Drummer Charlie Howe followed, because, said Mackie, he was already losing his hair.

'The photo on the *All Out Attack* sleeve is two punks and two skins,' he said. 'We had 'Oi! Oi! Oi!' in 'Someone's Gonna Die' but I never considered us as an Oi! band. We were lumped in. The 'Oi! Oi! Oi!' was taken from the Rejects – to me they were the best Oi! band. Nidge really loved Micky Geggus. But it wasn't like, let's shoehorn Oi! into the song because this is going to go somewhere. It was, oh that fits nice there, you can imagine the crowd, singing along. When Bushell said, do you want to be on an Oi! album? Yeah, of course we do, because it's going to sell thousands. You don't worry about that fallout after.'

Mackie said Bushell visited the band's hometown to write a feature on Blitz for *Sounds* and while he was there discovered quite a thriving little scene. Mackie's sister had a band called Attak (who signed to No Future and featured on the fourth Oi! album) and his girlfriend was in a band called the Violators (who also signed to No Future). 'Bushell made a bit of a joke about the town,' Mackie said. 'He put, it's like *Last of the Summer Wine* here why are they singing about "football scarf now stained red" [a line from 'Someone's Gonna Die'], but he always had our back. He loved us. The Rejects were just like Herberts, that's what he called them, football casuals – they'd just wear trainers and skinny jeans but we were two punks and two skinheads and that was his ideal. He was always behind us.'

I asked Mackie about the violent sentiment of the songs on the EP. 'We were bootboys and violence is happening but we're on the fringes of it and, it sounds a cliché, but we don't condone it,' Mackie said. He recited a lyric, 'We fight to live, we live to fight, we don't give a shit what's wrong or what's right' ['Fight to Live' from *All Out Attack*]. He smiled. 'But then you move on'.

Southall, he said, had a significant and detrimental impact on the band. 'It was difficult to get gigs afterwards, no one would touch Oi! with a bargepole. That was the front page of the dailies. We're not talking a little brawl in a pub here, the venue got razed to the ground. It impacted the bands involved a lot more but it would ripple out to us. You had to nail your colours to the mast. We did our best to distance ourselves – we didn't want anything to do with the far right or any connection with that. We played RAR gigs, Anti-Nazi League gigs. We played with The Business and Infa Riot in Sheffield on that [Oi! Against Racism] tour [a date that was tied in with a 'march for jobs' protest in the city, part of the Right To Work campaign]. That was really good, a different crowd, more clued up because of what it was. Those bands were doing the best they could to distance themselves too. We got on with Micky Fitz, he was sound. There were people who came to see him who certainly toyed with things on the fringes. I think The Business did a Sham; the original line-up had to stop because it was too heavy.'

In early 1982, Blitz played the two venues in London that would still routinely book Oi! bands: the 100 Club and the infamous Skunx. 'Twice we did Skunx,' Mackie said. 'That was scary. It was dodgy as fuck. The Blue Coat Boy pub, Islington. The crowd was baying for blood, they'd be Sieg Heiling, crazy shit. You'd say, cut that shit out. It's weird. You kind of knew what to expect. It was just a back room of a pub. We went down alright because the songs were aggressive. The gigs we did in London were all heavy. We did a gig at the 100 Club and Carl got hit by a bottle, blood all down his face. Nidge offered the audience out, who fucking wants it? I'll fight you all, you southern fucking cunts. Then Micky Fitz got on stage and he was saying [to the crowd], what you doing you wankers, and Micky made sure we got out OK and Carl went to hospital and he got stitched up and everything. Micky came with us to the hospital.

'Ian MacKaye, from Fugazi, Minor Threat, Dischord Records, massive hero of mine [Epic Problem were named after a Fugazi track], was at the 100 Club gig,' Mackie added. 'He was roadie-ing for Black Flag at the time. They were in London, they were looking for something to do. Ian told me they stayed for a couple of songs and then fucked off 'cos it was so heavy. I think the guy with him might have been mixed race or a bit Italian-looking and they said they didn't feel comfortable. Ian told me they loved all the British stuff. A lot of the early US hardcore bands definitely took influence from Oi!. Agnostic Front cover Blitz. If you watch *The Godfathers of Hardcore* (2017), Agnostic Front guitarist Vinnie [Stigma] has got our logo stencilled on the back of his leather jacket.'

Despite their debut album making the UK Top 30, Blitz broke up at the end of 1982. 'I left after a gig at the Clarendon in London,' Mackie said. 'Carl was really pissed; it was a shambles. Bushell slated us. Carl didn't want to play to that audience, he wanted to move on, he'd become a casual. He was moving at a million miles an hour.' Carl kept the name and put a new short-lived line-up together which soon faltered.

Nidge resurrected Blitz in the noughties with Red Alert singer Steve Smith on vocals. He was the only original member involved. Blitz, like The Business, had been another UK Oi! band given the Rancid boost. They covered 'Someone's Gonna Die' and Lars Frederiksen even had a Blitz tattoo. Tragedy struck, however, and Nidge was killed while on tour in Houston in 2007. Got run over. He was 48.

Mackie was also a beneficiary of Lars Frederiksen's passion for Oi!. 'He invited Epic Problem to see Rancid when they did the Academy [in Manchester] and we played with [Frederiksen's Oi! band] Old Firm Casuals a couple of times,' he said. 'He has always been great with me. We went to see The Last Resort play not too long back because Lars was playing guitar for them. He was living the dream, got to play guitar in a proper authentic English Oi! band. He was in his element, all his backing vocals were cockney. He loves it and he's got to be a millionaire, the money he's made off Rancid, but he'd rather do that – he'd rather play rhythm guitar for The Last Resort in the Hairy Dog in Derby.'

Mackie, who had designed all the band's graphics, explained how Lars had helped him establish a legitimate line of Blitz T-shirts. If you've ever been to Rebellion, you'd see why that might matter. If only you could get a royalty on tattoos!

You can't really write an Oi! book without speaking to Garry Bushell. I'd done my homework, read his autobiography *Bushell on the Rampage* (2010) and his book *Hoolies: True Stories of Britain's Biggest Street Battles* (2010) and his opinionated *The World According to Garry Bushell* (2008).

In the *Guardian* article when I'd mentioned his name in relation to the controversy surrounding *Strength Thru Oi!*, the subs had added 'then-music journalist'. I told them he still was a music journalist, having recently replaced Gavin Martin as the *Daily Mirror's* chief music critic. He is also Review Editor of the *Sunday Express* and TV columnist for the *Daily Star*. And he still records and gigs with his band The Gonads.

It's an easy mistake to make; to forget that Bushell is foremost a music journalist. After he left *Sounds* in 1984, he spent sixteen years at *The Sun*, under the tutelage and influence of editor Kelvin MacKenzie who is quoted as saying (on the subject of how he perceived *The Sun*'s target audience): 'He's the bloke you see in the pub, a right old fascist, wants to send the wogs back, buy his poxy council house, he's afraid of the unions, afraid of the Russians, hates the queers and the weirdos and drug dealers.'

Bushell found it easy to serve up stuff for that demographic, quickly promoted to be *The Sun*'s TV critic and a lead feature writer. This led to him becoming something of a hate figure. Boy George called him 'the Bernard Manning of pop'. *Viz* ran a cartoon strip called 'Bushell the Bear', a character obsessed with homosexuality, the scourge of political correctness and non-existent left-wing conspiracies to the exclusion of all else. He admitted in his autobiography: 'I parodied my own views, becoming a caricature of myself either for devilment or comic effect.'

In doing so he became a household name, a regular on TV, even had his own TV show for a while. Since then he'd had a go at most things: novels, autobiography, non-fiction, blogging (on his own website), ghostwriting (Jeff's Rejects book), radio presenting and politics, standing for the English Democrats in the 2005 elections. The party wanted to leave the European Union and establish an English parliament, and, I read, had attracted quite a few BNP voters. He was routinely critical of Labour and proudly patriotic, campaigning, for instance, for St George's Day to be a public holiday.

We began a dialogue via email in early June. It was clear he was aware of the book. 'Ha, yes, we were told your agenda was to establish that Oi! was a far-right plot, which of course it wasn't.' We chit-chatted a while. 'I'm glad to hear Mackie's well,' he wrote me. 'I loved Blitz. I remember they came down to my old council estate, the Ferrier, and were a little disconcerted because of the *Clockwork Orange* vibe. I did go up to see them in New Mills, quite a tough place in itself but much better scenery.'

I mentioned I'd come into contact with his friend, the Oi! poet Garry Johnson, when I wrote my Stone Roses biography, as Johnson had managed the Roses briefly in the mid-eighties. He was an interesting figure: dropped out of school age 14, been to borstal, and then been encouraged by Bushell away from his band Buzz Kids towards poetry. Johnson worked fast: wrote and published the first book about Oi! in a few short months after Southall. It was slim and speed-fuelled, called *Oi! A View from the Dead-End of the Street*. His poem on *Carry On Oi!*, called 'United', had been a plea for unity between black and white.

At the time I'd been speaking to him, Johnson was preoccupied in a heated marital issue which he was then chronicling on the internet. Bushell said it had ended up with Johnson being banged up in Belmarsh. 'Sadly, he's been ill for years now,' Bushell said. 'A great shame as he's a lovely man.'

Bushell was happy to answer my questions. Via email. I knew he was playing at Rebellion with The Gonads so I said hopefully

I could see him face to face down the line. I'm looking at the list of questions now, 17 in total.

I had two key thrusts: there were clearly strong links between many Oi! bands and the NF/BM, and that contradicted his long-held position that there was little or no far-right associations in Oi! (although he had admitted there was a far-right element among the audience, 'but this was 1980 when the far right was polling 15–20 per cent of the vote in inner city wards'). I suggested that while it was believable that *Sounds* editor, Alan Lewis, didn't know who Nicky Crane was, surely *he* did when he put him on the *Strength Thru Oi!* cover. I also asked why the same cover was used on all subsequent reissues of the album up to present day.

Maybe overly aggressive? He was riled anyway, writing back: 'Your angle is a lot like the old *News of the World* one: "Mr Bushell, I put it to you that you are a wife-beater". Me: "I've never beaten my wife!" *News of the World* headline: "Bushell denies he's a wife-beater". Public: "hmm, no smoke without fire."'

I thought I'd blown it. I explained my sources, said I was a fan of Oi!. Four days later he sent me a long defensive email. Some of the stuff I already knew – it was the same Oi! stuff he'd peddled elsewhere, about how from age 16 he was a committed Trotskyist (broadly meaning power to the people). I'd read about his background in left-wing politics in his autobiography. Born in 1955 into a solid Labour family in Charlton, south-east London, dad a fireman, mum a bank worker. How as a reggae-loving 15-year-old suedehead he was on the streets pushing the *Socialist Worker* newspaper, how at 18 he'd joined International Socialists attending many demos and marches. Then after he'd done his A levels and a degree in sociology at

North East London Poly he had taken a journalism course and started working for left-wing publications, *Temporary Hoarding* (the RAR magazine), *Socialist Worker* and its youth publication *Rebel*. This was when he began writing about punk, which led to his own punk fanzine, and ultimately to *Sounds* in September 1978, where he was openly political, urging readers to vote Labour in 1979 and 1983.

In his email he wrote about The Rejects battering the BM, plus an incident at a Poplar pub where BM skins were dispatched by Terry Adams ('Oi! the DJ, solid Labour'). He said there were a lot more Labour people around than right-wingers in Oi!, naming Dave Long (Syndicate Records) and Snaky John (Muir) the boss at Manchester's Babylon Books who'd published Johnson's Oi! book. 'They weren't in the audience, they were managing bands, getting deals and putting on gigs,' he said.

Bushell accepted Hodges, Hitchcock and Panther were ex-BM skins, said he had written about it himself several times in *Sounds* and beyond. The crucial part he said was 'ex'. Hodges, he said, was always Labour when he spoke to him, admired Jim Callaghan (Labour Prime Minister 1976–79).

'Was there a neo-Nazi skinhead problem in the late seventies and early eighties music scene? Undoubtably yes,' he said. 'But the bands who attracted them and had the most trouble from them were Sham 69, The Lurkers, Madness, The Selecter, Bad Manners and so on. Suggsy's closeness to Ian Stuart Donaldson is well known yet somehow that never seems to merit a book.' Bushell had written the article in *The Sun* in 1986 that had accompanied a front-cover photo of Suggs and Skrewdriver singer Ian Stuart together (headline: ROCK STAR'S NAZI PAL) but he said the photo was nothing to do with him. 'They [the likely pair who supplied the photo] wanted revenge on Suggsy for coming out for Red Wedge,' he said. 'They contacted the picture desk and news asked me to write it. I had nothing to do with the deal; they negotiated their fee with the deputy picture editor.'

He mentioned The Business and their anti-racism tour in the aftermath of Southall. How he and Lol Pryor had also met up with Red Action ('the most violent and effective anti-fascists in London') who started to put on their own Oi! gigs post-Southall. He might have mentioned his promotion, in *Sounds*, of anti-racist skin sects, 'Sussed Skins' and 'Skins Against The Nazis'. He could have referred to statements he made at the time such as: 'You can't just wave a Union Jack, you've got to have more to say . . . aim towards more purposeful rebellion.'

I think he'd been quite serious about finding purpose in Oi!. He had convened Mensi and Jeff and the 4-Skins for a *Sounds* feature, 'Oi! the debate' in early '81, followed by an 'Oi! conference' held at Conway Hall in June 1981, just six days before Southall, with fifty-seven people present including the Rejects, 4-Skins, Splodge, Infa Riot, Business and the Resort. The idea was to plan how Oi! could develop positively – talk focusing on arranging their own gigs, setting up their own label and playing benefits for working-class causes, such as striking workers and the unemployed.

Bushell was critical in print of songs such as 'Soul Boys' by the Resort, which advocated violence towards the subject, arguing it promoted division. There were concerns voiced at the conference about Oi!'s violent image and the fact it was getting too skinhead orientated. Bushell wanted to include anarcho bands such as Conflict and The Apostles, and Two-tone bands, on upcoming Oi! comps. 'Oi! is uniting punks, skins and everyone,' Roi said at the conference. 'Now we've just got to get away from football.' A prophetic statement. Later that day, at a gig in Southgate, north London, featuring Infa Riot and the Upstarts (who replaced the 4-Skins at the last minute) cops were called to break up a violent clash between Arsenal and West Ham hooligans.

In the email Bushell didn't have much to say about Southall. He wasn't there. He suggested that a minibus containing Business fans including Garry Johnson was attacked by Asians wielding swords. How there were a few black, Asian and Greek kids inside the venue. He had written in *Sounds* about 'at least thirty non-white skins' who were regulars at Oi! gigs, many half-Pakistani, others West Indian, an Arab and a Jewish girl, Danielle Lux (now a high-flying TV executive).

Later when the *Guardian* Crown Court article was published and he complimented me on its fairness, he had a couple of things to add about Southall. 'You called the SYM [Southall Youth Movement] "anti-fascist", but I was told by an Asian filmmaker from Southall that the mob's motivation was territorial rather than political. They didn't want other firms on their patch. There were genuine anti-fascists inside the pub along with apolitical kids. Calling the rioters anti-fascist seems like an attempt to make a mass arson attack seem heroic or justified. Secondly, you mention trouble in shops. There was one incident in one shop involving a few light-fingered teenagers from the Coldharbour estate in south-east London. The biggest crime the Oi! fans committed [at Southall] was being outsiders.'

When it came to the *Strength Thru Oi!* cover, I'd laid out the prosecution's evidence: what he'd said in the past; how he chose the shot in haste when a photo shoot with Rejects' road crew member Carlton Leach fell through; that he reckoned he had the Crane shot pinned up at work, thought it was a 'skinhead Xmas card'. He told the *Guardian* in 2010 he thought it was, 'a still from *The Wanderers*' (released in 1979 but set in 1963). This was as part of an article by Alexis Petridis looking back at Oi!, interviewing Bushell and Jeff for a piece headlined: 'Misunderstood or hateful? Oi!'s Rise And Fall'. Bushell was quoted as saying: 'It wasn't until the very last minute when Decca had mocked up the sleeve that the photo was sufficiently clear to reveal Nazi tattoos. We had the option of either airbrushing the tattoos out or putting back the LP by a month while we put the new sleeve together.' He admitted he made a rash decision and added: 'There was nothing else on that album or in Oi! that could possibly be construed as dodgy.'

He'd also stated that rather than the title being a riff on the Nazi slogan, Strength Through Joy, he was actually inspired by a Skids release called *Strength Thru Joy*, a limited edition second disc that came with copies of their 1980 album *The Absolute Game*. Singer Richard Jobson said he had got the title from a line in a Dirk Bogarde autobiography. Bushell said he was unaware of any Nazi connotations to the term Strength Through Joy. There was some debate around The Skids at the time, however: their 1979 debut album had a cover that was described by John Peel as 'Aryan' and 'Nazi wall posterish'.

Several people, I said, had suggested to me Crane was an infamous face, well-known by all in skinhead circles, and his various prison sentences were also well reported in the media. Also, the photographer who took the Crane shot, Martin Dean, was credited on the album sleeve and worked for *Sounds* photographing Oi! bands, so Bushell must have known who Dean was? I said I'd watched *The Wanderers*, and the 'baldies' gang in that movie were more comic than violent, didn't wear braces or Dr. Martens.

'I've been answering questions about *Strength Thru Oi!* for forty-one years,' Bushell said. 'Every time I do so, I am assured that my point of view will be put across fully. But inevitably, my answers are edited and used in part as part of a pre-conceived and false narrative. After the last time it happened (*Vive Le Rock*, 2021) I vowed never to speak about it again and see no reason to change my mind now. It was a cock-up, not a conspiracy.'

He did address one of my concerns over the *Strength* sleeve, regarding reissues. 'They're not mine to change,' he said. 'Captain Oi! [run by Mark Brennan] either licensed them years ago or bought the rights.'

He suggested the attacks on him, *Sounds* and Oi! by the *Mail* and *NME* at the time were motivated by industry rivalries – *Sounds* being owned by the Express group, the *Mail*'s then-biggest competitor, and beginning to outsell *NME*. He said Oi! had never had a fair hearing. 'Oi! wasn't skinhead. It was, by definition, for skins, working-class punks and football hooligans,' he said. 'And skinheads weren't all Nazis.'

Bushell said: 'Nazis only became our problem because of *Strength Thru Oi!* an' the *Daily Mail*'s distortions and hysteria.' He maintained his long-held line that the main problem Oi! had was football related. All the riots – he mentioned the Resort at Ladbroke Grove and Infa Riot at Southgate – were football/territorial battles. He also suggested the real scandal around Oi! was the links to crime, in some cases serious offences like armed robbery. 'Hodges did time for armed robbery, Roi's record meant he couldn't play America for decades,' he said.

He added that the general view of the BM at the time was they were nuisances, 'mugs'. In *Sounds* he'd called them 'cretinous', 'fringe crackpots' and 'pathetic'. He had been physically confronted by them several times; by 'the hardest of the hardcore at an early Rejects gig', saved from a beating by one of the Rejects' road crew. Garry Johnson, he said, had been beaten up in Peckham. Bushell's bandmate in The Gonads, Si Spanner, who was Jewish, was stabbed. He mentioned he'd been beaten himself by a BM mob at a gig at the 100 Club and attacked again by the same crew in early 1982. When he refused to cover Skrewdriver in *Sounds*, the hostilities stepped up. His address was published in *Bulldog* in 1983 and he was forced to move home, and there was a terrifying sounding incident at a train station where he was threatened with a Stanley knife.

There were some questions he ignored, such as when I asked about his own drift to the right and towards nationalism, and others I can't quite believe I asked. I wondered if he'd considered the implications of, when writing about his childhood and adolescence in his autobiography, his description of three incidents of black men mugging (twice at knifepoint) him and family members. This topic was what the NF had marched about in the seventies.

He concluded anyway, from my overall line of questioning (even though I had clearly stated I intended no offence and I was playing devil's advocate), that I was attempting 'to blacken the name of the bands involved' in Oi!. 'To smear us all and, in the process, undo all the good work we've done for forty years.'

I approached him at Rebellion anyway. The Gonads (who have released six albums since reforming in the late nineties) played late Saturday afternoon on the Pavilion stage. Bushell in his Motörhead shirt. I was reminded of the Oi! offshoot Bushell championed back in the day, he'd dubbed it 'punk pathetique': coarse comedy and punk energy from bands such as Splodgenessabounds, Peter and the Test-Tube Babies and the Toy Dolls.

Later that day I saw him in the front row of the Roi Q&A. Afterwards I introduced myself, but he didn't stop walking and headed for the down escalator. Weird. I saw him mouthing to the woman he was with, sort of exaggerated, what's he saying? I said, loudly, as he went down the escalator, 'wait at the bottom, I'll come down.' He didn't wait. I was done chasing. He'd told me he might write his own Oi! book one day. I don't know if he'll find the time. When I first approached him for an interview, his manager told me he was routinely working seventy-hour weeks.

He'd been nothing short of a phenomenon: he'd named Oi!, was the music journalist who championed it, put together the first two Oi! comps at *Sounds*, stuck by it after Southall in the face of fierce and hurtful criticisms, even formed his own Oi! band, The Gonads, and (with help from The Business) recorded songs for *Carry on Oi!!* and *Oi! Oi! That's Yer Lot!* The latter album, released by Secret in September '82, was advertised as the 'final instalment of the first phase of the popular proletarian punk phenomenon Oi!'. Bushell's name was not on the cover but he was clearly involved in the track selection: launching Frankie Flame, resurrecting Judge Dread, introducing The Blood (who he managed) and giving belated debuts to the East End Badoes and another east end/West Ham band (formed by another former Sham roadie and skinhead), Angela Rippon's Bum.

He might have been having some sort of breakdown. As Oi! became increasingly untouchable thanks to Skrewdriver and the NF/RAC rise (see chapter 8) he seemed to be in a frenzy, recording a deluge of tracks for his pal Dave Long who resurrected the Oi! comp idea for his Syndicate Records label, releasing *Son of Oi!* in '83 and the *Oi! of Sex* in '84. I've listened to these albums so you don't have to. Bushell was behind tracks by The Gonads, Gary & The Gonads, Oi! The Robot (with Frankie Flame), Prole, The Orgasm Guerrillas, Paranoid Pictures and Manic Youth (all with Steve Kent).

Syndicate went bankrupt in 1984. Bushell also left *Sounds* in 1984 and his wife left him (they had two very young kids). He writes in his autobiography that he tried to kill himself.

Here now I hoped to introduce you to The Oppressed, from Cardiff, formed by former borstal boy Roddy Moreno when he got out of prison. They were the final significant UK band to emerge from the initial Bushell Oi! scene (they made their debut with a track called 'White Flag' on *Oi! Oi! That's Yer Lot!*) and would become the Oi! band most closely associated with 'anti-fascism'.

Their debut album *Oi! Oi! Music!* released in 1984 (it included a cover of 'Chaos', the band also covered a Last Resort song live) was described by Stewart Home, in his book *Cranked Up Really High: Genre Theory & Punk Rock* (Codex, 1995) as 'one of the best skinhead records ever made'. Moreno was also active in booking Oi! gigs in Cardiff.

The Oppressed broke up in 1985 shortly after a gig Moreno organised in the city, featuring The Business, Indecent Exposure and Vicious Rumours (a new Oi! band who featured on both Syndicate Oi! comps) ended in a riot with a military surplus store smashed up and a policeman stabbed. I'm assuming the gig was targeted by the far right.

Moreno went on to run his own label, Oi! Records, one of the only outlets for Oi! music in the UK in the mid-to-late eighties that was distinct from the white power scene. The label's *This is Oi!* comp released in 1986 is a good example of the bands from this period, featuring Vicious Rumours, Condemned 84 and Section 5. Moreno was also the man who introduced the American SHARP movement to the UK in 1989, and designed the movement's famous Trojan Records-inspired logo. SHARP stood for Skinheads Against Racial Prejudice. Oi! Records released New York band The Press, outspoken anti-fascists, and the first group the SHARP scene rallied around in America. In 1994 Moreno reformed The Oppressed and they are now the world's foremost SHARP band.

I'd like to have asked about this and more but I missed The Oppressed when they played the annual anti-fascist festival 0161 in Manchester in early May and failed to recognise Moreno at a late-night pub gig in Blackpool during Rebellion. He was there, like me, to watch a SHARP band from Singapore called The Bois.

Instead, I'd like to introduce an erudite voice: Matt Worley, professor of modern history at University of Reading and co-founder of the Subcultures Network. He had written two academic articles specifically about Oi! that caught my eye: 'Oi! Oi! Oi!: Class, Locality, and British Punk' featured in the *Twentieth Century British History* journal (2013, Oxford University Press) and 'Hey Little Rich Boy, Take A Good Look At Me: Punk, Class and British Oi!' featured in the *Punk & Post-Punk* journal (2014, Intellect).

I also read one further article he wrote, 'White Youth: The Far Right, Punk and British Youth Culture, 1977–87', featured in the *JOMEC* journal (2016, Cardiff University), and a book, *No Future: Punk, Politics and British Youth Culture 1976-1984* (Cambridge University Press, 2021).

All good stuff – a mix of history, theory and sociology. Of course, I was looking for clues, leads and bits to nick. I didn't know, for instance, that the 4-Skins track 'Bread or Blood' from their debut album was about the 'East Anglian agricultural riots of 1816'.

Worley is a fan of eighties Oi!, of the opinion that it was driven by a mix of working-class social realism and street socialism, and argues that these aspects were buried beneath a mixture of middle-class prejudice, media misrepresentation and far-right encroachment.

We made contact, via a mutual friend, soon after Worley had attended an 'informal wake' for Lol Pryor (who had died in May 2022). He said he'd been talking to people who worked with Pryor and The Business. I explained I'd got off on the wrong foot with Bushell and feared that this was having a ripple effect. I'd recently been blanked in a pub by Steve Whale, Business guitarist. 'I know Garry [Bushell] quite well and have met a few others from that world,' Worley said.

We spoke for a couple of hours on the phone. Another Crown Court fan, Worley was born in 1970 and explained how he'd got into punk and Oi! when he 10 or 11, read *Sounds*, trying to understand what it was all about. Big fan of The Business, Infa Riot and Blitz. He recalled buying the *Son of Oi!* album in '83. 'At the time everyone was saying Oi! is Nazi, and I'm listening to this record where it's got an anti-racist song by Angelic Upstarts ['I Understand'], [an] anti-racist song by Newtown Neurotics and Liverpool poets like Mick Turpin talking about things I always think the left should be talking about, which is working conditions, wages and who makes the profits and who doesn't – inherently old-school socialism that people like Bushell still sometimes claim they adhere to. The poetry is where Oi! and the link to left-[wing] politics is clearest.

'Even at the time I thought, why is this record racist or Nazi?' he added. 'Almost all my life I'd wanted to write a corrective to that and I got to do that when I wrote the first Oi! piece. I felt I had the academic chops and research to do it.'

I asked how he'd gone about the research. 'I got in touch with people who'd been involved in Red Action, anti-fascists from the time who knew who was who and what was what. I never met Red Action's Mick O'Farrell, but he was quoted on an Oi! album sleeve. They'd recognised Oi! as a good thing. There's some bad people in it but it's a good thing because it's working class, it's a working-class culture and it's giving voice and space to working-class people. Then it was a case of reading the interviews from the time; looking what was actually said and done rather than taking accusations as fact.'

How had he got his 'in' with Bushell and co? 'I sent an email saying I always thought Oi! had been kind of so narrowed down and simplified in how it was interpreted, that the context was always missed and the wider picture was missed,' he said. 'I guess my gambit opened a door for me. I went and met Garry in a pub first of all, had a chat with him, followed-up again and he said he'd bring some people down, and there was Hoxton Tom, Lee Wilson [Infa Riot singer] and then he arranged a meeting with Lol. I met him a couple of times after that to follow up. I met Stinky Turner; he came down one evening.

'Garry is very wary because he gets it all the time, about Oi! being right wing or whatever,' Worley added. 'He's constantly having to have that conversation. There's certain homophobic things he said [in print], and I get why that's been criticised (and was at the time), but I never saw him say anything racist and I read so much [music press] stuff from that period. There was nothing at all. But he is very sensitive about it.

'It'd be hard to write about Oi! without mentioning Southall or the *Strength Thru Oi!* cover,' Worley said. 'It's an integral part of the history, but for it to become the determining factor of Oi! is missing the bigger picture. Garry used to get tonnes of stick for Oi!, but at the same time he was writing about Oi! his other obsession was Two-tone. Him and Adrian Thrills at *NME* were the main champions of Two-tone at the time, so in relation to accusations of racism in that moment, it didn't ring true.

'There was a lot of backward projection on his politics because of him later writing for *The Sun*. But in the early 1980s he was championing The Redskins and writing *Sounds* editorials telling people to vote Labour.'

Worley had written positively about the 4-Skins' music and I asked how he reconciled that with the involvement of faces such as Gary Hitchcock. 'I was talking to Lol Pryor about it,' Worley said. 'Lol liked his football rucks but he was also a trade unionist. He said something along the lines of, Oh I'd always have these kinds of conversations with Hitchcock, who had all these stupid views but he got things done on the music side of it. It is hard to get your head around if you didn't grow up in that kind of milieu – that's for people to work out themselves.'

I asked him what he made of 'One Law For Them'? 'Looking back, the song reflects Hodges, where he comes from and he had a BM background,' Worley said. 'The class element as I see it is the way in which it's perceived: if a black man throws a brick it's deemed to be a rebellious incident, if a white bloke at football throws a brick it's deemed to be hooliganism. Really crude, obviously, like a twisted 'White Riot' by The Clash, but that's the class bit; railing against middle-class views of black working class and white working class. But as it's through Hodges, it obviously contains racial overtones. At the time, most people saw it as about class, hence the cover image of toffs.'

And 'Brave New World'? 'Yeah, they are the two songs,' Worley said. 'That's Hodges' background coming through again or can be read in that way. They are ambiguous enough; he evidently didn't want to be too explicit about it but the signs are there for those who want them. There's an interview soon after Southall, when Hodges has left, where the band say their plan was to be anti-government: not party politics but the politics of street. Then [guitarist] Joe Jacobs says something along the lines of some songs having more meaning than they should have had.

'The thing for me is that class always predominated in Oi! – that's the thing that connects the bands,' he added, wrapping up. 'The politics vary. You can pick bits out – but why pick one song out over, say, 'Bread or Blood' or 'Out in the Cold' and 'National Insurance Blacklist' by The Business, or Garry Johnson's 'Boy About Town'? Oi! endeavoured to give voice to working-class people and that is a positive. It was a space to work out these politics. Try thinking of it as conversation (or a row) rather than any set opinion or position. Also remember how young they all were. I always think about these cultures as being contested spaces: a place where you try out your politics or argue your politics where it won't condemn you for life . . . though it obviously does in some circumstances.'

I also asked Worley what I wanted to ask Roddy, about the Oi! scene in the mid-eighties and the jarring mix of left and right-wing bands on gig line-ups? 'The scene was so small by then that a lot of them ended up gathering together wherever they could,' he said. 'I know certain bands and people now regret playing a couple of gigs and you get tarnished by association. I talked to one band who said they were the only gigs we could get, no one else was going to put them on.

'Again, it's really difficult for us to get our heads round where you could be in a room with someone with Nazi opinions and you don't just think, Right I'm leaving. But lots of people did back then, and not just in and about Oi!.'

Chapter 7

Paramilitary Is The Score: Combat 84

Combat 84. The infamous Combat 84. They were the final great Oi! band of the era, the next logical progression after Sham, Upstarts, Rejects, 4-Skins, Resort and Business. They turned everything up a notch: sound, lyrics, clothes. Singer Chris Henderson had a voice that was a mix of Fitz, Roi and Hodges, but it was not just a voice with this lot – the band swung in a way few Oi! bands did, and the songs stung.

They had nothing to do with Bushell's Oi!, didn't feature on any of the original four Oi! albums nor either of the next two on Syndicate. What made them (and sank them) was the BBC Two *40 Minutes* documentary they starred in, *Skinheads* (aired October 1982). It was filmed in early '82 and featured footage of a gig they did in January at Benny's in Harlow, west Essex. In total they were said to have only played live fewer than twenty times. They didn't record much, either (about eleven songs), but the band have been exhaustively repackaged over the years. I'm listening to *Complete Collection* on Spotify (Step-1, 2022) which collects all their tracks and adds live recordings. Their songs have been covered by Oi! bands such as Rise Up, B-Squadron and Lion's Law as well as the Dropkick Murphys.

Henderson, aka Chubby, was a young skinhead impressed by the BM skins and wanted recognition, preferably Leader Guard status. In 1981 he was 22, often hanging about the Last Resort shop. Derek Ridgers photographed him as part of a gang that were on the cover of his *Skinheads* book. He was the one with the Nazi slogan tattooed on his arm. 'He was OK when he was sober,' Ridgers told me.

The band played their first gig supporting the Last Resort and The Elite at the Walmer Castle in Peckham in October 1981. Roi was said to have produced their two-track demo featuring 'Soldier' and band anthem 'Combat 84'. Gary Hitchcock was a sort of band manager and attempted to get them signed to Secret Records. Bushell warned the label away, suggesting Chubby was a card-carrying BM member.

So bassist Deptford John, with the assistance of Dave Long, set up the band's own Victory Records and in 1982 put out the classic EP, *Orders of the Day*, which featured: 'Violence', 'Combat 84', 'Poseur' (Chubby's lyrics about the new romantics, specifically Steve Strange) and 'Skinhead'. It was said to have sold 10,000 copies.

Chubby died in 2013. In 2002 he'd brought out a book *Who Wants It?* that glosses over Combat 84 and chiefly focuses on his time, post-band, as a notorious football hooligan, a leading face in the infamous Chelsea Headhunters. He was arrested and acquitted in 1987 in a famous trial that was part of the government's crackdown on hooliganism. He spoke about the undercover police investigation on BBC news after the acquittal. 'A police conspiracy about legitimate Chelsea fans,' he smirked. I think he got compensation. At some point he relocated to Thailand and set up a bar in Pattaya, the Dogs Bollocks.

He was a polarising figure within Chelsea and Oi! circles, especially in relation to playing up for the camera. I got the impression he was troubled and impressionable, especially as a young skin. Stewart Home wrote that Chubby was playing at being a yob and had been educated at the exclusive Charterhouse school. In *Who Wants It?* Chubby admits he was once a public schoolboy, attended Seaford College in Petworth, West Sussex. Got expelled. Beat up the head boy.

It was Chubby's brother who went to Charterhouse. The pair were adopted. His mum was only 16 when she had Chubby. Their step-parents were rich; his stepfather had worked at Edinburgh University. After being expelled from public school Chubby went to 'special school' with 'seven people in a class', and then fell in with the wrong crowd, started drinking, robbed his mum's house (it is unclear if this was his real mum or stepmum – he ruminated on the confusion he felt about being adopted in the *Skinheads* documentary). Anyway, he went to court for it, got a two-year suspended sentence, and was put in care, in a hostel. I'd read somewhere his first intro to the music scene was when he got involved as security for Bad Manners and The Damned. It was clear he wasn't good at avoiding trouble, had been nicked twice for minor disturbances – one incident involved a fight on Carnaby Street, the police claiming he was seen 'kicking in windows, Sieg Heiling and pushing old women'.

I contacted Deptford John [Armitage] via his Guitar Hospital website. He has a workshop fixing guitars in Rotherhithe, south-east London. Post-Combat 84, after spells in the U.K. Subs and

The Exploited, he'd toured the world looking after the guitars of bands such as Iron Maiden, the Manic Street Preachers and The Verve, as well as for guitarists who played live shows with Take That, Spice Girls and George Michael. Other names he'd worked for as a guitar tech included New Order, Lily Allen, The Streets and Mick Jagger. On his site he has a glowing testimonial from Sir Paul McCartney: 'John is one of the most renowned guitar techs in the industry'.

He was happy to speak, and I called him one evening at the end of June. He said he'd heard about the book, knew people in the scene were suspicious but had nothing to hide. 'You're going to write the book anyway so I might as well try and get across our side.' He mentioned his wife was a tour manager and on tour at the minute with Jeff Beck, was somewhere on a private jet with Beck and Johnny Depp, so he was at a loose end.

I started off talking about Jimmy Pursey. John was at the Reading Festival gig in '78. 'I didn't go on the stage but I helped him drink the beer robbed from the beer tent,' he said. 'Jimmy was very much the figurehead for the working class. There was the Sham song that went, What have we got? Fuck all. And that was like the tune for Oi!. No one had anything. No one had any money. If anyone had a job they were mainly apprentices or basic low-wage jobs. There was a load of white working-class blokes who didn't really have any decent role models. It was no surprise that the Oi! scene begat football hooliganism.

'Oi!,' he said, 'was kind of the lowest common denominator scene in a way. You didn't have to be a good musician, no one had Gibson Les Pauls or a Marshall, they all had copies, their brother's amps. No one was really singing, people were shouting and screaming in rage, everyone was angry and it was really aggressive. There wasn't a lot of humour, it was very intense. It was like straight-edge hardcore . . . us against the world.

'The skinhead pubs were rough,' he added. 'If a fight started inside, we'd have to hold the doors shut so it didn't spill outside which meant the police getting involved and the landlord might lose his licence. I've seen loads of people stabbed in them pubs. But everyone was in a band; it was great. Every time you went to a skinhead pub you met someone who was in a band or you asked them to join your band if they could play an instrument. We got our guitar player Jim because one of our mates said he'd just bought a Les Paul on the catalogue. So, I said, do you wanna be in my band, then? I never asked him if he could play it. By the time we got our first rehearsal he'd sold the guitar because he couldn't afford the payments.' He said Jim, who played guitar throughout C84's lifespan, now lives in LA and runs a haulage company.

I asked about the name of the band. In Oi!, often numbers can be code. It does not take Alan Turing to crack the code (18 and 88 are the obvious ones, Adolf Hitler and Heil Hitler) but it can sometimes be confusing. I'd noticed 84 was also popular. 'The whole thing of the name was completely lost on everyone because of Column 88,' John said. I wondered if he'd meant Combat 18 and was confused but checked it out and Column 88 were another neo-Nazi paramilitary organisation that had been suspected of carrying out terrorist attacks in the late seventies/early eighties, including the arson attack that destroyed the Albany Empire in Deptford in 1978, said to be linked to the venue's support of RAR.

John continued: 'If you read *Nineteen Eighty-Four* by George Orwell, the dystopian version of the future, all the products are called Victory, that's why our label was Victory Records, and the

Combat was because we all wore combat gear.' He quoted the band's anthem, 'Combat 84: paramilitary is the score, we're the band, Combat 84'. 'That was all based on the book,' he said. 'George Orwell wrote about Combat 84.'

I said I felt the bass was a key part of the Oi! sound, a tractor rumble? 'Most of the songwriters were originally the bass players,' he said. '[Hoxton] Tom McCourt, me and Arthur from the Resort who lives in a retirement community 200 yards down the road from me. He's clean and sober and does counselling in prisons. He still writes for the Resort. The guitar players just followed the bass lines really to start with. It was very simple.' Hoxton Tom, he said, was 'one of my role models throughout the whole Oi! thing'. 'Me and him were both into a bit of Motown on the sly, the bass lines all came from that sort of thing, when the bass was a lot more dominant,' John said. 'Tom wrote some great songs.'

I asked him where he stood on 'One Law for Them'? His answer was quite oblique. 'Tom got stabbed and the police interviewed him, and while he was still sedated in hospital, he said, oh no it's OK [he wasn't going to press charges]. I got stabbed in the face, in the head and the leg after the New Cross fire [January '81, thirteen young black people aged 14–22 were killed in a house fire at a party]. I walked down to Lewisham Hospital and got sewn up and went to the police station and said, I'd like to report a racist attack, and they said, oh sorry we can't take that on board. Why not? There's no proof you didn't start the fight, off you go. Three blokes attacked me with knives at a bus stop in broad daylight, the traffic was stopped, I was stabbed three times.'

You're saying the song is about those sorts of situations, black gang assaults on white skins?

'Yeah, exactly,' he said. 'Now, if you listen to 'Brave New World', "rising from the ashes like a phoenix in the sky, birth of a movement 'cos the old one has to die." Now that one I would say had some slightly questionable undertones.'

Deptford John said he lived just down the road from Gary Hodges and they'd collaborated quite recently (2018) on a project called Mean Streak, releasing a self-titled EP. They were pals. Hodges was now considered 'grey zone' after a big comeback went awry. In 2007, he'd recorded two tracks for the *Kings of Street Punk* album, released by a new label G&R put together by Mick from the Rejects and Skully, fresh out of nick. Mick, Skully and H were involved in the recording of the new 4-Skins song 'Glory Days' and a reworked version of 'Chaos'. Also on the album were the Rejects ('21st Century Oi!'), The Business, Rancid, Red Alert, The Gonads and East End Badoes. Jeff even resurrected The Postmen and did a song called 'Oi! Along the Watchtower'.

Hoxton Tom was not interested in the reunion, said the band was 'about youth'. So, with the support of Indecent Exposure, who provided backing, Hodges' 4-Skins played three major festivals in 2008. In an interview published online to promote their appearance at the East Coast Oi! Fest in Pennsylvania (Indecent Exposure also played the festival as a standalone act), Hodges, soon to be 50, said: 'I left the band in late '82. We had all the shit and repercussions from Southall. I wanted to face problems head on, be true to myself and the people that used to support us. Other band members thought the way to combat this was to suck up to the left.'

Hodges' 4-Skins also headlined Punk & Disorderly in Berlin and the Rebellion festival in Blackpool. They then recorded a new album, *The Return*, released in 2010 by Randale. It was a mix of old songs re-recorded (including 'One Law for Them' and 'Brave New World'), a couple of Slade covers, and a few new ones. His voice was less potent and so were the songs. One, 'Soldiers Graves', was stridently patriotic with its 'Rule, Britannia!' chorus. However, it was 'Take No More' that critics swooped on; a song attacking 'illegal immigrants . . . begging in their gypsy mobs'. Hodges sang 'our country is full' and demanded 'we put our own people first'.

Deptford John said there was a misprint of the lyrics on the record's inner sleeve, which I took to mean that perhaps the word 'illegal' was missed out. You can pick this debate up online. Sedge of Indecent Exposure/Hodges' 4-Skins was active, saying the band were not racist just fed up with eastern-European immigrants. Challenged, he came back with a capital-letter diatribe: 'CRIME. TERRORISTS. NO.T NAZIS. STAND UP FOR OUR OWN.' *The Return* is still there to listen to on Spotify but the controversy generated put paid to Hodges. The past of Indecent Exposure was also part of the damning: their links to the eighties NF/RAC scene (see next chapter).

Deptford John stood by his mate; told me they might do a one-off Mean Streak gig at some point. John was still plugged into the Oi! scene, hence his call to the promoter of Cream of the Crop on my behalf. He knew Crown Court, The Chisel, Grade 2 ('I think they're going to be massive – the happy side of Oi!') and had helped out Rise Up with musical ideas and lyrics recently (he said Hodges was pals with the dad of the teenage singer in the band). John also knew Roi 'really well'.

'I got to know Roi through the scene in the early eighties,' he said. 'Roi produced our first demo except, he didn't – he just said I could tell people he had. We were mates when the band was fledglings and we still get on. He lives a couple of miles away from me. We go to the same tattooist. When I go to football [John also supports Millwall], I always see him. Roi doesn't drink any more. A lot of people from that scene are clean and sober or we wouldn't be here now.'

I asked about the early eighties Oi! scene in Deptford, his old stomping ground. He mentioned drinking with The Afflicted at the Fountain on Sunday night. 'The Fountain was a pub that served anyone,' he said. 'There'd be recruiters from the Ku Klux Klan in there, rastas, Hells Angels, punks, skinheads, mods. You'd all have your own bit. It was a place that would serve anyone – no one wanted to ruin it by causing trouble. There was another pub called the King's Head which is where I first met Nicky Crane.'

Oh, I said.

'Nicky Crane was also a neighbour of Garry's [Bushell],' he said. 'Dartford and Kidbrooke are on the same train line. Everyone knew who Nicky Crane was. Everyone I knew from that era knew who Nicky Crane was, whether they were a skinhead or a punk, he was known in south London. Garry backed himself into a corner when he said he didn't know who Crane was when he put him on the cover [of *Strength Thru Oi!*] but who gives a shit about that in 2022.

'The problem [for Bushell] is you're the architect of your own demise career-wise, really, by creating Oi! and then it becoming so right wing,' he said. 'And then the right-wing people thought you'd sold them out because you wouldn't support them. He wouldn't have us on the Oi! albums and by then he'd run out of bands to the point he was inventing bands!'

Did you hang out at the Last Resort shop I asked?

'Oh yeah,' John said. 'I used to like going there. I didn't have anything to do so I could go up there and hang about.'

Would you know the photographer Martin Dean?

'Martin Dean did all our Combat stuff. I don't know if he had a political agenda. I never got that from him . . . he was a really nice bloke.'

I asked John if he was at Southall? 'Chubby was,' he said. 'I wasn't. The trouble was Southall was another situation where it was just bad policing. There were the same people at the gigs as had always been at the gigs, but the people outside were told some skinheads had raped a woman or punched a pregnant girl. It's like small town rumours – you punch someone at the bottom of the high street, by the time you've got to the other end you've killed him. So they [the SYM] gathered up and in the end Chubby said the police were giving the skinheads shields, they were all standing shoulder to shoulder with the police – that never got mentioned anywhere.

'I'm not defending it,' John said. 'I'm just pointing out it wasn't handled as well as it could have been by the authorities. If you're going to let a gig like that happen there then you need to make sure the community as a whole is safe: that's the police's job, to keep order on the streets. To not have a strong police presence there, and when it fucks up, blame the victims whose pub was burned down is not right. They should have just told them they couldn't play. After the documentary, we had loads of gigs closed down by the police.'

The documentary: 'Four skins in 1982 London; their lifestyle and the skinhead culture' ran the blurb. The BBC filmed Combat 84 going about 'normal life', at another band's gig in Soho, in a tower block, on the tube, at a laundrette, in a record shop.

They were in camouflage combat jackets, camouflage combat trousers, black gloves, green flight jackets, large high boots, more closely cropped hair.

'People are scared of skinheads 'cos they are a force,' Chubby said to the camera. 'They stick together.' But, he said, violence wasn't a big thing to him, his main attraction to the scene was the music and girls. He came across as a bit cheeky, likeable. Then he said something quite shocking, but with a smirk. 'I reckon I hate the police as much as blacks, I really do hate them.' He recounted how a mate of his had got four months in prison for taking part in a riot in Battersea, caught with a bottle in his hand. He compared that to rioting blacks. 'They let 'em off,' he said. 'It's racial harmony but it's going too much on their side, which is unfair. What about us? It's our country.'

John, tall with mutton chops, wasn't in that particular segment of the doc. He had a section, where, dressed in a Crombie, he recited a political poem about unemployed youth called '1982' (later a C84 song).

'Skinheads,' he said on camera, 'had the greatest shock value' and he'd rather 'put aggression out through appearance than behaviour.' He was also filmed getting a tattoo, looked like a young Lal Hardy doing the inking.

'Politics holds no interest to me,' he said. 'Of course, I've been attacked for political reasons by West Indians who've been mugged into it same as everyone else . . . "all geezers with long-hair are commies, all skinheads are fascist". We've got a lot in common with blacks from the point of view we both get police pressure, spat on, can't get jobs, kicked out of places, them for their colour which they can never change and us for our appearance which we can change.'

The documentary's final five minutes focused on the Combat 84 gig at Benny's bar/club. The Elite were also playing. Combat 84 are happily surprised when they are filmed arriving at the club, by the large size and glitz of the place. They were then shown playing 'Combat 84', a small gang of their mates doing their violent dance thing down the front. 'We had a road crew of eighteen and no equipment,' John laughed. 'We had mates there because it was rough. And when you left your area, you took your mates with you . . . we'd take coaches to places just like The Business would. Just like the Rejects did. They were the same people you went to football with . . . it was a social thing, really. But there was definitely safety in numbers.'

The rest of the crowd look non-plussed and the band appear to abandon the gig. Someone says, 'clap or we go home'. You see John, in his Marlon Brando T-shirt, complaining about the 'big hard men around the side too scared to dance . . .' adding that 'the local mob are wankers'.

The music starts back up. But it's The Elite now on stage. Again, a small gang down the front doing the crazy aggressive dancing. This time, however, one of them gets punched, maybe accidently, because as soon as the bouncer steps in the whole gang square up to him. The aggression towards the bouncer seems to upset the local skinheads on the side, some wade in, a scuffle starts, calls for calm, a Sieg Heil, punches thrown. It sounds again like John over the mic now: 'Oi, you cunts, all you Harlow, leave it out, we're all skinheads, we're not gonna fight.' More fighting breaks out, more violent now. Same voice: 'Leave it out you fucking wanker . . . skinheads stick together.' Now it's Chubby on the mic: 'We're all white, OK, so stop fighting and stick together, don't matter who [which football team] you support.'

The fighting grows more intense, a real wild-west bar-room brawl in progress, about eighty people, punches thrown indiscriminately, chairs thrown. Over this chaos, the BBC put a voiceover. Chubby speaking from an earlier interview: 'People used to have pride in this country in Victorian times. Now we're just nothing. Great Britain? Should be pathetic Britain. We're patriotic. The young white youth has to try and get an identity – most are content to see this country slip down. People will follow anybody who stands up and they feel is strong. This three-party system is going to collapse, people will be looking for a new thing to follow and certain people will move in.' As he spoke the fighting was getting worse, someone brandished a chair leg, another had a metal pole, tables thrown. Combat 84's little mob looked to have the upper hand. The film ends with the police arriving.

'Chubby was the worst fighter I've ever seen,' said John. 'But he was the best one at starting fights, come on then, come on then, all that . . . next thing you know he's three rows back going, come on then, and me and Jim and Brownie [the drummer] are at the front. In the footage Chubby does a lot of gesticulating but in the end it's me and Brownie on the dance floor taking on all the local skinheads.'

I asked if the documentary was the end for the band?

'It was supposed to be the launching pad for the band,' he said. 'But we didn't know anything about how to conduct ourselves in front of a camera: there wasn't a lot of acting up but when they edited it, y'know, they put it out how they wanted it, which is what you agreed to when you signed the form. We went to see it at a studio and we all thought it was dead good because it had us in it and we looked good and there was a fight in it and we didn't lose. You're not really media savvy at that age, are you? Chubby was getting manipulated [during the filming] by certain people. When they knew a camera crew was coming to rehearsal some bloke turned up with all these T-shirts that said "Smash The IRA, Hang the IRA" and everyone started putting them on, apart from the people in the band who said I'm not wearing that.

'Oi! was a ripe recruiting ground for people who were looking for that generation's brownshirts to do their dirty work,' he said. 'From the Oi! scene there was an element of right wing but also left wing; most people weren't that interested in politics but because they were dissatisfied with life when these people told them whose fault it was . . . these were people from the lower end of education and some of them believed it and some of them felt safer taking that side because they looked scary, these people [in the BM Leader Guard].

'Later, after the band, we were going away with Millwall at Euston station, and some right-wing people came up to me and my little gang and said, you've got a bit of a firm there, son, have you ever considered doing something to help your nation?' John continued. 'I said, see this mob, that's our army, get your fucking own. That was it. I saw what it did to my band when one of them decided to flirt with it. I had to close it down. I'm still considered a right-wing person by [some] people but I'm considered a communist by others.'

I'd read about that: how he'd had serious repercussions from what he'd said in the documentary, threats of kneecapping. 'Oh yeah, because I compared white people to black people,' he said. 'I was told to go and apologise. The British Movement came to me at somewhere like the 100 Club and said, you compared us to black people, you need to get on telly and apologise for that.

I was like, how am I supposed to get on television, how do I do that? I was like, I don't think that's very realistic, do you? They were like, get it fucking done.'

I asked about Gary Hitchcock, the band's manager. 'He wanted to manage us,' said John. 'Chubby wanted him to but I definitely didn't. I didn't like the vibe off him. He just seemed like one of the angriest people I'd ever met. Honestly, for a bloke who was trying to sell himself as a manager, he was fucking scary. He singled us all out, one at a time, to campaign. He didn't meet us in the pub together, it was all done with a veil of intimidation – you know it makes sense – and all this. Then Lol Pryor got involved for a bit and said, you're gonna have to get a new singer. I said, I'm not getting a new singer, it's mine and Chubby's band . . .'

I said I thought Chubby sounded like Roi on 'Rapist', A-side of the band's second single, released post the BBC doc (the lyric went: 'we need a stronger government, bring back capital punishment'). 'Well, we reckoned he sounded a bit effeminate on the first EP, compared to Gary Hodges and Roi, so me and Jim said he sounded a bit twee . . . remember Chris is a public schoolboy and he was a Cypriot and he was adopted by a veterinarian,' John said. 'He was quite a complicated bloke but he was quite easy to wind up. Me and Jim, every time Chubby did something to try and make us look stupid, we'd go, at least I don't sing like a poof and all this. We'd go, did you have singing lessons off Marc Almond, and things like that, to wind him up. Also, me and Jim had deeper talking voices so we'd put on [a] high-pitched voice . . . childish pub stuff. That roar at the beginning [of 'Rapist'], I think Jim found it on a Bad Brains records. Me and Jim were always listening to other music whereas Chubby was always trying to publicise himself.'

Garry Bushell refused to write about 'Rapist' in *Sounds* so the band took action. 'One of Chubby's mates went up to *Sounds* with a samurai sword looking for him, a half-Indian rockabilly, wasn't even a skinhead, so I'm not sure why Garry thought everyone to do with Combat 84 was right wing,' John said. 'After that I said to Garry, I'm gonna come up and talk to you about this. I went up and we went to the pub, the Nag's Head, had a few pints, which he bought. He said, I really thought you were gonna attack me, I've got a hammer in my pocket. I was like, if I was gonna attack you, I wouldn't have told you I was coming, I'd have just waited for you and jumped you – he lived in an estate just down the road.'

The *Rapist* EP included two other infamous tracks. 'Barry Prudom' written by John, about the man famous in 1982 for killing two police officers and evading capture for weeks, which is quite vividly anti-police. There was also 'Right to Choose', a daft pro-nuclear bomb/anti-Greenham Common song which includes the line, 'It's better to be dead than fucking red'. I thought I detected a sense of humour in the songs, similar to how Graham Saxby had described 'Violence in Our Minds' as being tongue-in-cheek. 'Not really, there was irony but no humour,' John said.

Gigs were difficult to arrange post the documentary. It was suggested venues were subject to bomb threats from anti-fascists and band members received death threats, so they often played under an assumed name, 7th Cavalry. John said they played at the 100 Club with Skrewdriver 'when they first reformed' (in 1982 and were working with the Last Resort shop). Deptford John knew the band's guitarist, Frenchie. 'We started our apprenticeship together,' he said. 'I lost touch with him when he joined Skrewdriver.'

I asked about other bands they gigged with such as London Branch (who gravitated to the NF/RAC scene). 'London Branch always supported us,' John said. 'I went to football with two of them. And Vicious Rumours we often played with; their bass player is an ardent left-wing campaigner now.

'We used to put gigs on at the Blue Coat Boy pub [in Islington], Skunx,' John said. 'It was supposed to be part of the skinheads and punks thing: that was Dave Long and his business partner who also managed Splodgenessabounds. I used to help them book the bands for Skunx.' Opened in February 1982, Skunx was close to another pub, the 'Aggy', a well-known BM hangout, and Quartermasters, an army surplus store which sold German helmets, coshes, knives. The 4-Skins, without Hodges, played Skunx and Hoxton Tom DJed there, playing soul and reggae.

'Combat 84 did a gig there supporting Skrewdriver on Hitler's birthday,' John said. 'I didn't even know we were gonna play until about three hours before, some band had pulled out.'

Fucking hell, I said.

'We played the gig. Someone threatened me. I went home. That was the end of it. I got threatened by someone who thought they could make their name by threatening me . . . then whenever I saw them when they didn't have all their mates with them, they weren't interested.'

A lot of Sieg Heiling at that gig?

'Not an awful lot,' John said. 'There weren't that many people there. Seventy people standing in the corner. Someone sent me a picture recently of us at the gig and I've had to go on and stand next to Jim on stage, there's no room for me on the other side of the stage because of these enormous blokes in stupid T-shirts stood there [the infamous Skrewdriver Security].'

As for Combat 84? 'The whole thing fizzled out, the name became toxic, we couldn't get any gigs,' John said. 'I didn't want to do any gigs, not when your singer is inviting the audience to come upstairs and punch the bass player because he's a communist. The whole thing ran its course. It burned very brightly very briefly. The TV thing was just too much for people in the band in the current situation at the time.'

I'd read Chubby was on the door for the NF/RAC 'White Christmas' gig in '83 in Barking, which featured Skrewdriver – 500 people in attendance. By then Chubby was supposedly banned from the Last Resort shop. At the gig there was a riot, the area ransacked, cars turned over, windows smashed, beatings, Sieg Heils, carnage. I also read Chubby was trying to get Combat 84 signed up to the NF's White Noise Records launched in 1983 with Skrewdriver's first overtly political single, 'White Power'.

'I didn't even know there was a White Noise Records,' John said. 'A lot of stuff went on behind me. Chris was getting his head turned by the fact he'd been on telly. He had a couple of people he really admired, one of them was Hickey from the Chelsea Headhunters who used to be a roadie for the Anti-Nowhere League – they were into bootlegging, ticket touting, that sort of existence. Chubby quite liked the idea of having a phalanx of intimidating people around him, like Ian Stuart had – he thought if he behaved like that they'd all come and hang out with him. Me and Jim never discussed ending the band with Chubby, we just did the album and that was it.

'There was nothing to discuss with someone like Chubby,' he added. 'He was, I'm doing this, I'm doing this. We'd be like, nah, mate. He said, well, if we don't do this, there's no point having a band. We went, yeah, you're right, there's no point having a band because we want different things. We're not going to be here anyway, we're going on tour with U.K. Subs [both John and Jim joined the band], see you later, and he couldn't do anything without me because he couldn't do much organising. He wasn't a very organised person.'

The band's album, *Send In the Marines!*, was released in 1984, long after they had disbanded, made up chiefly of the tracks already released plus a live side done in the studio to bulk it out. It came out on notorious German label Rock-O-Rama, sold to them by Dave Long 'to get the money back so we didn't owe him any money,' said John. The label had also started working with Skrewdriver.

Combat 84 did record again. Around 2000, John and Jim made an EP called *Tooled Up*. Chubby wouldn't come back from Thailand so John sang. 'We were thinking about reforming,' John said. 'Me and Mensi always chatted, and I asked Mensi, if we reform C84 can we support you? He said, I wouldn't let you support us. I said, that's why I'm probably not going to reform 'cos all I ever wanted to do was support you. I'm a big Upstarts fan.' Deptford John created some controversy during this period, quoted online as saying: 'We believe in free speech, you don't have it in England any more but people should be allowed to say what they want, we don't support any movement as Jim said, but RAC should be given an equal platform as anything else.'

'I met Darren who runs Rebellion at an Argy Bargy gig a few years back,' John said as we discussed the band's place in the Oi! firmament. 'He came up to me and said, let me just be clear, Combat 84 will never play Rebellion. I said, the singer's dead mate, so I think we can both agree on that. Do you want a beer?'

Chapter 8

RAC

It begins in Leeds, but the main man was east Londoner Joe Pearce, from Barking, who established the Young National Front in 1977 when he was 16, producing the YNF newspaper *Bulldog*. It was the NF's first foray into winning over young skinheads. It was well known that NF leader John Tyndall (who was ousted in 1980 and formed the BNP in 1982) disliked skinheads but his lieutenant Martin Webster had seen how the BM, under Martin McLaughlin, had benefitted from an active recruitment drive of skins. Ironically the BM founder Colin Jordan, who McLaughlin replaced, also disliked skinheads, calling the second wave, 'mindless oafs' and 'nihilistic hooligans'.

Webster backed Pearce and the teenager hit on the idea of rating football hooligan firms in *Bulldog*, who had the best racist chant for example, and published this as a regular 'league of louts' feature. It meant *Bulldog* sold well at football grounds around the country.

'Chelsea was really bad,' Upstarts bassist John Woodward had told me. 'The racism at Chelsea was absolutely fucking terrible, the chanting of racist songs. When you used to go up the stairs into the old Shed, there would be a row of huge boneheads who would ask you to buy a copy of *Bulldog*, 50p. As an 11- or 12-year-old, when you've got some 24/25-year-old brick shithouse saying you must buy this before going in, you buy it. That's what they used to do all the time.'

In Leeds there was an NF-recruiter and punk fan, in his late 20s, who set up a scene he called Rock Against Communism (RAC) in '78, as a direct response to Rock Against Racism. His followers disrupted gigs by 'red' bands ('commie scum who hated Britain'), congregating around local band The Dentists. The band had songs with titles such as 'White Power', 'We Are the Master Race' and 'Kill the Reds'.

The NF had run electoral TV broadcasts for the May '79 elections but Margaret Thatcher had lured many of their potential voters to the Conservatives, who ousted Labour in the election, when she made a statement that Britain was 'rather swamped by people with a different culture'. RAC might have fizzled out but for Pearce who got right behind it, launched a quarterly music magazine called *Rocking the Reds* to cover the music that the 'scum' of the music press wouldn't touch.

He brought RAC to London and promoted a gig under that banner in August 1979, at Conway Hall, Holborn. The line-up was The Dentists, White Boss from Coventry (who I read had a bassist who went on to play in Coventry Oi! band Criminal Class who featured on *Strength Thru Oi!*) and Skrewdriver who were the big draw. They'd had a few records out in 1977 and in that period had attracted a strong but small skinhead following. Their single 'Anti-Social' released by Chiswick, home to Motörhead and The 101ers (Joe Strummer's pre-Clash band), showed a lot of promise, was a proto-Oi! belter. But their debut album for Chiswick was a disappointment, belying their roots as a Blackpool rock covers band. Singer Ian Stuart, however, had become a bit of a cult figure: he hated Teds, claimed he'd flattened Iggy Pop. 'I actually enjoy fighting,' he'd told *Melody Maker*. He slagged off Jimmy Pursey, saying he only wore Dr. Martens for gigs and was 'just posing'.

Gary Hitchcock was a big fan of the band in '77, called them 'the first real skinhead band', saw them supporting Sham at The Vortex, where 'everyone went mad, smashing things up'. The then 16-year-old Graham McPherson, aka Suggs, was another big fan, and became a roadie for the band, I read. Trouble besmirched their name: supporting the Boomtown Rats someone decked Bob Geldof, and at a gig supporting The Police a band member was said to require twenty-six stitches in head wound following a fracas with a black lad.

Stuart had left his civil service job for a shot at the big time and went back to Blackpool disillusioned in '78. He was recruited into supporting the YNF and became active in his hometown. This is when Pearce got hold of him. Stuart was 22; a new line-up of Skrewdriver based in Manchester (featuring future BBC radio presenter Mark Radcliffe) was going nowhere even though they'd undergone a radical change of musical direction, playing awful sub-bluesy country rock. Stuart even wrote to the *NME* to declare they were 'no longer a skinhead band'.

That had largely gone unnoticed in London and the Skrewdriver name attached to the NF-backed RAC gig at Conway Hall brought out their old London fans and others from the Sham Army. They were disappointed because Skrewdriver failed to show.

The gig attracted many protestors led by Rock Against Racism, said to equal the number of skinheads inside, approximately 200, with sixty police keeping the peace. The *NME* gave the show a large write-up but failed to get inside. In the immediate aftermath Stuart wrote a letter to *Melody Maker*, saying he didn't intend to do gigs for RAC while also pointing out RAR was backed by 'Communists and Marxists' who 'in their way are just as much a threat to the country as the NF or BM'. He said he had 'no interest in politics'.

He and Skrewdriver (with Deptford John's old pal Frenchie on bass) re-emerged in 1982 with a single, 'Back With a Bang!', on a new label, Boots & Braces, set up by Micky French at the Last Resort shop. With Roi's Resort folded and his new band The Warriors keen to move on, French had found a new band to use as figureheads for his shop and released a compilation album, *United Skins*, with a Micky Furbank-designed sleeve that showcased them.

On the 'Back With A Bang!' record sleeve Stuart was pictured sporting the then classic skin look: boots, jeans, braces and Union Jack T. He was definitely a skinhead now. I found a quote from French online saying: 'It was Suggsy that secretly funded the 'Back With A Bang!' single and the Skrewdriver comeback in 1982.'

It was interesting to see what Stuart had been up to after the Conway Hall no-show. He was said to have formed a short-lived band with the BM Leader Guard lad who played in The Afflicted, mixed with some of the hardcore West Ham BM skinheads, and attended NF/BM marches. I read that in July 1981, Stuart had planned to reform Skrewdriver for a ten-date tour organised by the NF but for some reason it never happened. He was also said to have spent three months staying in Suggs's mother's flat and to have roadied for Madness, who had a massive breakthrough in 1979 when their debut album went to UK number two. Madness had inherited a hardcore fanbase from Suggs's first band, North London Invaders (Gary Hodges was said to have thrown a photocopier through a window after an anti-NF film was shown at one of their gigs), and were accustomed to Sieg Heil salutes among their early crowd. There was a gig on the 1979 Two-tone tour featuring The Specials, Selecter and Madness at Hatfield Polytechnic that was said to have turned especially ugly with stabbings aplenty during skinhead clashes with the SWP's Anti-Nazi League. In fact, it was said to be a member of the Madness mob who'd pulled a blade on Jimmy Pursey and demanded he lead an NF march.

Suggs, at some stage, spoke vaguely about this. Said it started for many skins as 'a game' going down Brick Lane every Sunday for something to do, and how that scene could 'get a bit heavy'. He blamed the 'horrible perverts backing all these things', said 'the average punter doesn't know what's going on'. By 1982, Madness were stars, had scored three more top albums and ten or more massive Top 10 hit singles, and were in fact at number one with 'House of Fun' when Skrewdriver re-emerged.

'Back With a Bang!' was about being a skinhead in the summer of '78 when 'being patriotic was not the fashion, to fly your country's flag a crime' and how 'four years on' the skins were 'getting stronger every day'. *Sounds* reviewed it, mentioning the band's 'fascist past'. A little scene formed around the group, largely focused on their gigs at Skunx and the 100 Club. This was the scene Mackie had described Blitz finding themselves among in London – violent, heavy 'but weirdly more exciting for that,' he said.

Combat 84 were drawn in, so were London Branch and the Ovaltinees (who also gigged with Splodgenessabounds and attracted attention from Secret Records). A new band, Brutal Attack, were also part of this crowd. Deptford John said he was pals with the band's singer Ken McLellan. Blitz played a gig with them in Colchester, recalling them as Exploited-type punks (with 'liberty spikes') but they were now aligning themselves as a skinhead band.

The BM appeared to take over at Skunx, with a Leader Guard stationed on the door. The venue soon lost its licence under police pressure and was closed. Skrewdriver took up residency at the 100 Club and the BM appeared to take this venue over too. When Infa Riot played there, they were attacked backstage by Skrewdriver Security. The band spoke out in the press about the 100 Club booking right-wing bands, naming Skrewdriver and Combat 84, calling for a ban. Bushell also called for a press blackout on Skrewdriver.

At this stage the Skrewdriver set included a cover of 'Red London' by Sham 69, as well as Stones and Black Sabbath covers; Stuart wore a Union Jack flag as a cape on stage, and was routinely flanked by the Skrewdriver Security (SS), chiefly BM Leader Guard, who wore specially made-up T-shirts with their own logo. Black flight jackets replaced green flight jackets as uniform. Stuart began to intersperse the songs with short tirades, anti-reds, anti-Jews, anti-black, often anti-Bushell (Stuart routinely bad-mouthed Bushell from the stage). The almost exclusively skinhead audience would respond with Sieg Heils.

The NF's Joe Pearce was driving a lot of this, set the tone. He'd become something of a martyr figure, jailed for a six-month stretch under the Race Relations Act for inflammatory articles written in *Bulldog* and *Rocking the Reds*. He continued to stick the NF flag on Oi! ground. 'Oi! is music of the ghetto,' he wrote.

'Its energy expresses the frustrations of white youths, its lyrics describe the reality of life on the dole, it is the music of white rebellion. Bands who are not our friends are our enemies.' This was when he identified Bushell as the 'biggest enemy', put him on a blacklist and printed his home address in *Bulldog*.

He formed the NF-backed White Noise Records in 1983 with Skrewdriver the first release (a 7-inch single, 'White Power' backed by 'Smash the IRA'). Stuart had abandoned French and the Last Resort shop and, in his own words, decided to go 'all the way'. The White Noise logo was a Celtic cross (aka Odin's Cross/sun wheel/wheel cross) which became a key signifier among the scene.

Alongside White Noise, Pearce now began promoting gigs under the RAC banner in earnest, often around the Croydon area. Here the line in the sand was drawn: Brutal Attack were firmly on board, featured on a White Noise comp EP in '84, supplying 'The Return of St. George'.

From this point on gigs were clandestine, with only a meeting point muted, generally close to the venue, and violent – outside, if anti-fascists caught wind of the gig, and inside as new hierarchies formed, and weapons became commonplace. A chant, 'nigger, nigger nigger, out out, out' became popular.

The search for new bands to join the movement was on. Chris Mundie described how The Business were approached and refused. Presumably, Infa Riot also said no. An early coup was ABH who'd featured on the White Noise EP and on the concurrent *Oi! of Sex* comp. Stuart called out bands he said were too cowardly to join RAC or White Noise, 'for fear of killing their career'. McLellan said he'd formed Brutal Attack after 'all the skinhead bands' – he named Sham, Cock Sparrer and Menace – had 'let them down' with 'all the promises' forgotten. Stuart now took to the stage waving or wearing a swastika flag.

Nicky Crane, out of prison, became a menacing presence among the Skrewdriver Security. He and other BM Leader Guard faces continued to make their presence felt on the music scene: disrupting a Redskins performance at the GLC's 'Jobs for A Change' festival in Jubilee Gardens on London's South Bank in 1984. Crane was also said to have made the approach, instigated by Stuart, to new skinhead band Indecent Exposure who had released a seven-track cassette in 1984 that showed great promise. They were asked or told to join White Noise/RAC.

Indecent Exposure singer Milky was a Last Resort face with a great Oi! cockney voice, the band a continuation of the blunt force of Combat 84 with some obvious Rejects influence. They had a song calling for skinhead unity, 'Stick Together', on their demo, and an anti-glue sniffing skinhead song called 'The Fool'. The most controversial song on the cassette, surely the one that had attracted Stuart to them, was an 'anti-commie' song called 'Rocking the Reds'.

Two of the tracks on the Indecent Exposure cassette, 'Bank Holiday' and 'What's The Point?' ended up on a 1985 White Noise Records compilation *No Surrender!* alongside songs by Skrewdriver and Brutal Attack. The album was the final release on White Noise Records. It featured Sweden's Ultima Thule who had contributed a version of the Swedish national anthem. Their singer was a member of the neo-Nazi Nordic Realm Party. They would go on to be, and still are, a hugely popular band in Sweden, selling hundreds of thousands of albums and singles; their 'viking rock' much admired for its patriotic stance by the leader of the Sweden Democrats, currently in government, but who like the band have a history that links them to a far-right, racist organisation called Keep Sweden Swedish.

Indecent Exposure, who covered 'A.C.A.B.', 'Wonderful World', 'Bad Man' and 'King of the Jungle' live, were soon playing with Brutal Attack under the watchful eye of the BM Leader Guard. Former 4-Skins guitarist Paul Swain briefly joined the band before taking up with Skrewdriver. When the debut Indecent Exposure album was released by Rock-O-Rama in 1985, they seemed to have added some songs with patriotic/nationalistic overtones such as 'I Won't Let My Country Die', 'Save The Nation' and 'England My England'. I read they wanted out of the RAC/White Noise scene as soon as they were in, hoped to work with more mainstream Oi! labels. They soon broke up.

Skrewdriver had begun working with the German Rock-O-Rama label in 1984, releasing their album *Hail the New Dawn* via them rather than White Noise Records (sample lyric: 'They come here to this country from the jungles and from trees'.) Rock-O-Rama, run by Herbert Egoldt, started out as an offshoot of his record shop in Cologne, releasing punk and hardcore bands from Germany and Finland who were often left leaning or anti-fascist. It was now set to become the world's premiere and most infamous white power label, home to Skrewdriver for the remainder of their career and all the UK bands that came next, including Brutal Attack. It also began to release a wave of controversial German acts, most significantly Böhse Onkelz (see chapter 10).

Pearce had not entirely given up on his music biz ambitions. He created the subscription-based White Noise Club and continued to organise gigs, a series of which, beginning in 1984, were promoted as the 'RAC Summer Festival'. They were held at a farm in Suffolk that belonged to the father of future BNP leader Nick Griffin. Indecent Exposure played the first of these festivals, alongside Skrewdriver and Brutal Attack. In ads and merchandise for the event, Furbank's skin was corrupted, now flying a Celtic cross.

Links were being established across Europe and at the 1986 RAC Summer Festival it was estimated half of the 600 crowd were skinheads from Europe: Belgium, Holland, Germany, France and Italy. There was talk of building a White Noise empire in Europe.

I counted as many as twenty UK bands who became part of this 'white power' eighties Oi! scene, and if they were halfway competent they were soon fixtures on the Rock-O-Rama/RAC conveyor belt. One was Skullhead, formed by an NF organiser from Newcastle with a boot tattooed on his face, skinhead Kev Turner. He was said to have been radicalised after his best mate was brutally stabbed to death. They included Blitz's 'Someone's Gonna Die' and Cock Sparrer's 'England Belongs to Me' in their set and debuted in 1987 with an album called *White Warrior*. Their progress was blunted when Turner was sent down for four years for wounding with intent.

Most of these RAC bands referenced the classic proto-Oi! and early eighties Oi! bands as their musical influence, corrupted now to suit extremist ideologies. Offensive Weapon from Belfast for example: they featured Johnny 'Mad Dog' Adair, a prominent and active member of the paramilitary Ulster Defence Association. Croydon's Sudden Impact had a song called 'Nigger-Loving White Slag'. A band called British Born were maybe the first band to mention 'real Oi!' describing it as 'patriotic music for British youth'.

The scene was buoyed by a glut of fanzines, one of the most infamous being *The Truth at Last* from Paul Burnley. He became another infamous face on the scene. His real name was Bellany, son of acclaimed Scottish artist John Bellany. He and his brother John were noted for their commitment. Paul was involved with a White Noise/R-O-R/RAC band Public Enemy but sacked for being 'too extreme', often to be seen waving a swastika flag at their gigs. The Burnley brothers then formed No Remorse, named after the Motörhead album, who covered 'Chaos' live among a deluge of profoundly offensive and inciting material. They pledged their allegiance to the BM, said their mission was to 'spread the word of white resistance against treacherous government and alien forces dominating our existence'. A No Remorse T-shirt read: 'One day the world will know Adolf Hitler is right'.

Nicky Crane supplied artwork for their debut album (he did the Skrewdriver album covers too), which was released by Rebelles Européens [RE], a new French label formed in 1987. It was run by Gaël Bodilis, active in the youth wing of the French National Front. He was based in Brest, north-western France, and staged a festival in the area featuring No Remorse and Skrewdriver, alongside a handful of French Oi! bands including Bunker 84 and Legion 88 (see chapter 10). He tried again the following year with the same UK bands plus Brutal Attack but police stopped the gig, a riot ensued and eight black men were said to be injured.

Bodilis built a significant stable of UK RAC bands at RE including Violent Storm from Cardiff, English Rose from Leicestershire (they had a song called 'Stop the Invasion' and also included a cover of Cock Sparrer's 'England Belongs to Me' in their live set) and Lionheart (whose tracks included 'Bring Back the Rope' and 'Asian Invasion'). Bodilis said 'all these bands have a right to express themselves and music is an excellent way of spreading these ideas'.

British Oi! was another prominent UK fanzine covering the scene, unusual because it covered both 'Roddy Moreno's Oi!' (routinely referred to as 'commie Oi!') and 'White Noise Oi!'. A contributor to the fanzine was Alex Allui, an Oi! aficionado/nerd who formed the final noteworthy RAC band, Battle Zone, who signed to RE and named 'anti-social' French Oi! band Evil Skins as an influence. Allui was an oddity: he had a song about animal rights, saw himself as part of a new generation of European nationalists; anti-drugs, immigrants and gays. 'We could be labelled a racist, fascist, right-wing band and realistically that's what we are,' he said. He was soon wanting out of what he'd gotten himself into.

'When I was a teenager and started being a skinhead the only real scene was the RAC scene, so I naturally drifted towards that,' Allui said in an interview he gave to a Czech website around 2009, having completely abandoned the far right, had his tattoos redone. 'The skinhead scene in the middle-to-late eighties in the UK was very small. The non-political Oi! scene was almost dead, there were no ska bands. So it was very easy to get drawn to bands like Skrewdriver, Brutal Attack, etc. The music was powerful and the scene was very healthy. I was very young and gullible, I suppose. I had a lot of friends in the area I lived in Essex that were right-wing (RAC) skinheads, so I went to gigs with them, met more people and made friends all over the country, and little by little you find yourself believing the politics. I have to admit those days were exciting – some of the bands were great, the atmosphere was amazing. And it was the only place you would see hundreds of skinheads together. It was easy to get caught up in all the excitement.'

Throughout the decade Skrewdriver remained the dominant

RAC force and, in 1987, they abandoned the NF and formed an organisation called Blood & Honour, named after their 1985 album, often referred to as '28' (B being the second and H being the eighth letter of the alphabet). Stuart had risen to NF central London branch organiser, been jailed for twelve months for violent disorder and assault after a fight with three black men, but the NF had started to openly denounce neo-Nazism. Stuart's lyrics had become increasingly outrageous, his Hitler obsession in overdrive, the survival of the white race a paramount concern.

Brutal Attack, No Remorse and Sudden Impact all abandoned the NF and joined B&H. The NF said they had kicked the bands out for being a 'sordid and politically suicidal Nazi cult'. The first B&H gig in the UK, in Carshalton, Surrey attracted 700. Crane was on the door collecting the £5 entrance fees.

The neo-Nazi rhetoric and imagery among the B&H bands grew even more extreme, an impending race war being predicted, people declaring they were prepared to die to keep their country pure, plans said to be afoot to bomb Notting Hill Carnival. Stuart and Crane gave an interview to the *Sunday People* (headline: 'Britain's Sickest Band') where they expounded on their views about blacks, Jews and communists.

The gigs were lawless; fights over women, stabbings, even rape. There was talk of Gary Hitchcock forming a homegrown label, Viking Records, and a growing presence of football casuals on the scene. There was also an emerging link with America. WAR (White Aryan Resistance) in conjunction with the Ku Klux Klan and the infamous Chicago Area Skinheads were planning to bring Skrewdriver to America. Stuart was soon sworn in as a member of the KKK. No Remorse were obsessed with American white supremacist terror group, the Order, who'd attempted to found a 'homeland for whites' with money raised from a string of armed robberies (two members were jailed for murder).

Labour's Jeremy Corbyn was the first British politician to express concern about B&H, who were spreading, forging 'divisions' across Europe, the first being in Belgium.

This brings us back to Mensi and the Upstarts and the Main Event concert at the Astoria in '88. The Business were also on the bill for the gig. I read the whole thing was organised or funded by a central London shop called Cutdown which sold, behind its blacked-out windows, neo-Nazi records and associated merchandise such as 'Hang Nelson Mandela' T-shirts. A good pal of Stuart's worked there. Corbyn had tried to get it shut down. You have to presume the bands on the Main Event bill were unaware of Cutdown's involvement. Details are sketchy but Skrewdriver and B&H took the ransacking of the Upstarts as a major victory.

There were consequences with being so high-profile: Stuart was a walking target in London and in 1989 he was attacked by Red Action, requiring twenty-six stitches in a head wound. The scene was also now said to be under increased police surveillance, concerts more difficult to stage, a sense of paranoia spreading about informants within. Inner rivalries also intensified.

Increasingly the bands looked to Europe, where gigs went ahead and were well-attended, the major UK bands said to be able to attract up to a thousand skinheads in both Germany and Sweden. It's probably around now that Oi! as an influence on the RAC/B&H music became negligible. Stuart came out and said he disliked the Oi! 'tag', called it too close to punk, said Skrewdriver were a 'skinhead rock band'. They had a go at 'Sweet Home Alabama' and heavy metal, covering songs by

Judas Priest and AC/DC. Stuart recorded solo albums where he covered Elvis and The Who, had a go at Golden Earring's 'Radar Love'. He also released a rockabilly album as The Klansmen and formed his own heavy metal band, White Diamond. Brutal Attack were doing 'All Right Now'. When Skullhead's Turner got out of prison and became active again, they were doing 'Run to the Hills'. Lionheart did Guns N' Roses. Sudden Impact did 'Saturday Night's Alright for Fighting' and then released a heavy metal album. There was a growing fixation with Vikings. It seemed to be part of the white warrior lineage: skinheads, Nazi soldiers and Vikings. Nordic gods – Thor, Odin – were everywhere. No Remorse released an album called *See You in Valhalla*.

Nineteen ninety-two was a tumultuous year for B&H. In March four members of Violent Storm were killed in a car crash on the M4. In July, Nicky Crane came out as gay, taking part in a Channel 4 show, *The Skinhead: Fascist or Fetish?*, part of the channel's lesbian and gay series (the skinhead look had long been popular on the gay scene). He was 34. *The Sun* headline: 'Nazi Nick is a Panzi'. There were longstanding rumours circulating about him after he was seen on the door at west-end nightclubs such as Taboo and Heaven. There was huge unease among B&H, particularly at the top of the newly formed, breakaway, Combat 18, intended initially as a BNP street force, security for the party (as the BM Leader Guard had been for the British Movement). One of the reasons the NF had fallen out of favour with the B&H bands was the discovery that leading figures in the party such as Martin Webster and Patrick Harrington were gay.

Crane also told Channel 4 he was 'ashamed' of his political past and insisted he had changed. 'Everything I done was for Adolf Hitler' but 'the view I've got now is, I believe in individualism and I don't care if anyone's black, Jewish or anything. I either like or dislike a person as an individual, not what their colour is or anything.'

B&H warned gay skinheads to keep away from the movement for their own health's sake. There was a C18/B&H attack on a gay bar in London. Skrewdriver were being billed to headline a big Blood & Honour blow-out on Saturday 12 September and the temperature was rising. Called the Main Event 2, an RAC gig, with Cutdown again said to be involved, it was the band's first London gig for three years and it generated a lot of publicity. Stuart appeared on LBC, interviewed by Richard Littlejohn. Mensi appeared on MTV to condemn Skrewdriver. There was a report on BBC Two. Most of the British newspapers covered it.

Writing in the *Daily Mirror*, Tony Parsons said: 'Oi! as played by Skrewdriver and their kind is punk without the theatrical overtones, punk without O levels, punk that has never been to art school. This is the genuine voice of council estates. Real working-class music. Unlike every musician since Elvis, Oi! bands don't play with mythology of danger. They were and are the real thing. It isn't pretty.'

I noted that much later Bushell cherry-picked this quote, took out 'as played by Skrewdriver and their kind', and used it as a vindication of Oi! music from Parsons. I took it up with Bushell in the initial questions I sent him but he did not respond. At the time of the '92 gig Bushell wrote: 'Swastika junkies like Skrewdriver are a disgrace to our flag and country.' He also said Oi! had 'turned to shit'.

Other bands said to be playing at an undisclosed location included Brutal Attack, No Remorse, French band Bunker 84 and Sweden's Dirlewanger. About 1,200 tickets had been sold in advance, £10 a ticket.

On the eve of the gig Stuart was hunted down to a West Midlands pub (he'd moved out of London and was living in Derbyshire) and glassed by anti-fascists. On the day, trouble started early. At one of the redirection points, Hyde Park Speakers' Corner, a few hundred Anti-Fascist Action and Red Action gathered. Crane was said to have met a hundred or more German skinheads at Euston station to redirect them. Hundreds more skinheads gathered at Cutdown (which was later attacked with sledgehammers, all the stock destroyed).

Waterloo station was said to be another redirection point. Many of the hundreds of skinheads there had travelled from America and Europe to attend the gig. The BM Leader Guard were said to be split between holding the venue (rumoured to be in Eltham, south-east London) and providing support at Waterloo. When the B&H chief of security was arrested for carrying CS gas and removed from the station, there was much confusion among the throng gathered, said to number about 500, over what to do. Expecting trouble from anti-fascists, B&H had raised a heavy crew from various football firms to attend Waterloo (Chelsea, West Ham, Millwall and Portsmouth among them). This was an uneasy alliance of factions and by now there were said to be a thousand or more anti-fascists gathered at the station, including Red Action's hardest men. Fighting erupted about 3 p.m., all trains were cancelled and the station was closed at 5 p.m.; ultimately forty-four people were arrested, seventeen hospitalised. This was the so-called 'Battle of Waterloo'.

'We absolutely annihilated them at Waterloo and some of them said, what a great day, what a victory,' Mensi said. 'They turned defeat into victory.' The gig surprisingly took place but amid chaotic scenes. Outside, up to 500 riot police trying to keep back anti-fascists, many ticket holders denied entrance.

Even smaller shows were now incredibly violent and dangerous: nine people were hospitalised during a Skullhead gig and ten people were charged with violent disorder following a B&H gig, when Indian restaurant staff were attacked with baseball bats and bottles. Two prominent BNP/B&H members were jailed; in their van the police found a machete, an axe, CS gas, clubs, knives, knuckle dusters and a swastika flag.

Crane was beaten unconscious by AFA (three AFA members were jailed) and the police arrested the people distributing Skrewdriver albums in the UK, Skrewdriver Services, who were jailed for inciting racial hatred. C18 took over Skrewdriver Services and they attempted to breathe new life into the scene, but some bands appeared to be uncertain where this was heading. Battle Zone were desperate for an out. 'They visited my home and work with machetes,' said singer Alex Allui. Paul Burnley of No Remorse (who had become the first B&H band to play America) was allegedly terrorised out of the movement following a heavily policed Skrewdriver White Christmas event in Mansfield in 1992 with 500 fans present. A new Oi! band, Close Shave, who had released their debut album in 1988 on Link (*Oi! Kinnock Give Us Back Our Rose!*) were said to have been violently attacked by Skrewdriver Security and now appeared on the bill for what would prove to be the final big UK gig featuring Skrewdriver, on St George's Day, April 1993. Also on the bill were Brutal Attack, Skullhead, English Rose and Battle Zone. The event was said to attract 350.

C18 had plans for a Summer 1993 European Aryan Festival at a farm in Nottinghamshire with a bill to include Skrewdriver,

Germany's Noie Werte and English Rose with 2,000 predicted to attend. Having won their first council seat in the Millwall ward of Tower Hamlets in late '93, the BNP was beginning to rebrand itself, eager now, as the NF had been before them, to sever its associations with Skrewdriver, C18 and B&H.

The B&H bands again took to Europe, particularly Germany, where there was now a B&H division, and where Skrewdriver record sales were at their strongest. B&H had also forged strong links with far-right groups in Italy, Sweden and France. There were events advertised with names such as Hitlerfest (in Sweden) and a swathe of new bands in Europe now operating under either the RAC or B&H banner. Predictably there was violence: at a Skrewdriver gig in Germany, three band members were arrested after a stabbing took place pre-gig.

Then in September '93 after a night out in Burton-on-Trent the car Stuart was travelling in crashed, span off the road, killing him and another passenger. No other car was involved. Conspiracy theories flourished. He was 36. Crane died shortly after in December from AIDS-related illness. He was 35.

C18 organised a memorial gig for Stuart in January '94 featuring Skullhead and Brutal Attack, who released a tribute record, 'I Watched as He Bled', but the Becontree gig was cancelled (same as the Summer 93 fest). Skullhead split. Rock-O-Rama Records ceased to exist in 1994 after a police raid. It was said Herbert Egoldt had made himself a millionaire out of the white power music scene. Rebelles Européens was also out of business, their final release had been in '92.

Chapter 9

Pride: The Templars (American Oi!)

There is no question that The Templars are America's greatest and most influential Oi! band. What is even more admirable about them is when they started out in 1990, Oi! music and skinheads in America had as bad, if not worse, a reputation than in the UK.

Oi! had started with a flourish in America in the early eighties with a band called Doug & The Slugz from Los Angeles. Singer Doug 'Dagger' Kane was 15 in 1982 when he first got into Oi!. He was already a regular at gigs by Californian hardcore bands such as Black Flag and Circle Jerks whose members sometimes had skinheads and namechecked Oi! as an influence but who had developed their own separate scene. Bushell said Black Flag had actually offered up a track for the *Oi! Oi! That's Yer Lot!* compilation, but it was unclear why it wasn't included.

What initially turned Doug on to Oi! was the Blitz EP, *All Out Attack*. He picked it up at a hip record store called Poo-Bah in Pasadena which was close to where he lived. 'It blew my mind,' he told me when I called him one morning, LA time. 'There was a little picture of the band on the record sleeve and at the time a lot of the LA bands, like Black Flag and Circle Jerks, were growing their hair out, starting to look like Charlie Manson. I heard 'Someone's Gonna Die [Tonight]', the lyrics were aggressive and the sound was bringing me in. I decided I don't want to be this LA punk kid any more, I'm gonna shave my head and be a skinhead. There weren't many skinheads in LA at that time. Very few who wore Dr. Martens boots and bomber jackets and braces, maybe a handful, and LA's a big place. I was one of the youngest of that group in the beginning.'

Then he discovered The Last Resort 'through one of Garry Bushell's comps' and they became his favourite band. 'I loved them,' Doug said. 'I found out how to get their album through the Last Resort shop and I purchased it from there. Nobody had that record in LA It wasn't available in the record stores. When I got it, I played it to every punk kid in north-east LA and it was like dominoes falling – kids from Pasadena, South Pasadena, Highland Park, Alhambra were just coming to where we were hanging out and shaving their heads and finding Dr. Martens boots, and the next thing you knew there was a centralised area of skinhead kids and little by little an Oi! scene was developed in LA all because of The Last Resort's *Skinhead Anthems* album. That record created a lot of problems for the local police department,' he laughed.

Doug & The Slugz, in thrall to the Resort, Blitz, the Rejects, Sham and The Business, created an LA Oi! sound that was different to what was happening in New York, which is sometimes seen as the birthplace of Oi! in America. 'A lot of the NY skinhead stuff was based more around that hardcore sound,' Doug said. The most notable band were Agnostic Front who also namechecked the main UK Oi! bands as an influence. 'When we heard Agnostic Front's first 7-inch – and those guys are friends of mine – I didn't like the record, I didn't understand it,' Doug said. 'These guys are skinheads? It doesn't sound anything like a skinhead band.' Agnostic Front, however, became long-time supporters of Oi!. In 2000 frontman Roger Miret compiled a compilation, *The Worldwide Tribute to the Real Oi!*, with Agnostic Front and other hardcore bands such as Madball and Sick Of It All covering Oi! classics. A couple of Agnostic Front also currently have an Oi! band called The Take.

I asked Doug if he knew The Effigies from Chicago or Iron Cross from Washington DC, also bandied about as early American Oi! bands. Agnostic Front popularised an Iron Cross song called 'Crucified' and The Business also covered the song. 'I did know about them but even though those bands had a skinhead kind of look, the sound was different. I don't think we ever considered Iron Cross or even The Effigies as being Oi! bands.'

Doug & The Slugz's early set included covers of 'Chaos' and 'We Rule OK'. 'We just connected with those songs,' Doug said. 'It's so strange because some of it's so English. We don't really know about working class in America. We have class division here but we've always called that: rich, lower-middle class or you're just fucking poor. The California kids getting into being skinheads were really from a background of dysfunctional family shit. You're talking about broken apart homes – dad's gone, left mom and the kids alone, mom's working two jobs to support the kids, there's no parents around at all, the kids are in the streets at night, you're getting fucking drunk, smoking weed, you're getting in fights.'

I wondered if another difference was the early Oi! scene

in LA was mixed race? 'Exactly,' he said. 'I had a mulatto guitar player [Scott Graham] and then the second drummer was half-Mexican, looked like a little Mexican kid. Our area was filled with Latino kids and black kids and white kids and even some Asian kids: the skinheads from our scene in '83 and '84 were all these different colours so the whole racist thing . . .' Doug paused. 'When we became aware of that through Skrewdriver, that was actually quite upsetting to us. We couldn't understand that. What? We're not supposed to like one another or hang out with one another? Fuck that. This was before SHARP, we're just skinheads, but when the whole Nazi thing or "white power" skinhead gangs formed in the suburbs of LA, we beat those guys up if they came to our area or if they came to our parties.'

The Slugz, he said, quickly developed a strong following in their area. 'Was there violence involved with it? There was,' Doug said. 'We were really just young teenage boys and aggressive. Wherever we went to play all the skinhead kids from my area, the North Side Firm, would go, similar to Cockney Rejects and the Inter City Firm. These kids followed us wherever we went and then we would just trash the clubs and fight with anybody. A lot of the other punk and hardcore bands in LA didn't want my band playing. In the beginning they didn't want any skinheads around anyway, skinheads were trouble for them, skinhead kids mobbing their shows.

'For a while we had two local venues where we played all the time and then one of them shut down,' he said. 'The city closed it down because there was so much trouble going on. Pretty soon we were struggling to get gigs because everyone knew Doug & The Slugz as being affiliated with the North Side Firm.

'One of the last shows we played was at the Cavern Club, Hollywood Boulevard,' Doug recalled. 'A skinhead show we wound up headlining. It was one of the first skinhead shows with just skinhead bands and it was packed with about 200 people in there, and outside in the parking lot there was all these brawls going on. The LAPD was out there, taking kids to jail: it was just wild.'

Doug & The Slugz recorded music in the mould of the Resort, songs such as 'Skinhead Faction' and their anthem 'Doug and the Slugz'. 'Just demos,' Doug said. 'We'd make cassettes and sell them at shows or give them away.'

He laughed. 'I'd send those cassettes to Micky French at the Last Resort,' he said. 'I'd call him from my mom's apartment and my mom would slap me in the face when she got the phone bill. Micky would be telling the other skinheads in the shop, hey there's these skinheads from LA on the phone, man. He said, I love the cassette. I said, put me out on a record, I wanna make a record deal. He'd be like, maybe I'll put you on a compilation when I put out another comp. I thought that was cool. I didn't want to be on an American punk label at that time – why would I want to be on with those bands? I didn't like those bands. I liked this stuff. I was sending the tapes to No Future Records never getting a reply. We were so young, we were just having fun . . . there was no business, we'd get our tapes, we'd sell them or give them to all the other little skinheads.'

I'd read that Doug left the Oi! scene around 1985 after getting heavily involved in the LA gang scene. I asked if the North Side Firm started as a skinhead gang and then became a more serious street gang?

'That's exactly right,' he said. 'It was all skinhead kids and then at some point the gang just started. They were constantly fighting with other punk gangs at gigs. Suicidal Tendencies had their own gang, then there were the LADS, LA Death Squad, one of the oldest punk gangs, mainly based around Hollywood, and another gang, the FFF, Fight For Freedom, up in the Valley. Those brawls were becoming real dangerous and then it became on the street. I also had problems with the Cholo gang that were not far from where we lived and the Crip gang started to come down – they were jumping out of cars and cracking skinhead kids over the head with pipes, breaking skulls, or they were shooting at us. It was bad. It was challenging to be a skinhead; you run into a Crip gang member on the street in those early days and this was before the whole Nazi thing or white power came along and they were definitely hostile.'

Doug got out of the gang scene, formed a punk band, Schleprock, who had some success in the nineties following the Green Day/Rancid American punk explosion. He has recently reformed Doug & The Slugz. Another band he had called The Generators were working with Randale and the label released the old Slugz tapes in 2018, reviving interest. Doug found guitarist Scott, who was homeless, having been in and out of prison for most of his life, including serving seven years in Folsom State Prison for attempted murder, and put the original line-up back together, recording most of the songs they had back in their original set for a new album on Step-1/Longshot in 2020, *Smash! Hits Vol. 1*.

'Among the four of us we were able to bring it back to life again and better than when we were kids because we were noisy and pretty bad when we were kids,' Doug said. 'We were able to make it a little better-sounding than it would have been back then.' Garry Bushell included one of the songs, 'Friday Night in an

Old Town', on *Oi! 40 Years Untamed* and the band are becoming increasingly popular in the current Oi! scene. 'I told the guys what we need to do is exactly what we would have done when we were 15,' he said. 'Keep it simple, keep it straight, keep it raw. That is honest and that got a lot of people attracted to the [reformed] band . . . it's different to what a lot of the newer American Oi! bands are doing these days.'

After Doug backed out of the LA Oi! scene circa 1985 he avoided shows by new Californian Oi! bands such as The Bootboys. They covered 'Violence in Our Minds' and 'Police Oppression' and featured on a 1988 Link compilation called *U.S. Of Oi!* which, for many in the UK, was a first introduction to American Oi!. The Bootboys would quickly become engulfed in controversy. By 1989 they were calling themselves Youngblood, said to be affiliated with the gang Doug mentioned, LA Death Squad, signing to R-O-R with a debut album called *Final War.* They were one of the many American skinhead/Oi! bands who fell under the spell of the RAC/B&H scene and moved increasingly towards a white power/neo-Nazi stance.

White Aryan Resistance [WAR], the white supremacist neo-Nazi organisation who had visited England to see Skrewdriver play, were at the heart of this, based in California. Founder, former KKK Grand Wizard, Tom Metzger, now approaching 50, said: 'We are an openly white-racist movement – skinheads, we welcome you into our ranks'. They organised an 'Aryan Music' festival in 1988 where the Skrewdriver-influenced Midtown Bootboys from Tulsa played. A member of that band, aged 21, was jailed for four years for attacking 'minorities' with a baseball bat soon after. WAR were also linked to the murder of an Ethiopian man by three white supremacists.

In New York, Youth Defense League (YDL), another band on *U.S. Of Oi!*, covered Skrewdriver and affiliated with RAC. And Doc Marten, from New Jersey, active since circa 1987, covered the 4-Skins, the Upstarts and Rejects. Their shows were synonymous with violence and they also released material with R-O-R.

There followed a glut of American Oi! bands from various states who began to identify as RAC and released records via R-O-R: New Glory (who were on the *U.S. Of Oi!* album); Arresting Officers (who namechecked Skrewdriver and Combat 84 as influences); Allegiance (who namechecked Sham 69 and the 4-Skins). These groups and more were gathered together in 1989 on an album called *The Spirit of Oi! American Style*.

A homegrown network emerged. Initially a firm called Romantic Violence imported and distributed Skrewdriver albums in America. It was run out of Chicago by the notorious Chicago Area Skinheads (CASH) gang, founded by Clark Martell in 1985, and openly neo-Nazi. In 1989, aged 30, Martell was jailed for 11 years and a new CASH leader emerged, Chris Picciolini, then just 16. His band called Final Solution began releasing records through Rebelles Européens.

A new label, White Terror Records, superseded Romantic Violence to become the official label for B&H America. They were based in Minnesota and began releasing homegrown American Oi! by acts such as the Midtown Bootboys, The Voice and Das Reich. Another band linked to White Terror, Fight For Freedom, formed out of the eponymous FFF, the other feared LA punk gang Doug mentioned.

Resistance Records, however, became the key label. It was formed by 20-year-old George Burdi, singer with Toronto band RaHoWa (Racial Holy War), when a deal with Rebelles

Européens for his band fell through. He was familiar with the UK scene – RaHoWa had played with No Remorse on their first visit to America at an open-air festival on a farm near Ottawa, playing to a couple of hundred skinheads. Canada had its own RAC acts, alongside RaHoWa – Cross, who also appeared at the festival (and signed to R-O-R) and Aryan who were formerly Vacant Lot, another Oi! band signed to R-O-R.

RaHoWa had a song called 'Third Reich' which had the lyric 'kill all the niggers and gas all the jews, kill a gypsy and kill a commie too'. Bizarrely, they also covered the Upstarts' song 'Solidarity' about the Polish trade union movement.

Resistance Records was based in Michigan and soon had fifteen bands attached including Aggravated Assault, which featured a former member of Doc Marten, Nordic Thunder and Bound for Glory. A joint effort by the American and Canadian government shut down the label and RaHoWa around 1997 under provisions against promoting hatred.

Bound for Glory from Minneapolis, featuring a former YDL member, were the first American RAC band to play Europe, in Germany. When No Remorse returned to America to play the 'Aryan Festival 92', which took place at a secluded desert camp outside LA Bound for Glory were also on the bill (as were Dirlewanger from Sweden). The singer in Bound for Glory was shot dead by a member of SHARP in Portland in 1993. He was 21. The band continued, releasing a split album with Brutal Attack in 1994 and are still going. Brutal Attack, alongside No Remorse, were the other UK RAC band most active in America: they played the 'American-European Unity Fest' in Pennsylvania in '92 which featured Nordic Thunder, Aggravated Assault, Das Reich, Max Resist and the Hooligans, Bound for Glory and Aryan.

In 1988, an American organisation called the Hammerskins emerged from Dallas and seemed to be a homegrown version of B&H. It spread rapidly. Formerly Haken Kreuz (meaning appropriation of the swastika by the Nazi party), Max Resist and the Hooligans were associated with the notorious Westside Bootboys, aka the Detroit Hammerskins. Picciolini merged his Chicago CASH gang with the Hammerskins. A member of Bound for Glory was said to run a chapter in Minnesota.

The 'leaderless' neo-Nazi organisation was said to have nineteen Hammerskins chapters across America by 2000 (such as Canada's Northern Hammerskins) with many other chapters throughout the world today. I heard whispers of one 'grey zone' band in the UK who were said to have links to them. The Hammerskins have been linked to numerous racist murders and attacks over their history, most notably the 2012 Sikh temple mass shooting in Wisconsin (six dead, four wounded). The man behind the shooting, 40-year-old Wade Michael Page, was a Hammerskin and played in neo-Nazi bands.

They hold an annual festival, 'Hammerfest', to mark the anniversary of the death of the singer from Resistance Records band, Nordic Thunder. The band, formed in Delaware in 1991, average age around 17, namechecked British RAC bands as inspiration. The singer was shot dead after playing a memorial festival for Ian Stuart in 1994.

It was difficult to gauge how popular this underground scene was in America; a few hundred skinheads, maybe, at these 'Aryan' outdoor gigs in the desert or secluded farmland. Their impact on the national psyche was enormous, however. There were a couple of infamous TV incidents: in 1988 on an episode of *The Oprah Winfrey Show* debating skinheads, a member of the Aryan

Youth Movement called Winfrey a monkey, and while being led off set was seen Sieg Heiling. It made national news and is still referred to by Winfrey today. The skinhead went on to form a Californian Oi! band called Extreme Hatred, became a WAR organiser and played the Aryan Fest in 1992. He namechecked Battle Zone and Skrewdriver and his band were linked to both White Terror Records and Resistance, featuring on the latter's '96 compilation album *A Tribute to Ian Stuart And The Glory Of Skrewdriver: The Flame That Never Dies*.

The other infamous American TV incident in 1988 was on the Geraldo Rivera show, *Geraldo*, where a discussion about white supremacy escalated into a full-scale brawl in the studio after a SHARP skinhead attacked Tom Metzger's son. Rivera had his nose broken in the mêlée.

Phil Templar sighed. 'It was these nerds involved in paramilitary racist organisations engaging in domestic terror getting all the media attention,' he said. 'So to most people when they see a skinhead they assume they're involved in some sort of racist weirdo activity. You also had skinhead bands in America who played gigs and hung out among themselves without any trouble. That tends to get ignored by the media. But if you smash up a synagogue, it's going to make the news.'

I saw The Templars play the 100 Club in August 2022. Crown Court's Trevor Taylor introduced me to Phil, the band's black co-founder and drummer. He works as a doctor, a foot & ankle specialist. The band were in their 50s now, singer Carl Fritscher (the first Oi! musician I'd seen in Nike trainers) was married with kids, they all had careers (bassist Perry Hardy, who studied geography at University of Illinois, works in urban planning,

Carl studied Scandinavian languages at University of Washington) and were spread about the country. They came together when they could, as friends, more for fun than anything, a break from their normal reality. This was their only UK date of 2022.

There were four of them on stage but it felt like five; two guitars blasting. There was no rock posturing, or really any posturing. They'd cut seven or eight or more albums, a stack of singles and EPs – I was still catching up with their catalogue. 'The Sixties Are Over' was a song I recognised. Carl dedicated another, 'War on the Streets', to Taylor. They started to heat up the longer they were on stage. 'Victim' and 'Skinheads Rule OK' had the thick attack I associated with the band. About half an hour in they played 'Clockwork Skinhead' by the 4-Skins and everyone started with the crazy dancing down the front. They did 'Violence in Our Minds' as a final song and about twenty other skinheads and fans (there were quite a few normal-looking young people at this gig), were up on stage, all sharing the mic, singing and having a laugh. The band were encouraged to play on and they belted into Cock Sparrer's 'Runnin' Riot'; Carl left it to others. It got quite chaotic. Everyone was smiling, having a good time.

About a month later I caught up with Phil on the phone. He was living in Barcelona, moved there earlier in the year. New York was not the same any more, he said. All the clubs the band grew up playing in, or watching bands in, such as CBGB had closed down. 'Cost of living steadily going up, less safety as well,' Phil elaborated. 'It was time to look elsewhere otherwise I'd just be in NY paying a lot of rent complaining all the time and getting older doing it.'

I said I'd read Spain was quite hot for Oi! now. 'You've got lots of bands in Barcelona and its outskirts spread out through Catalonia,' he said. 'You've got bands in Madrid, [and] in the Basque area, and they are damn good as well. It's not like Paris, though. Paris is like the fountain of youth in terms of Oi! music. But Barcelona is doing pretty good at the moment. A lot of young bands, which is good and keeps the scene vibrant.'

Phil mapped out a late eighties American Oi!/skinhead scene that was distinct, in fact initially opposed, to the RAC/B&H/Hammerskins scene just outlined. I'd watched a recent documentary called 'The Baldies: Anti-Racist Skinheads Fighting Nazis', about a gang from Minneapolis who were influenced by UK skinheads and developed into something called Anti-Racist Action and organised on a national scale. In New York, of course, SHARP was founded in the late eighties.

'SHARP let people know not all skinheads were just going around beating everyone who is not white,' Phil said. 'I was a black kid and there was plenty of other black skinheads in NY at the time. Finally, we had a voice. Skinheads can be black. It was important for me to have people acknowledge black people had a direct hand in creating the original culture, alongside the white youth in Britain, with the clothing style, the Ivy League style, and [the] attitude, Jamaica music genres, American soul music. At the time, SHARP was significant for me. Finally, there was something good people were talking about in relation to skinheads. When it hit the news, it was cool. Something new and refreshing. Not your typical country-bumpkin concert in some sort of hick town barnyard with a bunch of rednecks in overalls calling themselves skinheads running around beating each other up.'

The Templars are all about Phil and Carl. They met in 1990, aged 21 and 18, respectively, lived a short walk from one another in small towns on Long Island. They were both Anglophiles, loved British Oi!, early obscure punk and sixties beat groups. Phil's family had Caribbean roots and he spoke French naturally, so he was also listening to French Oi! bands like Komintern Sect. 'All the old bands from the Chaos Productions label in the early eighties,' he said (see next chapter).

Neither could play instruments but that didn't stop them picking up the drums and guitar Carl's elder brother had left laying about in the family garage. The two became oddly insular, developed this bleak, raw, tough sound. Carl was the first American to have a voice that could compete with the English greats. They recorded the music themselves, crudely lo-fi in Carl's garage on home equipment. 'It was crazy because I'd found someone who lived near me who liked all the same bands that I liked,' said Phil. 'That made everything easier for us [when it came to] writing songs.'

They played their first gigs in 1992; one, at an Oi! Fest in Washington DC, opened their eyes to the fact there was a nation-wide scene developing, bands like Patriot (who I saw at Rebellion) and Anti-Heros prominent. 'I was like, there's an Oi! band in North Carolina? [Patriot],' Phil said. 'I was completely shocked. Hearing about bands in Atlanta [Anti-Heros] shocked me even more. There was no internet, so the scene was all snail mail for fanzines and records.

'We were living in our own little bubble of New York, with CBGB,' Phil explained. 'To us, New York was the music capital. There was an Oi! scene in NYC and the north-east, established bands like Forced Reality, The Press, The Bruisers, YDL, The Radicts [released alongside The Press on Roddy Moreno's Oi! Records] and some others. You also had a lot of bands playing in the hardcore scene that listened to Oi! music. It wouldn't be strange to go to a hardcore matinee at CBGB and see members in a hardcore band wearing a 4-Skins or Angelic Upstarts T-shirt or the infamous "crucified skin" [Furbank] T-shirt. American bands like Negative Approach incorporated a cover of 'Chaos' in their set.'

From the first single, 'Poor Knights of Acre', in 1993, The Templars were righteous. They went boots in on the far-right scene. The first line of the first song, 'I've Heard It All Before' went, 'I've heard your politics and your views, they sound like shit.' It went on, 'I read your pamphlets and they seem like a fucking joke, the fools that follow you ain't old enough to vote.' Carl upped the equipment in his parents' garage to an eight-track, and this was their own studio, Acre, where all their early material was cut. Carl in control, a Long Island Joe Meek. With no one to stop him, early tracks such as 'Bovver Boy' pushed Oi!'s brickwall sound almost into the avant-garde.

Phil was DJing, organising gigs, printing T-shirts and a little Oi! scene formed around The Templars in New York City. They often played with another new NY band Oxblood; the two released a split EP in 1994 (The Templars continued to release split records throughout their career and it has become commonplace practice now in Oi!). 'Oxblood was a band that Carl and I played with sometimes in the studio,' Phil said. 'Out of New York in the early nineties, it was always us and Oxblood playing gigs together. All good friends and inseparable back then. Lots of laughs and funny memories. There were bands from New Jersey as well in the early nineties that were part of the scene: Those Unknown and The Wretched Ones from the [New Jersey] Headache Records stable.'

The Templar's first album was split with, rather incredulously, Sunderland's Red Alert. Gaz Stoker was in the band at this point. 'We loved Red Alert and all the No Future bands like Blitz, Violators, Partisans – we grew up on those bands,' Phil said. The album came about after Phil set up three local club dates for Red Alert around NY with The Templars as support. 'Because it was so special for us,' said Phil, 'we were like, let's take them to Carl's house and record some tracks before we take them to the airport. They banged out six tracks live and then we took them to the airport.'

The Templars' next album, *The Return of Jacques De Molay*, also released in '94, remains an all-time classic. Still sounds incredible. 'We wanted to play Oi! but we wanted to be a band that is not like every other Oi! band,' Phil said. 'I'm a self-taught drummer. Carl learned guitar later in life. We didn't just want to play three-chord songs, simple songs . . . we had to do something different, we had to play different, we had to do it different from everybody else. Most importantly, we didn't want to fade into obscurity.'

Phil recalled a significant moment for the band, when they were first invited to California and found they were headlining a sold-out show. They also played with The Business in 1995 during their first tour of the US. A change in the Templars' outlook occurred when they agreed to record in a proper studio, for their third album, *Omne Datum Optimum* (1998). This was at the nudging of Mark Noah, former Anti-Heros singer and now in charge of his own GMM label. At the time the Anti-Heros were national news because they were featured in the film *American History X* starring Edward Norton as a rehabilitated white power neo-Nazi skinhead. The producers had used the

Anti-Heros name as sort of a visual shorthand for white power Oi! music, and they featured on tattoos and posters. The band won a well-publicised lawsuit and the movie had to be re-edited.

The Anti-Heros were an influential Oi! band, featured on Link's *U.S. Of Oi!* compilation, and Link had released their first couple of albums in the UK (the first song on their debut 1986 album went 'Anti-Heroes, Oi! Oi! Oi!'). And GMM were one of the most significant American Oi! labels. Their 1993 comp *The U.S. Of Oi! Volume II* is an excellent start point to explore what this scene was all about. The label also provided an outlet for European Oi! bands such as Condemned 84 and Oxymoron alongside American acts Dropkick Murphys and The Ducky Boys.

'When Mark [Noah] approached us, he said that GMM would release our new record but only if we recorded in the studio to see what our full potential was,' Phil said. 'Carl and I were not sure but we were good friends with Mark – and still are – so why not trust him. He's one of our greatest supporters. Back then you had a lot of people who either loved our lo-fi raw sound or who said they loved our music but wished we recorded in a real studio.

'We did it twice,' Phil said. 'We did two albums [in the same studio]. 'For the next one, *[The] Horns of Hattin* [2001], we made it sound rougher. That was the album Lars Frederiksen wanted to produce. Mark was in town, working on the [new Anti-Heros] album that Lars was producing. We were at a bar and Lars came down to meet us. I told Mark, no. I inferred that we have a certain way of playing and we didn't need anyone to help us with our sound. I wasn't trying to be offensive but told him, thanks, but no thanks.'

When Phil joined German band Stomper 98 (see next chapter) as a side project to The Templars, he and Frederiksen would eventually work together. 'Stomper 98 added him to replace one of the guitarists and on the last full-length Stomper 98 album [released 2018], both Lars and I play on it. Lars is a solid guy. He's one of the guys who needs to be respected. He has done a lot for Oi! music and he didn't have to. He could've just settled with Rancid and lived his life and ignored the new wave of bands coming up. Instead, he helps bands get gigs, pulls the older bands to support him when Rancid comes through.'

On *The Horns of Hattin*, The Templars did a Skrewdriver cover, a song called 'Backstreet Kids' (from the band's debut '77 album) and this ushered in the first sign of internet controversy that still sometimes attaches itself to the band. I knew Phil was an admirer of the 'Chiswick sound' and had already mentioned several obscure bands – The Stukas, The Rings, Johnny Moped, Little Bob Story and Count Bishops – signed to the Chiswick label alongside Skrewdriver. 'All those bands had a rough, great sound, and that was an influence too,' Phil said. 'Yes, Skrewdriver happen to be on the label. OK, fine, who cares, it is what it is . . . nothing we could do about it.'

I said it wasn't an issue for me: I'd recently discovered Negro Terror's immense 2018 track, 'Voice of Memphis', a Skrewdriver corruption of 'Voice of Britain'. It remains one of my favourite American Oi! tracks. There's an excellent film on the band called *Negro Terror*, released 2019.

'They also did that [Skrewdriver] song, 'Invasion', which is hilarious,' Phil said. 'With 'Voice of Memphis', they took that song and made it their own. They took a song that was completely political and made it their own sound with their own message. When we did 'Backstreet Kids' we called it 'Blackstreet Kids'. We did it as a play on words years before *The Horns of Hattin*. The Anti-Heros were supposed to do a split with us. The Anti-Heros doing a version of 'Anti-Social' but calling it 'Anti-Hero'. A totally anti-racist single, just a slap in the face to all the idiots out there following all that stupid shit. But it never was released so we had this track in limbo and we just put it at the very end of the album as a hidden track. And we got a lot of flak for it, flak we are still dealing with to this day. And I'm like, do you not see the make-up of the band? We've been against racism since the first EP.

'Then Negro Terror cover a Skrewdriver song and everyone's like, oh this is a fantastic cover. I'm like, wait a minute, when we did it, it was a problem. When they did it, alright, no problem at all. I guess life is funny like that. Rest in peace to Omar [Higgins, singer with Negro Terror, who died in 2019 aged 37]. Omar was a great guy and I'm glad they didn't get any flak off it. They're an ace band. We know where we stand, and we've always known where we stand regarding racism.'

The Templars continued to record for GMM but returned to Carl's garage, their old Acre Studio ways, for their next album *Outremer* (2005). There was a prolonged gap between then and the band's final album to date of new material, *Deus Vult*, released by Pirates Press in 2017. But they had done enough by then to be considered Oi! royalty.

I asked Phil why the prolonged break in the noughties/early teens? 'There was a time where we didn't play in our own city for three or four years,' he said. 'We just spent time playing elsewhere. We did a lot of European shows, which was awesome. We played Rebellion a few times. But New York for a while was really dead meat. It was around the time there was loads of violence at gigs and a lot of places were avoiding Oi! gigs or being shut down. One big thing that caused problems was all the political shit [see chapter 12]. All the political stuff mixed in with social media was a recipe for disaster. People sabotaging shows, just a lot of unnecessary nonsense.'

I got the impression nonetheless that The Templars had fun in the decade between albums, playing 'pretty much most of the planet,' Phil said. 'When we play gigs abroad, we always tell the promoters we have a monetary guarantee, accommodations for the time we are there, and we always do a day of culture and sight-seeing if we have the time.' He is a West Ham fan and he told me how promoters had taken the band to see football matches in Brazil and Mexico. He also mentioned playing with the Rejects in Las Vegas, having Roi join them on stage to do 'Violence in Our Minds' when they supported The Last Resort at the Boston Arms in London. 'We pay tribute to all these bands we grew up listening to; without them, there'd be no us. On some of our old flyers we'd put "Grandsons of Oi!". I've always said we're an Oi! band and I've always tended to criticise bands that call themselves "streetpunk". Oi! is not a dirty word.'

At Rebellion, as well as Patriot, I'd seen two newer American Oi! bands, Suede Razors and Ultra Sect.

Mike Josephson was in both bands. We spoke on the phone in late September. He was in Tacoma, just south of Seattle. Mike was also the founder of Longshot Music, which has been for the past twenty-five years the most significant Oi! label in America. It was Mike who'd introduced me to Doug & The Slugz. Sometimes he's credited on records as Mike Thug.

He said he had started Suede Razors in the early noughties, based around the Bay Area, San Francisco (first release, 2014).

Although they loved Last Resort and the 4-Skins, Mike said they tried to tap into some rock'n'roll glam, Slade or Sweet, and some Australian pub boogie rock, Rose Tattoo, to come up with what has been described as 'Bootboy Glam' or 'Bovver rock'. 'Not strictly Oi!,' he said, more a sub-genre.

Ultra Sect were formed more recently (debut EP released by Longshot in 2018) because Josephson (and Suede Razors' youngest member Bryan Zimmerman) wanted to do a band with more of a 'traditional Oi!' sound. They have recently released a split single with another hotly tipped American Oi! band, and fellow Californians, Vis Vires (who feature Perry Hardy from The Templars).

Josephson was generous with his knowledge and his time. He said the drummer in Suede Razors and Ultra Sect, Eric Owens, had also played in The Bootboys. 'He was a young drummer on the LA music scene and it was a band he got involved with briefly [before they became Youngblood],' Josephson explained. 'The Bootboys were one of those bands who became dubious but they weren't one of the untouchable bands. As a kid I would never listen to Bound for Glory or RaHoWa, but a band like The Bootboys . . .' he trailed off. 'It's like Condemned 84 [in the UK], they for some reason get a lot of heat. I always grew up thinking they were a hard Oi! band, I didn't lump them into a category of like, say, a Skrewdriver.'

Josephson was Canadian, from British Columbia, part of a small town skinhead crew as a teen. He said Mark Noah and the Anti-Heros were an early influence. 'He stood up to the stereotypes of skinheads being Nazis,' Josephson said. 'Some of their stuff was unabashedly patriotic, they got accused of being nationalists, this that and the other, but Mark wasn't a racist or a bigot – he sang about issues that had to do with America. Ultra Sect do an Anti-Heros cover now.' Josephson was also an early supporter of The Templars. 'I used to write letters to Carl a lot,' he said 'Exchange ideas. The Templars are *the* iconic American Oi! band, there's no two ways about it.'

Longshot started putting out records in '97, shortly after Mike moved to Vancouver (he moved to America in 2003). 'My very first releases were "tribute" records because everybody likes to do covers, it's fun,' he said. 'I was just getting [North American] bands I knew or bands I would reach out to to contribute. The first one I did was The Oppressed [The Templars contributed] and then I did a Cockney Rejects one and then a Cock Sparrer one.' The Dropkick Murphys, who enjoyed a run of four Top 20 American albums between 2007 and 2017 and were recently featured on the cover of *Rolling Stone* magazine, contributed to the latter.

'The early incarnation of the Dropkick Murphys was definitely cut from the cloth of an early streetpunk/Oi! band,' Josephson said. 'They were from Boston, part of a strong New England scene of bands: The Bruisers, The Ducky Boys, Lenny Lashly was there doing a band called Darkbuster. They were not straight-up skinhead Oi! bands but they put that American spin on it – it's where the term "streetpunk" comes from. It's a morph between the American style and UK Oi!. TKO Records from the Bay Area was around in the late nineties and they were putting out a lot of that "streetpunk" brand.'

He added: 'There was that real blurry thing in the nineties and 2000s where Oi! was pushed aside and everybody was saying "streetpunk" – nobody wanted to use the term Oi!. Even at Longshot, I used the name "streetpunk" [for a multiple-volume series of comps, *Oi! This Is Streetpunk*].'

Longshot were behind a whole new wave of US Oi! bands, a year zero being the label's 2012 compilation EP, *A Better Tomorrow (The Next Generation Of U.S. Oi!)*. The standouts were Noi!se and Razors in the Night (named after a Blitz song) but Mike also mentioned Antagonizers ATL, Harrington Saints and 45 Adapters as part of this scene. Longshot also distributed a host of modern Oi! bands from around the world. 'One of the bigger ones would be Marching Orders from Australia,' Josephson said. 'I put out their first record and we're working on a complete singles package right now [see chapter 11].'

Longshot also introduced new wave UK (Booze & Glory, Crashed Out, Argy Bargy) and European (Lion's Law and Stomper 98) Oi! bands to America. 'A lot of what I was putting out was co-releases in partnership with another label, so a lot of that stuff was brought to me,' Josephson said. 'I like the music but it was put out by European labels and if they didn't really have a distribution outlet for North America I helped. They would reciprocate if I had a band from Canada or America who wanted to release their music in the UK/Europe. A lot of Longshot was built on that mutual co-operation.'

Those European labels are Contra, Rebellion, Randale?

'Also Step-1,' Mike said. 'Those are the four major players.'

We talked a little about the latest wave of exciting new Oi! bands. Josephson was involved with Rude Pride from Spain and Brutal Bravo from Germany and rated Violent Way and Castillo from America. He also mentioned Mess from Mexico City and Crown Court (Longshot had distributed one of their early singles). 'Have you heard of Rixe?' he asked. 'Wattie [Lion's Law singer] plays bass and sings in that band. People love that band here. They spend a lot of time touring, they were just here in North America, up and down the west coast two months ago. Popular and influential. There's a lot of bands who play shows but don't travel so don't tie the scene together. If you want to have your mind blown just look at Paris – there's probably about ten bands in Paris that are very interesting, one of my favourites is Squelette [see next chapter].'

Josephson reflected on his long association with Oi!. 'The scene comes in waves, peaks and troughs; some of those American bands Longshot released [in the noughties/teens] helped carry the genre through some slightly less glory days, but right now we're hitting another surge of new bands,' he said. 'Last month I had three releases from new bands: the one I'm urging people to check out is called Slugger, younger guys been bouncing around playing in other bands for years, definitely, unashamedly a skinhead/Oi! band, really exciting.'

I spoke to Josephson's bandmate in Suede Razors/Ultra Sect, Bryan Zimmerman, at the end of October. Early morning in San Francisco. He'd been partying the night before, a little groggy. After Rebellion, I'd seen him in Oi Oi The Shop and then later the same day at The Templars gig in London. He was ten to fifteen years younger than Josephson, late 30s. He said the Bay Area, where he grew up, had a rich history of melodic 'street-punk' bands and he was a teenage fan of the bands on local label, TKO, and the bands they released such as The Bodies and Reducers SF. 'Also I'd go see [Headache band] Those Unknown who relocated to Santa Rosa, the town where I grew up,' he said. Templars and Anti-Heros became two of his favourite American Oi! bands and they led him to discover British Oi!. 'It was actually Link Records and their [multi-volume] *Oi! Chartbusters* comps that first sucked me in,' he said. 'Bands like

The Business, Last Resort and Blitz. Also when Cock Sparrer first came over here in the late nineties they only did three or four shows and one was San Francisco, so we were exposed to that. They are the biggest small band in the world.'

Zimmerman formed Suede Razors he said to play 'skinhead rock'n'roll' as opposed to the 'streetpunk' of his former bands. He described this period as 'the biggest resurgence' of Oi! he had ever personally experienced in the Bay Area Oi! scene. '2010–2013,' he specified. 'It was the first time I can remember when it was "cool" to be a skinhead, not only were the shows really explosive with a lot of local bands and great crowds, but we had killer reggae DJ nights. We also had promoters bringing in a lot of skinhead reggae artists from the late sixties/early seventies. It was a time when there was a ton of energy in the Bay Area scene. The thing that made it even better was that it was happening in Europe too, so we were touring and experiencing the scene over there and taking notice of the youth in their scene.'

Ultra Sect (and tracks such as 'Turn up the Oi!'), he said, was a reflection of his love of hard aggressive British Oi!. 'Mid-tempo and in your face.' I asked him how today's scene compared to that period he described when the Suede Razors first formed? 'The thing I've noticed, and this is a general statement,' Zimmerman started, '[is] I've felt my generation is the last generation in the USA that was really into the music. Are there other younger people in America doing it? Of course, but impactful, large group of people – it's felt like we were the last. But going over to Europe [with Ultra Sect] I immediately noticed there was a ton of young people, and that's what breathes life into the scene – having new kids coming to the shows.'

He said social media was now the biggest driving force on

the Oi! scene. 'It's really made it an international scene,' Zimmerman said. 'We have these communities and friendships that are worldwide now. That's a positive thing and something that hasn't been there on the same level in the past: the friendships among people, bands and fans. The fact we're even talking about a new wave currently happening is cool: there is now youth, early 20s, mid 20s, a new generation playing Oi! and there's enough of them to be making an impression. It was on your radar and it's on a lot of people's radars.'

Finally, for this American chapter I spoke to Greg Huff of Bishops Green, one of the most significant bands to emerge from Canada and hugely popular in Europe. They are another Longshot band. Huff was in Vancouver. I spoke to him in mid-November. Earlier in the year Bishops Green had played a twenty-date European tour, breaking new territories such as Athens and shoring up their following in Germany and France 'and picking up some new young fans,' Huff said.

He'd been playing in Oi! bands since the mid-to-late nineties when his first band the Glory Stompers released a split with The Templars. He'd also formed popular Vancouver Oi! bands Subway Thugs (which featured Josephson), The Lancasters and Alternate Action.

Bishops Green had been advertised to play Rebellion and I was disappointed, and confused, when they hadn't. 'Yeah, life happens,' Huff said. 'Maybe next year, we'll see – it's a great festival!'

Despite his look, heavily tattooed including on his skull, and his music, he was disarmingly polite and sweet, softly spoken. He mentioned the Subway Thugs playing an Oi! festival in '98 in Phoenix, Arizona, with the Anti-Heros and Templars. 'Those were interesting times, little bit of craziness and violence thrown in there, lot of fun – lot of good people,' he said. 'I'm still friends with a ton of people from that time.'

I asked about the Canadian scene in general. 'Every city had its own scene because it's so spread apart,' he said. 'Calgary, Montreal, Toronto. The Prowlers [part of a left-leaning contingent based around the Canadian label Insurgence whose compilations are called *Class Pride World Wide*] were on the east coast. I would travel to go hang out with the skinhead/punk Oi! scene there. They'd throw great parties. Rob Horseman who was in the Subway Thugs did a Canadian Oi! comp [called *Oi! Let's Go . . . Canada!*, 1988]; it's a harder to find comp but pretty good, a good eye-opener for the Canadian Oi! scene back then.'

He said he preferred the term 'streetpunk' over Oi! for Bishops Green. 'It's punk rock really,' he said. 'It's how the songs matured, it's the sound that comes out of us, I guess – working-class punk'. Has Huff also developed a more mature vocal style over the aggressive bawl of the Subway Thugs? 'Yes, a little smoother around the edges,' he laughed. We talked about the band's popularity around the world. 'We played Bogotá, and Mexico City and Guadalajara and the scenes there were absolutely amazing!' Greg said. 'I was blown away how big the scene was in Bogotá.'

Despite the popularity of Bishops Green – 1.4 million Spotify streams in one hundred countries in 2021 – they were not on a level to pack in work. Vancouver is a notoriously expensive city to live in. And work meant they could not commit to the extensive touring that might lead to the band turning pro. 'It is a catch-22,' Huff said. 'As much as we'd love to do this full-time we all have to work. That's just the scenario I have to accept.

Our jobs are flexible enough that we do get time to tour but the extent of our touring is limited for sure. I'm passionate about it and love playing music but I do have to work my day job.'

Chapter 10

For My Clan: Lion's Law (European Oi!)

Wattie, the voice of Parisian band Lion's Law, was the only fella I met who made a living out of playing modern Oi! music. Had done for the past six years. 'Luckily,' he said. I figured Wattie made his own luck: played in five bands, toured endlessly, booked gigs in Paris for other bands, ran a radio show. 'The minimum salary, but I'd rather live with the minimum wage and do something I like to do,' he said.

His real name is Victor Lapprend and for the past ten years he's been Oi!'s most recognisable young face, since Lion's Law's video for their song 'For My Clan' became a YouTube hit (7 million views) and he appeared in a cameo role in a Beyoncé video for 'Flawless' (98 million views). He's 32 now.

Crown Court's Taylor, who'd known Wattie for the best part of a decade, introduced me to him at the 100 Club when Lion's Law were supporting The Templars. It was largely through sheer force of Wattie's stage presence that he made the Lion's Law show an event it was a pleasure to be at. I didn't think it was going to happen at first. They were a five-piece, in old-school adidas trainers, youthful but definitely past their first flush, adult. Wattie had boots on and a deep, growling, booming voice tinged with an unmistakable French accent (the band sang mostly, but not exclusively, in English). By the fifth song, 'Layafette', Wattie had everyone onside and in the moment. 'Un Jour', tipped them over. Wattie had his top off, revealing a torso covered in tattoos, and so did many in the crowd.

Lion's Law were touring America in October (twenty-or-so dates, west and east coast), so I figured I'd leave Wattie until that ended. When it did, I saw he was touring again with one of his other band's, Bromure. We spoke one Friday morning while he was home in Paris. He was warm, big-hearted, spoke English well, mentioned he spoke Spanish and Italian too. He said the recent Lion's Law visit to America had been the seventh or eighth time he'd toured the country, including several times with his other main band Rixe, and that this latest time they'd taken eighties French Oi! band Komintern Sect along as support (the two bands, despite their age difference, share a drummer).

'It's funny because if you ask any punk or skinhead in France they would know a lot of songs by Komintern Sect by heart, they are a true classic, but when we go to the US, Lion's Law is bigger than Komintern Sect,' Wattie said. 'We were playing club shows for 200–250 people [on the tour] and people were saying that Komintern Sect were great, and I was saying, yes but if you really want to see them in their element come to Paris. Every year we do a show, us and them, and a ska/skinhead band called 8°6 Crew and every year we need a bigger venue. The last one we did we sold out 1,500 tickets.'

'Every time I go to America, I see more and more people wearing French Oi! band T-shirts,' he added. 'It seems like a part of the US punk [scene] just discovered the *Chaos* compilations [called *Chaos En France Volume 1* and *Volume 2*] of early French Oi!, '83, '84, with all our best bands – Camera Silens, Snix and Komintern Sect.'

I'd read Wattie talk about being a fan of Snix (from Lille, 1982–87) before. I was curious because Gaël Bodilis had put them on at a French RAC gig with Skrewdriver and they'd released an album on Rock-O-Rama. 'Snix was a nationalist band, but the lyrics don't really talk about this so . . .' Wattie, started and paused. 'There was a lot of bands from the eighties in France that were patriotic or nationalist but they were strongly not Nazi,' Wattie continued. 'A lot of those band would be super-proud of being French but they would never have Nazi-sympathising lyrics. They were just being provocative, being silly and super-patriotic because they were copying the English skinhead movement which was always waving the flag. Bunker 84 and Legion 88 are the real French Nazi bands [from that era]: only racist lyrics, super hateful. You can't compare Snix to Bunker 84.

'The past is the past and now it's fine if we listen to bands like Snix as long as you are clear on your stance,' said Wattie, who had emerged in the noughties as a figure in the SHARP skinhead scene in Paris. He explained that he loved Snix because they were one of the early eighties French Oi! bands who, although influenced by the classic English bands, had helped forge a distinct 'French Oi! sound'. 'It doesn't sound like Last Resort,' he said, 'If you listen to Snix it's very particular: it's one of the bands that made French Oi!. That's why I always speak about them.' What he was talking about essentially was saxophone, part of French Oi! DNA. 'Saxophone is very much linked to French Oi! – the main bands from the eighties [including Snix] all had at least one song with saxophone,' he said.

'Something else [with French Oi!] is when you listen to bands like Camera Silens or Snix, the lyrics are really personal and deep and it's why the saxophone works because it's way more melancholic and poetic.'

I wanted to drill down a little bit deeper into the eighties Oi! scene in France. I asked Wattie about Snix playing gigs in France with French RAC band Brutal Combat who had links to NF's White Noise Club circa 1985. 'Everybody played with Brutal Combat,' he said. 'In the early eighties everybody played together. Before making a turn to the right wing, Brutal Combat played with Camera Silens, Komintern Sect . . . all those guys know each other. French Oi! bands just started to be a bit too dumb and that's what killed the first wave of French Oi!. If you speak to first-wave [French Oi!] bands like Swingo Porkies [Paris, 1979–83] or Komintern Sect, they stopped because they didn't want people making Nazi salutes at their gigs. It changed after '84, but all the bands from '79–'84 knew each other.

'Gaël Bodilis is one of the guys who brought the heavy politics into French Oi!,' Wattie added. 'When Brutal Combat signed to Rebelles Européens it changed the whole band. I also think there was a change of line-up because some of the guys were not that interested in releasing political music.'

Lion's Law had covered an Evil Skins song, who I read were another French neo-Nazi Oi! band from the eighties. Was that similar to Negro Terror or Templars doing Skrewdriver, I asked? 'We changed the lyrics and made it ours,' Wattie said. 'But you have to know something about Evil Skins: I am 200 per cent sure when I say this. Everybody in France, from left to right, know every Evil Skins song . . . it's such a classic. I grew up and was way more into the left part of skinheads and we were blasting Evil Skins all fucking night. Let's say 95 per cent of the lyrics are just really aggro and funny, they also had that ambience with saxophone. It's [the] really typical sound of French Oi!.

'They were also one of the toughest Nazi gangs in the eighties,' he added. 'When you speak to the guys now, they are all active in cleaning up what they did in their past. The guitar player is a Buddhist monk, he runs a temple in Normandy and is preaching for non-violence; he goes to schools and tells his story about the eighties, him being one of the bad guys and how much he regrets this. I had a chance to speak to those guys and they were not even like super-Nazis; going to [political] rallies and stuff. They were just beating people up in the street and what they found to be the most provocative thing was being a Nazi skinhead. People would look at them like, oh my god! I'm not giving them an excuse but if you listen to their story, it's just that for a few years of their lives they were being the worst people ever.'

We talked briefly about other French Oi! bands from the eighties such as Tolbiac's Toads, so-called 'because they were wearing the green bomber jackets,' Wattie said. 'One of the really early Oi! bands: not a Nazi band but they were super-patriotic and nationalist. The singer was gay but he was one of the scariest skinheads in Paris, so when people were being stupid and homophobic they wouldn't say shit to him. His boyfriend was one [of the] big pop singers from France back in the eighties.'

I asked about another band I'd read about, L'Infanterie Sauvage? 'I love them,' Wattie said. 'Early eighties punk/Oi! band from Paris. Everybody loves them but the singer is dead. After L'Infanterie Sauvage was over the singer went into that

Nazi shit; he went a bit crazy and he ended up singing with Legion 88. He started to love Ian Stuart – there's a picture of him with Ian Stuart. Legion 88 is the only French band [that was] welcomed to England and played with Skrewdriver; they played the RAC gig in the barn. The singer bombed the Communist Party local club. He went to jail for that and when he got out he admitted he was going too far and doing stupid shit and then he drowned. He died when he was 24.'

Wow, I said, if L'Infanterie Sauvage were a UK band with that history they'd be firmly in the 'do not touch' pile. 'They were all doing crazy shit because they were lost,' Wattie said. 'Strange times. I'm too young to judge but I love talking about it.'

Wattie said that during the nineties, although there were some notable French Oi! bands such as The Herberts and the 8°6 Crew, the Oi!/skinhead scene wasn't as big as it had been in the eighties. 'The Nazis were in strength – that's where the SHARP influence was born,' he said. In Paris, he explained, there were actually three distinct groups of skinheads: RASH (Red and Anarchist Skinheads), the neo-Nazis and SHARP, who were seen as being in the middle. At some point during the decade a neo-Nazi skin murdered a RASH skin and both scenes (Brigada Flores Magon were the big RASH band) largely quit Paris. Wattie said that nowadays there were very few neo-Nazi Oi! bands left, and those that continued were very secretive, playing gigs in the woods in northern France.

In the late nineties a new Parisienne Oi! label began to reinvigorate the Oi! scene: Une Vie Pour Rien. It grew out of a fanzine of the same name run by two friends, David and Ben, the latter also playing in Oi! bands, Lutece Borgia and Moonlight Wankers. The label released bands like the HardxTimes, The Janitors,

Bombardiers and also the 8°6 Crew (a ska/reggae outfit who had an Oi! band on the side, Survet Skins). 'Ben is still one of the key people today,' Wattie said. 'He's a good friend. When he releases something [on Une Vie Pour Rien] you can buy it with your eyes closed – you know it's going to be good. People from all around Europe know about this label.'

Une Vie Pour Rien released Wattie's first band the Maraboots after he moved to Paris from Lille in the noughties. Alongside another band, Street Kids, Maraboots led a resurgence of French Oi!. 'Street Kids were great, younger than us but unfortunately they never released anything on record,' Wattie said. 'But together we kickstarted a new generation of SHARP. There was other Oi! bands around, but for SHARP Parisians we were the young kids. I think a lot of the older generation didn't really believe there would be another generation, so when they saw a lot of 18-year-olds kids wearing the same style, playing the same music, they were really happy and proud to see that.'

Lion's Law, formed around 2012, was a collaboration between Louis from Street Kids and Wattie. 'We said, we want something different together but how are we going to do something different when we already do two bands, so we said, let's sing in English. Street Kids had an English name but sang in French.' Was that a deliberate move to appeal to a wider audience, I asked? 'We were already playing outside of France but I think it helped,' he said. 'But to be honest, if you do a quality band, even if it's in French, you can tour wherever you want. In Rixe, we only sing in French and we've toured Japan twice, Australia, South Korea, four times [in] the States, Mexico. So that's not something that's going to block the band from growing – if it's good, it's good. People don't really care.'

All photos on this page: Phil Templar

Game changers: The Templars. The band's founders Phil Templar (left) and Carl Fritscher started out in 1991, in a garage in Long Island, New York. Their raw sound, insular recording technique, defiant attitude and clear anti-racist stance begat the whole modern Oi! scene.

Mike Josephson

SKINHEADS AGAINST SHARP RACIAL PREJUDICE

Doug 'Dagger' Kane

Hard, fast and fun: Bishops Green from Vancouver (top) are currently one of Oi!'s biggest bands.

SHARP (Skinheads Against Racial Prejudice) was founded in New York in the late eighties. Their logo was designed by Roddy Moreno of Welsh Oi! band, The Oppressed.

The very first American Oi! band was Doug & The Slugz (centre right) formed in LA in the early 80s. They did not release a record in their heyday.

Mike Josephson

Ultra Sect (right) from the San Francisco Bay Area, featuring Mike Josephson (second from right) and Bryan Zimmerman (far right) are leading lights of a thriving new wave of American Oi!.

Karl Khal

Victor Lapprend

European sons: Modern German Oi! band, Brutal Bravo (top), with Karl Khal (left).

From Paris, the towering Lion's Law (bottom) and friends. Singer Wattie (real name Victor Lapprend, right) remains the leading light in the anti-racist Parisian scene.

Osvaldo González

Al White

Luis Português

World Oi!: (Clockwise) Worker Sweat from Chile, 80s/90s south American Oi! champions.

Debut album cover of Australian band Marching Orders, Australia's best-known Oi! band. It features a shot of a 1960s Melbourne 'Sharpie', a widespread subculture that pre-dated skinheads in England and is now an Oi! cultural touchstone worldwide.

The Rotten Boys (middle) from Brazil, who broke into their country's mainstream rock culture in the 80s.

Marching Orders (right), singer Al White in the centre.

Al White

Chris Wright

Green shoots: The Business (top left) in their final lineup. Front man Micky Fitz RIP (right).

Lars Frederiksen of Rancid fame being tattooed by Chris Wright of Crashed Out (top right).

Grade 2 (left), hotly tipped young Oi! band from the Isle of Wight.

Early shot of Jamie Flanagan (bottom, black Fred Perry shirt), singer with new-wave UK Oi! band, Tear Up.

Sarah McCauley

Solid rock: Jeff Geggus (top). He told me the Cockney Rejects' recent world tour would be their last. Jeff and band co-founder (his brother Mick), plus bassist Vince Riordan, are Oi! royalty.

Cock Sparrer's founder and drummer, Steve Bruce (bottom left), holding copies of their most recent album, *Forever* (2017), in Oi Oi The Shop.

Oi!'s biggest band (although they prefer the term 'streetpunk'), Cock Sparrer (bottom right). From left: Daryl Smith, Colin McFaull and Steve Burgess.

Legends: King of Oi!, Roi Pearce of The Last Resort (top).

Style and staying power, Graham Saxby fronting The Warriors (middle).

Bill Bennett and Sarah McCauley (left), the husband and wife team behind Oi Oi The Shop, a thriving, positive hub for the current Oi! scene worldwide.

Keith Altham Estate

Everlasting: promotional shots of Cock Sparrer in their 1977 incarnation (top and bottom left). Songwriter and guitarist Garry Lammin (centre in both shots) drove the band toward a 'bootboy' football hooligan image.

Oi Oi The Shop, Camden Market (bottom right). 'We're not going to give you a good kicking and tell you to fuck off. Come and see what it's all about, talk to us.'

Lion's Law were another band offered support from Lars Frederiksen. 'Lars played half of the solo on 'For My Clan',' Wattie said. 'We booked a show with Stomper 98, who love French Oi!, and Old Firm Casuals and on the same weekend we were recording the first Lion's Law album. On the afternoon before the show we took them to the studio and asked them to play. Half of the guitar solo is by the guitar player from Stomper 98 and the other half is Lars. Not a lot of people know that. He's been supporting us lots . . . he's cool.'

I asked Wattie if 'For My Clan' had been a big hit in France? He laughed. 'It was not a hit,' he said. 'Nobody in the streets would know 'For My Clan'. But people who are just listening to rock or punk rock would know that song and they see me and say, oh that's the guy from 'For My Clan'. YouTube helped it get through to a lot of people.' After the video for the song blew up, Lion's Law toured hard and became the biggest new Oi! band around the world.

Their latest album, their fourth, released in 2020, *The Pain, the Blood and the Sword*, had sold an impressive 6,000 copies worldwide via an almost familial network of independent Oi! labels (in countries including Japan, France, Germany, America, Brazil, Malaysia and Canada), all corralled in this instance by Spain's HFMN, based close to Barcelona.

'There's not a lot of bands from our generation playing a lot of shows, so that's why people ask us to come everywhere, Asia, Brazil . . . because we are a super-active band; we do a lot of shit and we're still young,' Wattie said. 'I never felt Lion's Law was a big band except when we were in Bogotá. There are maybe five or six skinhead shops in the city – it's one of the biggest skinhead scenes in the world. When we played there it was a crazy show. Even when we were walking the streets, in the parks, there was nothing but skinheads and they were calling us, singing, trying to take pictures.'

Germany is another country where Lion's Law are popular. 'Germany has always been a rock country,' said Wattie. 'When I was younger, we'd travel there to go to festivals and you'd see Cock Sparrer headlining and you'd have 20,000 people, huge punk/Oi! festivals. In France you'd never see this.

'Spain is great too, still very active,' he added. 'A bit of a smaller scene than Germany but people go crazy at shows. There are a ton of new good Oi! bands in Spain and they had lots of good bands in the eighties too. I love it because I've spoken fluent Spanish since I was 16.'

And Japan? 'I've been to Japan four or five times touring and people say, wow, man, it must be crazy,' Wattie said. 'We always have a great time because Japan is something else, a different universe, but really the shows are regular club shows with 150–200 people. They had a pretty strong Oi! scene in the nineties, even eighties, but now it's always the same people at shows – guys from the nineties – there's no younger generation.'

Which brings us back to France, to Paris and Une Vie Pour Rien's remarkable *Paris on Oi!* compilation released in 2022, featuring a dozen of France's new, young and thrusting Oi! bands such as Squelette, Cran (with a female singer) and Bromure (another of Wattie's bands). 'That was something that me and David [from Une Vie Pour Rien] planned,' Wattie explained. 'Just before Covid I did a list of all the Oi! bands that are actually playing in Paris and there were at least twenty-five active bands. Wow, it's big. David said the scene in Paris has never been this big. So we decided to make the compilation as a snapshot – we think it's important to let people know the energy, starting with younger bands. Lion's Law is not on the compilation because we're ten years old – too old. The comp represents the new breed of Paris bands.

'There are also a lot of Oi! bands in other cities of France, so it is very active right now,' Wattie added. 'The new wave of French Oi! is super-Oi!, like eighties Oi!, not mixed with hardcore or American [streetpunk] stuff.'

Even so, he said the Oi! scene was still 'super underground' in France. 'It's not that easy to find skinheads in Paris,' he said. 'We just have two or three pubs where we meet; it's very small compared to the size of the city.' I expressed surprise when Wattie said that no mainstream French media had picked up on what was happening in Paris, the success of Lion's Law. 'It's still maybe because of the skinhead bad rep,' he said. 'It's a very bad reputation but, well, what have we done? I don't know.'

Lion's Law are still pushing, though. They've played twice at Hellfest, the biggest rock and heavy metal festival in France, with 55,000 tickets sold annually. 'That is helping us finish the bad rep associated with skinheads and Oi!,' he said proudly. 'When they see us live they are like, whoa they're actually good.'

Many European countries had their own, usually colourful, Oi! histories. Italy, for example, had their own iconic act, Klasse Kriminale, formed in '85, in north-west Italy, and who, sixteen albums later, are still going, having released split singles with bands such as The Oppressed, Angelic Upstarts and The Old Firm Casuals.

Italy also seemed to have had its own Southall moment, in 1983, at the Raduno Oi! festival in Toscana. It was the third such annual Oi! festival, all in some way organised by Nabat, the country's Oi! pioneers from Bologna. They also ran their own label C.A.S. and released the country's first Oi! comp *Skins e Punks = T.N.T.*

At the '83 Raduno Oi! fest, there was some neo-Nazi infiltration, Sieg Heils shouted from the stage, and a big riot involving football hooligans, skinheads, punks and locals. From here, Italian Oi! bands found it difficult to get gigs and a more hardcore far-right Oi! scene took root. Veneto was the first region to have a neo-Nazi scene centred on the band Plastic Surgery, but I could name five or more other Italian RAC bands who emerged. Nabat disbanded, but before they did, C.A.S. put out Italy's definitive Oi! comp, *Queli Che Urlano Ancora* (translation: *Those Who Still Scream*) in '85, the so-called *Chaos en France* of Italian Oi!.

Nabat's guitarist went on to play in Skrewdriver. Klasse Kriminale also had a controversial member, Antonella, who left to join UK RAC band Battle Zone. The band's singer Marco, however, was a key figure in re-establishing Italian Oi! as a positive force. He formed his own Oi! label, Havin' A Laugh Records, and released a series of compilations in the nineties, including *Oi! It's a World League* in '93, which featured Oi! bands from around the world and is another great snapshot of that period, *Oi! Against Silvio* in 1994 and *Oi! Against Racism* in 1998. Marco also released Oi! bands such as Asociale, who put out a single called 'Tom Hoxton For President' in 1992. Asociale's singer Ivano Bergamo also worked with The Templars.

I never got a chance to see Klasse Kriminale play, although they were still quite active. 'Italy is a bit dead now,' Wattie said. 'It used to have a good skinhead scene in the eighties and they had good quality bands, and [in the] nineties too, but now it's a bad time. Sometimes it's like a wave, it's down but it's going to be big in a bit. I love Italy but there's not that many people in the scene any more – a few good bands, of course.'

The best was Iena from Florence, who'd been recording since 2018, and were tipped by the influential writer Freddy Alva, the man behind the seminal 2009 hardcore compilation, *New Breed*, and the first journalist to publicise the 'new wave of Oi!' in 2014, tipping Crown Court and Suede Razors. I saw Lumpen, from southern Italy, play at Rebellion, a three-piece band from the noughties, two brothers up front, socialists and Ultras. They both pulled off their tops before they started to play, showing their beer-bellies and tats. They looked good, whipped up an entertaining, quite light-hearted, storm, rolled on Jenny Woo for a cover of 'Que Sera, Sera' at the end of their set. Woo was one of the few female Oi! musicians I saw play in 2022, a Canadian skinhead who'd recently released a split single with Klasse Kriminale.

I also saw Los Fastidios, from Verona, a SHARP Oi! band, formed in '91, at Rebellion. They were super-active in the UK in 2022. They played the main stage at Rebellion, early afternoon on Saturday. Enrico De Angelis from the band had formed KOB Records, one of Italy's most notable newer Oi! labels. They had released the new Lumpen album, and Silvero Tucci from Lumpen had played in Los Fastidios for a few years too. I got a sweaty hug from Silvero and left it at that.

Spain, I heard, had a new wave of modern Oi! but sadly I never saw one Spanish band in 2022. Phil Templar had mentioned Bloody Gums (Tarragona), Cuero (Bilbao), Reconquesta (Catalonia). Freddy Alva was tipping Join The Rejects from Valencia and several people mentioned Rude Pride (from Madrid). Bloody Gums were signed to a record label called

Tough Ain't Enough, from Madrid, who in 2021 had released the excellent compilation *Chaos in Basque Country*, which featured twelve contemporary Spanish Oi! bands. Cuero's *Black Metal Skinheads* cassette is a favourite of mine, released by Mendeku Diskak, a new Oi! label, based in the Basque Country. Mendeku Diskak had also released several new upcoming Oi! bands, including Mexico's Mess, LA's Castillo, Brux from Barcelona and an Italian band, Scalpo.

I read an interview with the label's owner Eduard on DIY Conspiracy, a hardcore punk zine that originated out of the Balkans. He was a former RASH skinhead and he explained there was a big self-supporting Oi! scene in the Basque country. There was another great Oi! label in Spain, Common People, active since 2010, based in Barcelona. They were behind a 2014 compilation *Chaos in Catalonia Vol. 1*, and had worked with some UK acts such as Red Alert as well as much local talent; the latest being a band called Revanche. Of course, there was also HFMN in Badalona, just north of Barcelona, who had released the latest Lion's Law album and many others since 2006. Wattie had mentioned a Spanish Oi! band called Crim who had worked with both Common People and HFMN.

Spain, like France, seemed to be bursting with fresh blood and the country hosted the popular annual three-day Oi!/ Streetpunk festival Beach, Beer & Chaos ('racists, fascist, pc idiots not welcome') in Badalona. The 2022 festival featured many of the newest and best Oi! bands from around the world. The country also had a rich Oi! history, beginning in the eighties with the pioneering band Decibelios, and progressing through the familiar issues with the far right: the singer with Spanish RAC Oi! band División 250, formed in 1991, went on to be the leader and spokesman for Democracia Nacional, a far-right Spanish nationalist political party.

The Netherlands also seemed active. They had Evil Conduct, an eighties band, reformed in 1999 who were one of the biggest Oi! bands on the circuit worldwide, as evidenced by some of their split releases: The Old Firm Casuals, The Oppressed, Marching Orders, Agent Bulldogg (Sweden), Anger Flares (Japan) and Dedo Podre (Brazil). I saw them at Rebellion. The Reapers were a far fresher Dutch proposition, debuting in 2019. They featured Ronny Hamersma who also played with Crown Court and a couple of other pan-European bands. His first Dutch band Discharger, circa 2015, had featured singer Tim Steinfort, now in the contentious Haymaker (see chapter 12).

The scene in the Netherlands was very much tied to Rebellion Records, founded in 2002 by members of Dutch Oi! band Razorblade. The label has put out over 400 releases to present, been home to many nineties European acts such as Ultimo Asalto from Italy and Oxymoron from Germany. They'd also released American acts such as The Templars and Old Firm Casuals and many UK bands such as Last Resort and Crown Court. I particularly liked their *Oi! Aint Dead* series of comps, seven in all, starting 2012.

If you had to pick one European country where Oi! truly flourished, however, it was a no-brainer: Germany. Two of the biggest labels, Randale and Contra. One of the most active promotion companies, M.A.D. Popular bands including Oxymoron from the early nineties and Stomper 98 (the band who feature Lars Frederiksen and Phil Templar) who emerged in the late nineties and are still going strong (splits with The Templars, Maraboots and 45 Adapters). Stomper's singer Sebi has a controversial history on the far-right scene (see chapter 12) while the band's guitarist, Nudel, plays in a second band called Toxpack whose most recent album, in 2022, went Top 5 in Germany.

The biggest German Oi! band of all are, of course, Böhse Onkelz. Evil Uncles. They have sold over five million records in Germany, nine platinum and twenty-four gold albums. Since 1998 they have been on a consecutive run of six number one albums. Singer Kevin Russell has a British father and a German mother. He is also a tattooist. A former heroin addict and alcoholic. In 2010 he was sent down for two years following a hit-and-run, driving under the influence of drugs, two people seriously injured.

The band were formed in 1980 and started out with songs such as: 'Turks Out', 'SS State' and 'Kill The Hippies – Oi!'. There was a protest outside the Rock-O-Rama shop after the label released their debut album in '84, a request made to put the album on a list of 'Publications Harmful to Young People'. The official report stated that the group's songs 'openly or covertly incite racial hatred, glorify violence or threaten violence against those who think differently'. They had one song called 'Germany for Germans'.

They were linked to the NF's White Noise Club and played a RAC festival in Germany. Indecent Exposure were also on that bill. Böhse Onkelz quit the white power scene around 1986 and the Oi! and skinhead scene at the end of the eighties. A close associate of the band was stabbed to death in 1990. Less than a decade later they were signed to Virgin, had shaken off much of their past, and in 2003 they supported The Rolling Stones in Hanover. On their own stadium tour in 2004 they attracted the largest crowd to an open-air show in Germany's history: 120,000. They have since spoken out against extremism.

I discussed this with a friend of a friend, Markus Erling, who lived in Berlin and had been a skinhead in the early eighties. 'Here in Berlin in the beginning of the eighties the first four Oi! compilation albums were very important, [they were] our focus and reference,' he said. 'There was no right-wing relationship to Oi! in Germany until Ian Stuart and Skrewdriver decided they were going white power. That was the moment when all the already right-wing people and youth said, OK that's our new movement, and they stole the skinhead movement and Oi! music and transformed it into a right-wing thing.

'Böhse Onkelz were a punk band [who] then switched to an Oi! band,' Markus recalled. 'They bunkered here in Berlin together with a band called Kraft Durch Froide, Strength Thru Joy, the Nazi slogan. Those two and a band called Endstufe [who also signed to R-O-R and are still going] were the founding bands of the right-wing Oi! movement. In the beginning the audience for Böhse Onkelz and Skrewdriver was the same.'

Markus also mentioned 'extremely right-wing skinheads' in East Germany who congregated in clubs called 'Schwein clubs': pig clubs. He mentioned an East Berlin band called Unerwünscht from 1982 and their song 'Oi Oi! Oi! Destroy'. It features on 2020 compilation, *Too Much Future – Punkrock GDR 1980–1989*.

I asked Markus about Rock-O-Rama. 'One of the most important punk labels at the time: my impression was they were at first tolerating right-wing bands and then discovering we can make money out of it,' he said. 'In the beginning the label was releasing bands that were not right wing, but those bands became considered as right wing because of the reputation of the label.' A perfect example of this, he said, was OHL, Oberste Heeresleitung (German Supreme Army Command in the

First World War). 'They had soldiers in tin hats on the sleeves, so immediately people think it's a right-wing band, but if you listen to the lyrics it's clearly not,' Markus said. 'They were really walking on the small path between the left- and the right-wing thing and playing with it.'

Markus said he quit being a skinhead after the riots at an infamous football game between Turkey and West Germany in Autumn '83 (Euro qualifiers in Berlin). 'All the right-wing skinheads from all over West Germany came to Berlin to fight mostly the Berlin Turkish community,' he said. 'After the match the skinheads left Berlin, went home, and we Berlin skinheads who had nothing to do with football were left here. So, you can imagine; when entering into a subway, for instance, and a Turkish guy sees you, he identifies you immediately as a right-wing hooligan skinhead. After some months I could not continue to explain to everyone who saw me that I'm not right wing and that I do not have anything to do with football or the hooligan scene – it was exhausting.'

The political schism that opened up in the early German Oi! scene had a defining moment: July '83 in Hanover, at an event protesting the state's aggressive clampdown on punks that erupted into violence. The organisers had called for a coming together between punks and skinheads: 'From now on we should be united! Oi! Oi! Oi! not Sieg Heil!' Right-wing skins instead went on the rampage. A similar event in '84, also in Hanover, again attempted to reunite the skin and punk scenes, but erupted into similar violence. Nonetheless these so-called 'Chaos Days' in Hanover became an annual tradition that ran up until at least 2013, often attracting a huge police presence.

Germany equalled, if not eclipsed, the UK RAC scene in

terms of the number of bands involved in the eighties and nineties, and also in their popularity, judged by numbers at gigs, and extremism (a band called Radikahl had a song called 'Wogs Out'). Many released albums with R-O-R or Rebelles Européens and then when those labels were closed down, another German Oi!/RAC label emerged, Dim Records, to facilitate their music.

In late 1992, the Ministry of the Interior estimated that there were about 6,500 skinheads in Germany, of whom 4,500 were right wing. By 2003, the number of skinheads had risen to 10,000, based on police estimates. Sometime in the late nineties authorities began a clampdown on the scene. The German division of Blood & Honour was outlawed in 2000. German neo-Nazi band Landser became the first music group recognised as a criminal organisation and their singer, Michael Reneger, was sentenced to three years in jail. In 2004, a court banned Nordfront's debut album *Throw Them Out!*

'The eighties was before my time,' says Karl Khal, founder and guitarist of Brutal Bravo. 'But I have friends from the time and as far as I know it wasn't that different to how it was in England – many German skinheads turned to Nazism and the right-wing stuff.' I'd been listening to quite a bit of German Oi! but hadn't found any I liked. The Court's Taylor suggested a newish band, Brutal Bravo and introduced me to Khal who told me he'd been playing in Oi! bands for about fifteen years, since he was 17, while also promoting shows in Germany, was friendly with Wattie, connected to the scene all around the world. I asked if he could maybe give me the guided tour of German Oi!. 'I think Germany is a little special and complicated, but I will do my best to give you the feeling,' he said.

I was interested in the handful of Oi! bands who were on R-O-R in the early to mid-eighties, pre-dating but sometimes crossing over with the label's roster of German and UK RAC acts. One band was Cotzbrocken who featured on the label's influential 1982 compilation LP *The Germans Are Coming*, alongside OHL, the band Markus mentioned, and Die Alliierten, who had anti-fascist songs. 'The very first skinhead band was Die Alliierten, and they did have a song against Nazis on their first album [1983's *Glory and Honour*],' Khal said. 'I love OHL. They're still putting out albums. Many skins liked them. It's true Rock-O-Rama were a notorious label but [they] had a lot of punk bands as well.'

I asked about Böhse Onkelz. 'The history of the band is well known,' Khal said. 'They started out as a punk band, got skinheads, were involved in the early skinhead days and when all the nationalism got big they were involved in that. They used to play shows where Nazis showed up – there were many Nazi skinheads at that time. They did a fast turn when they realised it was not exactly what they wanted to do. They were very young and they were not a full neo-Nazi band like the nineties bands. The same with Endstufe who are still playing shows – if you listen to the lyrics and the albums they don't have any nationalist or racist lyrics. That has never been the problem with Endstufe. It is all the people around them; the shows they play are very right wing but they still try to represent the skinhead style and scene. But in terms of sound and attitude, [the] very first Endstufe album, just like the first Böhse Onkelz album, is very important for German Oi! music, the same as Vortex [another R-O-R from the early/mid-eighties] or early Daily Terror or Alliierten.'

I'd read about Daily Terror on the *Creases Like Knives* site; they played the 1983 Chaos Days festival that ended in a riot and courted controversy for the next decade until they split. Singer Pedder Teumer was a much-discussed character, a football hooligan, with associations on the right of the Oi! scene that meant sometimes Daily Terror shows could explode in violence. 'Daily Terror were playing with Endstufe early on but there were also very left-wing bands playing the same shows along with rockabilly bands,' said Khal. 'Daily Terror just didn't care so much actually; they were very influential.'

I asked Khal if Oxymoron were the first German Oi! band in the nineties that were left wing, a sort of rehabilitating force at a time when the right-wing Oi! scene was dominant. He said it wasn't as clear-cut as all that. 'It depends very much on the city,' he said. 'For example, from my hometown of Freiburg, skinheads in the eighties and nineties used to go to shows of Nazi skinhead bands even though they were calling themselves SHARP or anti-racist just because it was a skinhead show. On the other hand, I know people from the same time who were always very strict, didn't want to get involved.' Khal explained it was not just left wing versus right wing either, there was a hangover from the Chaos Days riots and an over-arching 'punks against skinheads' sentiment in Germany. 'The special role for Oxymoron in the German history of punk and Oi! was they were uniting both scenes, punks and skins,' said Karl. 'The two subcultures were fighting all the time but Oxymoron had a punk and [a] skin and they were able to connect both.'

I asked about Stomper 98. A controversial band, I suggested?

'No, I wouldn't say they are controversial,' Khal said. 'Not at all.'

If I wanted controversial, Khal suggested 'the whole Scumfuck [roster of] bands'. 'I think if you want to understand German Oi! music you have to look up Scumfuck Records [active 1989–2007],' he said. 'It was founded by Willi Wucher, the singer of Pöbel Und Gesocks, who used to be the Beck's Pistols, and he was also part of Body Checks which was more a right-wing band but that was more a little sidestep from him. Beck's Pistols was another band connecting punk and skinhead culture and very important.'

I had never heard of Scumfuck, so I asked Khal again about Stomper. I thought they were maybe the breakout Oi! band in the noughties, a sort of Lion's Law for Germany?

'This is sort of the days when I started to be a skinhead, around 2005, and the scene was huge,' Khal said. 'In my small hometown there were, like, sixty skinheads and we had a bar just for us. Stomper 98 were one of the main bands and they played really big shows. That was a sort of a revival, and they started touring; they are very [well] known and they are very connected. Touring was a new thing for Oi! at that time.'

By huge shows, I asked, are you talking two or three hundred?

'No, the big shows that came around 2010, there was 600 at Oi! gigs,' Khal said.

Khal started playing with Freiburg Oi! band Gewohnheitstrinker ('habitual drinkers') in 2008. They formed in 2001 and were a Scumfuck band but switched to Randale in 2010; their excellent sixth album was released in 2021.

'When I was a young skinhead this was the big band,' Khal said. 'The members were all nineties skinheads. Me and my friends were the young thugs around when they were playing. Then when one guitarist couldn't play, they asked me to join the band. I was 17 and they were all in their 30s. They already had two albums out [both on Scumfuck]; they were my favourite band.'

I asked what kind of crowds the band were playing to when he joined? 'If you look at the German Oi! scene now it's very strict, but at this time the groups were together more,' Khal said. 'It was clear we were a skinhead band and not a right-wing band but the boundaries weren't so clear as now. Bands we were playing with were never left-wing or anti-fascist bands, they were skinhead bands, a little edgy maybe but not problematic. At this time in Germany, there weren't openly right-wing people around, some of them were more attracted to the right than others but they weren't being political, we were all in one room, all into skinhead music. Maybe years later some of the bands turned more right wing and some of the skins started to be attracted more to the right-wing bands.'

Is this why and when the term 'grey zone' pops up, I wondered?

'Yeah, around that time,' Khal said. 'A few years later, actually. That was maybe something of a reaction to that scene.'

We talked about newer German Oi! labels. 'If you look into today's Oi! you should mention Lionheart Records, Steeltown Records, Try and Stop Me Records, and if you look back a little more there is Knock Out Records [1989–present]; they put out the Loikaemie stuff, also Bonecrusher [and Oxymoron].' I asked about Randale? 'Randale is from the south, close to where I grew up, so we used to go to their shows as kids, a lot of fun actually,' Karl said. 'The Randale HQ used to be deep in the Black Forest and they put on great shows with very special bands – it was hard to catch them anywhere else, you had to drive deep into the forest to see them.'

That sounds dodgy?

'Sometimes it was a little,' Khal said. 'But the vibe was great. And Contra Records is from eastern Germany and they are still very strong.'

I asked if there remained as big an audience in Germany for Oi! bands now? 'There is a big, big audience,' Khal said. 'If Lion's Law plays in a German town, even on a weekday, the club is full. Lion's Law draw people who are interested in rock music or who grew up with Böhse Onkelz and like skinhead music a little but are not strictly skinheads. Over the last fifteen years there developed a sort of second-skinhead scene called "Deutschrock". Maybe I'm being a little arrogant here, but they are not skinheads; they are not what we do.'

I thought maybe he was talking about the 'Streetpunk' scene. I'd written down the names of ten or more German Oi! bands from the noughties and teens who I'd not got round to listening to, some of whom I assumed must have aped the American sound. 'Deutschrock'?, you mean sort of 'streetpunk'?, I said.

'No, not at all,' said Khal. 'When the Böhse Onkelz split up in 2004 [after their farewell tour; they have since reformed] there were bands forming who tried to fill the gap. Starting around 2010 many Böhse Onkelz fans, some from the more conservative side of the skinhead and Oi! scene, formed groups who called themselves Oi! bands but they were just Böhse Onkelz cover bands like Frei.Wild. That's Deutschrock; it's a huge scene, a lot of bands [I found a perfect example, Martens Army and their latest release, 'Skinhead Rock'n'Roll']. They have a different style and attitude and play different music to what we do. It's a very, very German thing.'

I was disappointed to learn that Brutal Bravo, who started to release records in 2017, had recently split. They sang in English and were modern, fast and hard new-wave Oi!. Khal hadn't wasted any time forming two new bands: RumpelstilSkin and Collaps. 'I moved from Freiberg to Bochum, the Ruhr area,' he explained. 'RumpelstilSkin is more a band influenced by German late eighties/nineties Oi! music. Collaps is picking up the modern sound of bands now, like Rixe. Wattie was a game changer for many new bands coming up.'

Paris seems to be the city, I suggested. 'Yeah,' Khal said. 'The French scene is one of the most active right now. They do things differently than we do, that's maybe because the French punk and Oi! [scene] never had Böhse Onkelz. It's tough because there are not that many German bands now. We have a huge network and Oi! bands like to tour here but there are not that many new bands in Germany. There are some youngish people coming up again, though, so maybe there will be a new wave.'

Chapter 11

Days Gone By: Rotten Boys/Marching Orders/ Worker Sweat (World Oi!)

In the mid-eighties, Garotos Podres ('Rotten Boys' in Portuguese) put Oi! on the map in Brazil. Their debut album, *Mais Podres Que Nunca* (More Rotten Than Ever), released in 1985, sold 50,000 copies. Via email I interviewed the band's drummer and founder Luis Português. He didn't speak English, so the process required intermediaries and translations and took months.

I knew there was a strong and thriving Oi! scene in South America, countries with their own unique relationships with the music, but it was difficult to navigate. It was clear Colombia, specifically Bogotá, had a strong Oi!/skinhead scene in the noughties and teens, as evidenced by the 2012 compilation called *Chaos En Colombia* which featured local Oi! bands such as The Adhocs, Skandalo Oi!, and was still thriving.

At Rebellion, I'd seen Sudor Obrero from Chile, on the small stage, an anti-fascist Oi! band. I thought they were pretty good. Had a skinhead girl dancing with them. After the gig I asked if any of them spoke English and someone scribbled down the name Cristian Blich [White]. He replied as Cristian Dentone, a journalist, ran Hersham Boys Records in Argentina, an Oi!/ska label. He said he also promoted Oi! gigs in Argentina. I'd heard of an eighties Argentinian Oi! band called Comando Suicida who were controversial, possibly football hooligans with far-right leanings, featured on the first Argentinian punk album in 1988, *Invasión 88*. Cristian suggested I might want to speak to Rod from Espiritu Callejero who 'as many in Latin America say are the Argentinian Cock Sparrer' or Sudor Obrero's singer Osvaldo. Unfortunately, they didn't speak English.

I mentioned to Cristian I was in the process of trying to interview Luis from Garotos Podres and he said he knew him well, was 'a great Brazilian friend'. I'd got hold of Luis via Henrike Baliú, from Blind Pigs, a big band in Brazil, sort of the country's Rancid. Henrike said Luis was also the founder of Rotten Records, a pioneering Brazilian Oi! label. 'Oi! in Brazil has a very unique, troubled and infamous history with the street gang, Carecas do Subúrbio,' Henrike added.

When I'd interviewed Jeff Geggus in Manchester, I also mentioned I was trying to get a Brazilian Oi! band for the book. He said he knew Luis, said his latest Brazilian Oi! band, Sindicato Oi!, were good lads. Jeff's wife was Brazilian, and the Rejects were playing Brazil in 2023 on their farewell tour.

Luis sent his replies to my questions in February 2023. He explained the Garotos Podres had started out as part of a wave of Brazilian punk bands who were influenced by Oi! in the early eighties. He mentioned Neuroticos (members of whom were now in Inocentes who were supporting the Rejects in Brazil) and Dose Brutal. Brazil was under military dictatorship from 1964 to 1985, and punk, Luis said, 'always contested all the problems we were experiencing at the time – police violence, misery, unemployment – the police were very violent with society as a whole.' The punks were an 'easy target' of repression due to their looks.

Skinheads, he said, first appeared in Brazil in São Paulo. 'The first skinhead gang were Carecas do Subúrbio,' Luis said. 'They started in the punk scene and appeared in a photo on the cover of the first Brazilian punk compilation *Grito Suburbano* in 1984. After a few years skins began to appear in other Brazilian states. We lived in a time when information arrived with delays or was distorted, we didn't have internet, only letters, and we received some 'zines from abroad. Most bands didn't understand English so they depended on someone translating. Carecas do Subúrbio were inspired by the skins of England in the look but they created their own rules: in the beginning, they didn't drink alcohol, they did bodybuilding and they weren't involved with soccer. They began to have fights with the punks at the time, and this division grew and they were appearing more and more in the newspapers. This fame attracted people more interested in violence than in the true skinhead culture, and other gangs emerged in other states and cities.'

Luis came from an industrial region called ABC, just south of São Paulo (named after three cities: Santo André, São Bernardo and São Caetano), an area known for its car manufacturing. 'The Labour unions were very strong in the region,' he said. 'So much so that the Workers' Party [PT] of current president Lula started in the city of São Bernardo do Campo, where most of the car factories are concentrated.'

Garotos Podres were the first band to assume Oi! as a definitive musical identity in Brazil and Luis said they were influenced by all the classic UK Oi! bands. They had a popular song called 'Anarquia Oi!' (Anarchy Oi!), clocking in at 1 min 42 secs, on the debut album. Luis, however, said he considered the band's second album *Pior que Antes* (Worse Than Before) released in 1988, the 'most Oi!' of all the band's releases. It sold around 25,000 copies.

'When our first album came out there was a wave of rock bands in the country, with influences from English punk like Buzzcocks, The Jam and The Clash, on the radio stations and TV shows and our music was also played on the radio,' Luis said. 'In the beginning we played at underground punk festivals in São Paulo but after the band started to be on the radio and reach all kinds of audiences we participated in big concerts. The biggest audience we played to was around 30,000 people at a festival in the city of Florianópolis in the nineties.'

At the end of the 1980s, Luis explained how a 'white power' Oi! scene emerged in Brazil and divisions opened up between racist and non-racist skinheads who were known as the 'Carecas'. 'As in Europe, the Brazilian far right tried to recruit young skinheads to serve as shock troops in street demonstrations,' he explained. 'Organizations such as the Brazilian National Socialist Party, the nativist movement and the Brazilian Integralist Action had skinheads in their ranks. In 1989, some skinheads participated in a demonstration in honour of the 100th anniversary of the birth of Adolf Hitler, held in São Paulo.'

The early 1990s was a troubling time for the Brazilian Oi! scene, Luis explained. 'There were several groups claiming the term skinhead for themselves, almost all of them extreme right wing and street gangs. We had to stop playing in the city of São Paulo for six years in the nineties due to fights involving the punks and skinhead gangs.'

Luis was instrumental in rehabilitating the scene when he started Rotten Records in 1994, 'showing the real face of Oi!' he said. His partner in the label was writer and poet Glauco Mattoso, who translated the book *Spirit of '69: A Skinhead Bible,* written by George Marshall (see chapter 13) for release in Brazil. Luis said the book was important 'to combat stereotypes'.

'Gradually, people began to understand that the skin culture was not born racist, nor linked to extreme right parties,' he said. 'Our first Rotten release, back in 1995, was the CD *Oi! Um Grito De União, Vol.1* (Oi! A Cry For Unity Vol 1) with Histeria, Virus 27, Bandeira de Combate and Mata-Ratos from Portugal as a guest band. This was the first compilation of Brazilian Oi! ever. New bands were emerging and there was a greater mix between cultures – punks, headbangers, rockers – that until then were at war with anyone who claimed themselves to be skinhead.'

Garotos Podres played in Europe, supported Oxymoron in Germany in the nineties, and Rotten Records built links with Oi! bands and labels around the world, importing and distributing Oi! into Brazil. He was proud of the compilation his label put together in 1999 called *A Volta ao Mundo em Oi!tenta Minutos* (Around the World in Eighty Minutes) which featured Anti-Heros, Oppressed, Business, Section 5, Nabat and Oxymoron. 'The best release, in my opinion,' he said.

From the 2000s, UK Oi! bands began to play in Brazil: Cockney Rejects, Business, Cock Sparrer among others. While anti-fascist collectives formed by punks and skins emerged, Luis said the Garotos Podres and Rotten were part of an apolitical scene, 'without involvement with the extremes.'

He added: 'We ended up creating a scene with bands, labels and friends who just wanted to have fun and feel good, and this was frowned upon by both sides – right and left – and they labelled us as ambiguous or fence sitters [or 'grey zone', see chapter 12],' he said.

I asked him how the scene was nowadays in the country. I'd noticed Firm Records (who were involved with the most recent Lion's Law album release) had released the compilations *Brasil Oi! Vol. 1* and *2* in 2014 and 2015, with *Vol. 3* arriving in 2019. These albums had been released in conjunction with a reformed Rotten Records and Sindicato Oi! featured on them. Luis was friends with Firm Records founder, 'Tuca', who had been inspired to start his label by Rotten.

'Those compilations show the new bands of the time,' Luis said. 'A new crop of bands and people listening to streetpunk and Oi! The best period for the Oi! scene in Brazil was from 2014 to 2020. Henrike [Baliú] helped promote the bands with his internet radio show *Semper Adversus*. At the same time, 7 Produções [an event management company] emerged and we organized some concerts in São Paulo [for acts] such as: Jenny Woo, Lion's Law, The Templars, Haymaker, Komintern Sect and Facção Opposta [from Portugal].'

Were Sindicato Oi! now as popular as Garotos Podres, I asked? 'No,' he said. 'Sindicato Oi! is more underground. What happened to Garotos Podres in the eighties is practically impossible to happen again with a band coming from the punk scene. These are different times. Sindicato Oi! have managed to make a name on the Oi! scene with our records released on vinyl in Germany and Portugal. We also played at the Rebellion Festival, at the Skinhead Reunion in Brighton and in Germany at the Boots United Festival.'

I asked about Brazil in relation to the wider scene in South

America. 'I see that in Chile, Argentina and in Colombia they continue to produce records, concerts and new bands pop up,' he said. 'At the moment I believe that the Brazilian Oi! scene is not as strong. There are few concerts and not a lot of new bands. Oi! is still quite marginalized in Brazil because of the violence, and it is still considered by most Brazilians as a neo-Nazi scene.'

The language barrier also made it difficult to negotiate contacts in countries in south-east Asia where I knew there were strong Oi! scenes: China, Singapore, Malaysia, Indonesia, Taiwan, South Korea and Japan. I kept looking at Japan: the Rejects were touring there in early 2023 as part of their farewell tour, supported by Anger Flares, a Japanese Oi!/streetpunk band from the early 2000s. The promoters of the Rejects gigs were Bootstomp Records, a label founded in 2004, who released a series of three Oi! compilations under the title *Bootboys Stomp*.

I had stumbled on a compilation called *Oi! of Japan*, released in 1985 by AA Records. There were some great bands on there. The Cockney Cocks track 'I Don't Care' seemed promising. The Wanderers sounded good too. AA Records had also been home to Cobra who had formed in '82, an early if not the first Japanese Oi!/skinhead band. I'd noted Cobra due to their extreme skinhead styling. They had crossed over into the mainstream in the nineties, played the Budokan in '91, signed to major label Pony Canyon, releasing an album called *Oi Oi Oi*. In 2011, AA Records released *Oi! of Japan Vol. 2*, another belter.

I'd read that the UK RAC bands such as Skrewdriver did good business sending records and merch to Japan in the eighties, and a handful of Japanese nationalist Oi! bands had formed in their image, known as the Japanese Movement. From out of this something called the Samurai Spirit Skinhead bands had emerged. Sledge Hammer were first and best known. They appeared on an infamous album, *Werewolfen: The Japanese Samurai Compilation* released in 1995.

The Oi! scene in Japan never recaptured its nineties fervour but new bands continued to emerge in the noughties such as Anger Flares and Bulldog Samurai who had their song 'Oi Oi Nippon' featured on a 2006 comp Phil Templar put together, *Anti-Disco League Vol. 1*. The RAC scene seemed to continue too. A band called Aggro Knuckle hooked up with long standing American white power band, Bound for Glory, for a tour and a split single.

Malaysia was another country where there was a strong Oi! scene. 'In 2000 it was the biggest skinhead scene in the world,' Wattie told me. There were two main bands: A.C.A.B. from Kuala Lumpur formed in 1994, anti-racists, debut album *Eastern Oi!* in '99 (selling 10,000 copies); and Roots 'N' Boots who featured on a comp called *Oi! It's a Malaysian League* released by Strange Culture Records (who A.C.A.B were also signed to) in 1998. 'When I was looking at the live shows, they were playing in stadiums.' Wattie said. 'I have friends who went there in the 2000s and they saw 10-year-old kids in bomber jackets and boots, it was big youth culture and street culture.'

There were Oi! bands called No Man's Land and Ten Holes in Indonesia, and a new Beijing Oi! band called The Brewers. South Korea, who hosted the Korea-Japan Oi! festival in 2004, has bands such as Captain Bootbois, Attacking Forces and The Brigade. Singapore has The Maniacs and Hard Steel Comrades as well as The Bois.

*

I didn't see any African Oi! bands but I wouldn't be surprised. There's a scene in Israel that looks interesting. I did make contact with a band in Australia, Marching Orders. The country had a thriving Oi! scene in the eighties. Unfortunately most of the bands I read about such as Order of the Boot and White Lightning (who signed to Rebelles Européens) were RAC acts. The guitarist in White Lightning went on to play in a number of other white power acts such as Fortress in Australia and No Remorse in the UK. Fortress became the mainstay of neo-Nazi rock in Australia in the nineties, signing to Rock-O-Rama initially and then America's Resistance Records. Australia was also among the first of many foreign franchises to be established by Blood & Honour. The country also established a Hammerskins division, Southern Cross Hammerskins, in the late eighties.

The best known early Australian skinhead band were Quick and the Dead from Perth. A band member went on to join Skrewdriver around 1984, and another guy from the band was in a militant white supremacist organisation called National Action. Quick and the Dead became White Noise in '85 with a song 'Sieg Heil We're Back Again', hooking up with Rock-O-Rama for a debut album in '88. White Noise reformed in 2007 for an Australian memorial gig for Ian Stuart.

I watched a great piece of archive news footage from Australian TV in 1984 discussing 'a skinhead revival' in Sydney. The report said there were two types of skinhead in Australia: 'Ska skins' and 'Oi! skins'. The latter were violent, racist and wore Skrewdriver and Union Jack Ts and everyone was scared of them. They hated Asian immigration and loved the 'mother country' (half of the 'Oi! skins' in Sydney were said to be English, or of English parentage).

Mike Josephson at Longshot introduced me to Al White, the singer in Marching Orders – Australia's biggest modern Oi! band. White and I spoke one morning in late October.

White was born in Northampton, England. His family then emigrated to Australia in the seventies when he was a baby. 'I got into being a skinhead around 1988,' he told me. 'I was at Flinders Street train station [the main station in Melbourne] and I saw this huge group of skinheads, girls and guys, older than me but only 14-, 15-, 16-years-old. I just thought, wow, this is what I want to be.

'There were mentions of Oi! but it was probably more Two-Tone, as that was the thing then,' he said. 'Madness and The Specials were popular and you had the Australian bands like Strange Tenants who played ska. You could say it was a fashion craze at the time – there was always groups of kids of that age hanging round in the city square at the train station, or any train station. You didn't have social media then so people used to meet up around the station a lot.'

'Back then it wasn't a case of, alright I'll cut my hair and go along to a show – if you did that you'd get yourself in trouble,' he said. 'You had to prove you were genuine, authentic; that you were worthy of being part of that sub culture. If you didn't you'd cop a beating and they'd take your boots off you. That used to be a really big thing – they called it getting rolled. Even people who weren't part of that scene would say, watch out for those skinheads, they'll roll you for your boots or they'll take your Harrington jacket off you. And everything cost so much back then, mostly it wasn't available: if you wanted to get a pair of Dr. Martens you probably had to save for a couple of months. And when you did have them, people would chase you and take them. I got my first pair when I was 13, a pair of black Dr. Martens shoes, and several times when I was coming through Flinders Street station the groups of skinheads and rude boys would say, oi mate, what size are those shoes? You either had to be a really good fighter or a fast runner. We were just little kids back then. Ten blokes chasing after us, we'd turn and run pretty quickly. There were lots of stories of people getting a beating and having to ride the tram home in their socks – it was on the news a few times.'

I said to White that all the eighties Australian Oi! bands seemed to be right-wing ones? 'Let's not call the Nazi bands Oi!,' he said. 'The skinhead scene I knew, there wasn't a lot of politics, it was more about small gangs – we didn't call them gangs, but I suppose that's what they were.' He said there was a small Oi! scene not affiliated with the right-wing movement.

'The eighties Oi! bands from Melbourne were Justified Hatred and No Remorse [not the English band] but I don't know much about them as very little info or music is around now,' he said. 'There were recordings done but probably onto a cassette and then lost, and there's not a lot written about them. I run a small label called Grudge Match records [mainly importing and distributing English and American Oi!] and I've often thought about trying to put together a compilation of Oi! bands from the eighties around Australia, there were a few but it is quite hard to find recordings.'

He added: 'But it was mostly ska bands that attracted the skinhead crowd in terms of the anti-racist side of things: Strange Tenants, Loonee Tunes, No Nonsense and The Allniters. There were loads and loads of skinheads in that scene. But in terms of the media, it was like anywhere – as soon as the word Nazi comes up that's what they will focus on. Blood & Honour always had a presence in Melbourne, even if it wasn't in big numbers, [and] they'd be all over the media. In the early nineties there was a bunch of murders within the scene and that's what people saw as skinhead – several of those guys ended up in maximum security and some may still be there today. So, whether their scene was bigger or not didn't really matter – they definitely stole the limelight.

'And then of course you had *Romper Stomper* [an Australian film from 1992 starring Russell Crowe], loosely based on some of those people,' Al said. 'After that movie and those murders, if you had a shaved head and boots you could barely go anywhere without ordinary people wanting to have a go at you. It was a pretty tough time to look like that.'

Nonetheless, in the nineties an Australian Oi! scene started to re-emerge, in Sydney. Al mentioned Stanley Knife, Drop Zone, Bedlam Beggars and Sydney Guns. 'I'd travel up to Sydney for festivals,' he said. 'You'd have ska bands, Oi! bands and crust bands all on the same bill. It'd be a two-day festival and the scene was small enough that most people [from across Australia] came together. Then towards the end of the nineties you had bands like Charter 77, No Idea, Hippy War Generals, GGF – maybe more punk bands but they did have skinhead members. It wouldn't be uncommon for them to do a 4-Skins cover.'

White started playing Oi! with Marching Orders around 2001/2002 when he was in his mid-20s. 'One of my motivations was I didn't think Australian Oi! had been truly represented,' he said. 'You'd have a lot of politics from both sides of the fence, and it seemed to me there wasn't really a band who said, we're not interested in politics, we want to be skinheads and play Oi!

music with our mates, drink a few beers and that's how it is. That's what Marching Orders was originally, we didn't want to be part of any political movement at all. We wanted to start off a new wave of Oi!. The plan was definitely to take influence from The Business, Cock Sparrer and 4-Skins and all the bands we'd grown up listening to, but we also wanted to include a bit of the uniquely Australian sound which came out of the Sharpie movement. It wasn't something that was well known and we just wanted to show off what had been [happening] in Australia.'

This was a sound American bands such as the Suede Razors had later tapped into, and the look associated with the Sharpie cult was something modern Australian punk bands such as Amyl and the Sniffers and The Chats had adopted.

'Sharpies were not specifically skinheads but a very similar thing,' White said. 'They actually pre-date skinheads, started up around 1960/1961 – there's even mention of Sharpie gangs going back to 1959 in the media. It can be quite tough to find information. It's not like the UK where subcultures are celebrated. I think a lot of people who were Sharpies in their youth in Australia want to try and pretend they weren't and hide it. In recent years the Sharpie scene has come more into the light; it always used to be talk and smoke tales that you'd hear around the traps. Now there's probably four or five books: the ones about the Thomastown Sharps are fantastic reads.

'The original Sharpies had short hair, crest-knit tops, similar to a polo, these pants [trousers] called flag pants, chequered pants,' White continued. 'If you look on the front of Marching Order's album *Days Gone By* [their debut, released in 2010, by Longshot], the guy on the cover is Rod who was an Oakley Sharpie, and the photo we used was taken of him and his son in the sixties. When

Days Gone By was released there'd been one book, *Top Fellas* by Tadghe Taylor, written about Sharpies but not much else. We wanted to try and bring that Australian culture into the public eye a little.'

Sharpie was chiefly a Melbourne scene?

'Yeah, there was a scene in Sydney of Sharpies but it was predominantly Melbourne,' Al said.

The main Sharpie bands were Rose Tattoo, Coloured Balls and the Aztecs?

'They were the main three but from different eras,' White said. 'Rose Tattoo came about in the late seventies, alongside AC/DC and the Angels, '77–'79, just after punk. It was very much the Sharpie scene that spawned all those bands and gave them the popularity they had. The seventies Sharpies were more similar to the UK style; the glam/bovver rock style – shaved heads and braces but they had the rats tails or the mullets. That was the uniquely Australian look and it was that era that gave rise to bands like Buster Brown. Angry Anderson [of Rose Tattoo] was the singer of Buster Brown and members of AC/DC were in that band as well. But the main Sharpie band would have been Lobby Lloyd and the Coloured Balls and of course you had Billy Thorpe and the Aztecs as well. The Coloured Balls album, *Ball Power*, which was early seventies, is the iconic Melbourne Sharpie record. I think they were only around from '72 to '74 because there was so much violence at their gigs, a lot of trouble.'

The Sharpies were known for violence, I asked?

'My memory of the Sharpies was you'd see these guys in striped skin-tight cardigans and they'd have short hair with tails at the back and probably one of their front teeth knocked out,'

White said. 'There were big groups of those guys around in the early eighties. It wasn't a small thing, there were literally thousands of them, every second suburb would have gangs of Sharpies and every main street would have them hanging around the local milk bar or fish and chip shops. If you read the Thomastown Sharps books, they describe how the scene grew increasingly violent, started with little scuffles here and there and then towards the tail end of the Sharpie scene, end of the seventies, early eighties, it ended up in shootings at houses. Then the Lebanese immigrants had various gangs and they came up against the Sharpies as well. Shoot-outs and nasty stabbings. That's what caused the scene to disappear.'

The reception to Marching Orders was initially positive. 'A lot of the young skins and punks would come along,' White said. 'We would play a gig and we'd have two or three hundred people coming along. We could even go out to the suburbs and play in local town halls to all the local kids and have a couple of hundred people coming. That was 2004/2005. The guy who did Rebellion did a festival in Australia: must have been about seven hundred people and that was really good. In 2008 we played in America, played in New York and then a festival called Oi! Fest in Pennsylvania [the year the 4-Skins played]. In 2011 we played Rebellion, did a bit of a tour of Europe. The scene was really healthy in Australia for a couple of years and then it sort of died.'

Why, I asked? 'We were the only skinhead band around and people would start saying, those guys must be Nazis,' White said. 'We had patches where people started boycotting us, chit-chat around the internet, things that were made up about us as well – we did get a hard time from a few people.'

The band did a Combat 84 cover early on, was that part of the controversy? 'That's a band I'd always liked – they certainly were controversial but we never did anything that should have made any controversy surround us,' White said. 'But you have people who get on the internet and say, this band is dodgy because this person knew this person and I heard they did this and this . . . We don't have anything like that now but there was a patch where that did happen. There are always going to be people who just rubbish Oi! bands and they're going to say things no matter what – they're not interested in looking at the truth.'

Marching Orders inspired a new wave of Oi! in Australia. They were followed most notably by Plan of Attack from Brisbane (debut album *Stick to Your Guns*, 2013, on Rebellion) and Rust from Sydney. 'In Brisbane you also had Mouthguard,' White said. 'You'd have the odd band in some of the other states but not really so much until recently. Plan of Attack are good friends of ours – we did lots of shows with them, we used to go to Brisbane and Queensland. There's been lulls, it's been up and down.'

White started other bands, notably RazorCut, a streetpunk/Oi! band featuring a unique two-female/two-male line-up, who were popular in the mid-teens. 'There was a pretty healthy local scene again in Melbourne around then,' he said. 'But probably the most interest we got for that band was from the crowds in Europe, especially Germany. When we toured, every show was sold out bar one. There's a [new Australian Oi!] label called Stun Grenade and [in 2018] they released a compilation of Australian Oi! bands [*We Come From A Band Down Under: Aussie Oi! & Streetpunk Volume 1*] and that featured RazorCut, Rust, Plan of Attack and all our current bands. It's a good representation from a few years ago where the scene was. A lot of the bands are still going: The Knock Backs, The Clinch, The Opposition, Nö Class.'

Melbourne band Nö Class, in particular, were the contemporary Australian Oi! band people were talking about. 'They're a great bunch of guys,' White said. 'I go to see them when I can. At the moment there is a bit of a revival going on. After Marching Orders finished and Plan of Attack went quiet and Stanley Knife broke up, things did die off for a while. You had bands in Brisbane still going and down in Melbourne you had The Clinch and The Opposition, so it never died completely, it kept going, but it's only really in the past two or three years you've had Nö Class and a few others that have really started to bring the scene back again.

'Those guys, if you go along and see them, there'll be various punk bands on, it's a mixed bill,' White said. 'They also started having shows in Footscray Park, open-air shows . . . that's really kicked things off again. And for the first time you're starting to see new skinheads in Melbourne. For a long time it was just the old guys, people like myself. But recently there's a small group of guys, 17- 18-year-olds, and they're getting into Oi! and ska and dressing to the original skinhead style and they've started hanging around some of the older guys as well and coming to shows. Things like that make me think this is great, something new is kicking off.'

White said he saw Amyl and the Sniffers as part of this new wave. 'They're not a skinhead band but you can definitely see the Aussie rock'n'roll/Sharpie influence, and the singer Amy had a feather cut for a while,' he said. 'I went to an Amyl and the Sniffers show in Melbourne and there were huge crowds there but what really impressed me was there were all these younger kids who looked about 18 all singing along and loving it. I haven't seen younger kids like Oi! or rock'n'roll for a long time in Melbourne. Something is really starting to happen. The general revival of guitar-driven music and rock'n'roll music is definitely kicking off round the world now. In the coming years I think the scene is going to be really healthy. Punk, Oi! and rock'n'roll – hopefully they'll cross over a bit and create a better musical environment.'

At the eleventh hour, in mid-April 2023, Cristian Dentone in Argentina sent me a long, written piece by Osvaldo González, the singer in Sudor Obrero (which translates as Worker Sweat), the Chilean Oi! band I'd seen at Rebellion. Dentone translated both ways, gave González the gist of my questions and then translated what he'd written. It took us about five months.

'In the eighties the atmosphere in Chile was full of fear and desolation,' González wrote. 'Often you could kiss death around the corner; the young people were without any hope. Hunger and misery were a daily and common theme. The dictatorship of Augusto Pinochet lasted almost two decades.

'The skinhead scene started in the fifth region [of Chile, in the port city of Valparaiso] as well as in Villa Alemana [a city in Chile's Zona Centrale]. Valparaiso and surroundings would be the cradle of Chile's "creole skinheads",' he explained.

González listed the first Oi! bands in Chile: Division Gamada, Los Suspensores, Frente Opuesto, Golpe Frontal and 'the most emblematic' Ocho Bolas. 'The first generation of Oi! bands were linked to nationalism,' he wrote.

'Music [vinyl] was hard to get in Chile at the time,' he added.

'Records either came from: England through the port of Valparaiso; were imported by those from the wealthiest neighbourhoods of [the capital] Santiago; via the ports of southern Chile; or from the German colonies in the south of Chile, populated by people that escaped from the Second World War. Records were exclusively for the wealthiest families of that time.'

'The first Oi! records in Chile were sent by Roi Pearce of Last Resort and 4-Skins,' González wrote. 'He sent a lot of material to spread the music.'

González said the first skinheads in Chile were just kids, aged 13 to 17. 'They didn't know what it really meant to walk around with shaved heads, boots and [*Clockwork Orange*-style] jockstraps . . . They just adopted it according to their life experience. Some were anti-racist, others simply hated being born.'

There was a strong togetherness; a culture of sharing what tapes and vinyl they could get hold of, all chipping in to raise money to import more Oi! records to Chile.

In 1989, Ocho Bolas released a cassette called *Al Servico* [At Your Service]. González said it is one of the only existing audio recordings of Chilean Oi! from that period. 'This wave only lasted until 1993 or 1994,' he said. 'The first vinyl Oi! record in Chile was *Trabajo Duro* [Hard Work] by Ocho Bolas, released in 1991 by the German label DIM [who also recorded Frente Opuesto].'

González mentioned another late eighties, early nineties band, Santiago Rebelde; the first ska band in Chile and the first to bring together skinheads and rudeboys en masse in Santiago. He said the city also had a RAC scene, called it 'Skinhead NS [National Socialism]' and said the main band was Rockanoi (the band later changed their name to Odal Sieg). 'In Santiago the meeting points of the Skinhead NS were the Persian Bio Bio,

Maipu and San Bernardo,' he said. The RAC scene in Chile was strengthened by *Romper Stomper*. 'In the mid-nineties the film was shown on open television,' González explained. 'The ultraviolence and the music blew the minds of many young people who were looking for their identity between hatred, alcohol and hard drugs.'

SHARP was born in Santiago in 1996, González said. 'Led by Nico Sharp and Daniel Negrete, they took the time to write fanzines in order to clear the name of the skinheads'. The SHARP crowd inspired more left-leaning political bands. Total Desacuerdo, a hardcore skinhead band led by Pablo Velazco and Mauricio Farias, were the most important. 'They mixed hardcore and Oi!,' González continued. He also mentioned a late nineties Oi! band from Santiago called Curasbun, who emerged from the anarcho-punk scene and released their debut album in 2002.

He said that for a few years from 2001, Oi! had a golden period in Chile. In Santiago, there was not only Sudor Obrero, but Criminalskin, Los Kolegas, Ateos Gracias a Dios, Yo te Afirmo Proletarios Oi!, Destroi!, Aversion Social and Skaparate. 'A great time, full of fights, drunkenness, gossip and drug addiction,' he wrote.

The scene was derailed when, in Valparaiso, a neo-Nazi gang known as Martillos del Sur attacked an Oi! band/skinhead venue. 'This was the detonator of several confrontations around the country that led to deaths and lasted more than a decade,' González said.

He brought up Laurel de Hierro, formed 2003, Chile's first female skinhead organisation. 'They were able to organise several concerts, publish several fanzines and above all beat up anyone who crossed their path,' he wrote. 'They were lovers of boxing and ultraviolence.'

In 2004, he said a band called Oi! Bastard, made up from Criminalskin musicians, blew up. 'It was an avowedly apolitical crew that turned into a very successful production company,' González said. 'They brought bands like The Business to Chile and established a small Oi! circuit in the country. Sadly, after Oi! Bastard split up, many skinheads who were apolitical went over to the more ultra-nationalist side, followed bands in the south of Chile like Orgullo Sur, Mac & Los Guarenes Korps, Golpe de Botas. In Santiago they followed Pelea de Ratas.'

González wrote how the Oi! scene revived in the late noughties, with newer bands such as Santa Blasfemia, Bootboys and Konducta Anti-Social all forming. In 2015, González formed his own record label, Oi! Fin Del Mundo, who in collaboration with Bar Crew Records, released a 2021 compilation, *Oi! Fin Del Mundo – Vol. 1*. It features all Chile's best bands (including Sudor Obrero). González was also active promoting gigs in Santiago by visiting Oi! bands such as Red Alert, Komintern Sect, Garotos Podres and Lion's Law.

He signed off by saying the Chilean Oi! scene was very much alive and in good health: 'The most recent bands that have come out are Cada Vez Peor, Exaltus and Los Problemas and all are very good projects.'

Obrigado e boa sorte a todas.

Chapter 12

'Grey Zone'

ISD (Ian Stuart Donaldson) Records was formed by Combat 18 in 1994, after the collapse of Rock-O-Rama and Rebelles Européens. A compilation, *Blood & Honour Volume One*, shored up the UK bands still associated with the organisation, and the label took control of the Skrewdriver back catalogue. ISD released an album called *Barbecue in Rostock* by No Remorse, said to be the most extreme neo-Nazi record made to that point.

There was, however, in-fighting within C18 and it culminated in a murder in 1997, with life imprisonment for two leading figures in the cabal. This was followed by police raids on many more connected to C18. ISD Records faltered, and the UK's RAC scene was disrupted.

Sweden became a focal point for the far-right scene. The country had established a formidable RAC scene in the eighties with Ultima Thule, Dirlewanger (named after an SS officer) and Vit Aggression (White Aggression) prominent. Ultima Thule and Dirlewanger both featured on a 1995 C18/ISD compilation, *White Resistance Vol 1*.

Two Swedish record labels emerged: Nordland and Ragnarock, which was linked to C18 and was formed by a former SS volunteer (Ragnarök was the final battle in Norse mythology). The label's offices were raided by police in '98. Two fully loaded automatic guns and hand grenades were found. Ultima Thule were linked to the label. In 2000, the band's studio was torched.

A third Swedish label, Midgard, formed in '94, became the powerhouse for the scene and it remains operational. Today on the label's website, they advertise prominent links to organisations with names such as European Brotherhood, Keep It White (Blood Honour Loyalty), Fasci Nation and Ansgar Aryan. They provide an outlet for the main UK white power bands left standing, Brutal Attack and No Remorse, plus a clutch of America's most notorious and long standing bands, Bound for Glory, RaHoWA and Max Resist.

Ultima Thule albums continue to feature high up on the Midgard list of homegrown releases, alongside Vit Aggression and a band called Svastika. The label has also made four volumes of a compilation called *White Pride Worldwide*. Perhaps most shocking of all was the label's link to Anders Breivik, the Norwegian terrorist, who in 2011 gunned down and killed seventy-seven people, chiefly at a Workers' Youth League (Norway's largest political Labour Party youth organisation) summer camp. In a manifesto he published online he named Saga as an inspiration, 'the world's best and most talented English-speaking patriotic musician'. The Swedish white nationalist had released three volumes of her tribute to Skrewdriver's music on Midgard. Her cover of the band's 'The Snow Fell' was specifically mentioned by Breivik.

Blood & Honour also remains active today with around twenty divisions or sections across the world. They have a no press policy; their motto: 'Run silent. Run deep. 28.' The anniversary of the death of Ian Stuart, on the 'third weekend of September', remains the most significant date in their calendar (memorial events have been held in places such as Melbourne, Budapest, California, Sweden, Poland, Italy, France and Ukraine). The B&H website also lists other important markers, including London Calling, which commemorates the 1992 'Battle of Waterloo' gig, White Xmas and events to mark the deaths of Violent Storm members.

In 2013 Channel 4 News reported on a secret Blood & Honour weekend gathering to mark the twentieth anniversary of Stuart's death, held in a large makeshift venue in a field close to Upper Heyford in Oxfordshire. The report predicted as many as 5,000 neo-Nazi sympathisers were to attend. At the time B&H was said to have twenty-eight divisions worldwide. Bands slated to play included Brutal Attack and two new UK names, Whitelaw and Section 88 (who released an album, *Ain't No Black* in 2008). At their own estimation there were 2,000 in attendance; photographs printed on the B&H site suggest there may have been fewer. One band, presumably linked to B&H Scotland played in kilts.

Oi! is still listed on the B&H website in a tick box for 'favourite genre of RAC music', alongside RAC Rock, NSBM (National Socialist Black Metal[1]), NSHC (Hardcore), ballads and punk.

---

1 NSBM has now usurped Oi! as the key music genre in the white power movement. Until the war with Russia, Ukraine was the country most associated with this music. The band Sokyra Peruna, formed in the late nineties, started the Asgardsrei festival in Kyiv, which became the most popular annual neo-Nazi event of the year: 'Two days, 14 bands, 1,500 places, 0 tolerance'. Several of the organisers and band members had been convicted of murders, assaults and other hate crimes.

B&H also produce a magazine and run a regular podcast which was started in 2010 under the name *28 Radio*.

Atrocities continued to be connected to B&H: in 2012, four B&H members in Florida were convicted of the 1998 murder of two homeless men. The same year B&H and C18 members in the Czech Republic, where a prominent RAC Oi! scene developed in the nineties with Buldok a popular band, were said to have firebombed a building occupied mostly by Romani families.

The B&H/RAC influence across Europe was scary to look into. In Russia, from the mid-nineties, there was a growing Oi! scene associated with the movement and a band called Russkoe Getto, later renamed Kolovrat, reached cult status. In 2012, the Russian Government banned B&H. Canada followed suit in 2019, banning B&H and Combat 18.

In Poland, a nineties RAC band called Legion was linked to the National Rebirth of Poland party and helped recruit skinheads to the political cause. In 2002 the singer of Polish 'neo-Nazi Oi!' band Honor, who were associated with RAC, was arrested for spreading hate. The B&H division in Belgium was associated with Fight-Action (who covered 'Chaos') in the nineties and the country had a notorious noughties RAC band, Kill, Baby . . . Kill! In Sweden the RAC remained strong into the noughties with bands such as Pro Patria, Endless Pride and Pitbullfarm (who covered 'A Case of Pride' by Skrewdriver) emerging.

There was also Brigade M from Holland, Oi-Kor from Hungary, Mistreat from Finland. The latter had a 2023 gig featured on the B&H website under an 'axis' of events section. All events advertised for 2023 were in Europe: Hungary, Estonia and Germany (where eighties band Endstufe continue to be popular figures on the scene). On this 'axis' page are banner ads for the British Movement and the secretive The League of St George, spawned from the Column 88 terror group.

In the UK, No Remorse continued to release new albums with titles like *Oi! Monkey* and *18 Was Right* until at least 2012 but seem to have now disbanded. Brutal Attack remain one of the biggest UK names. They released a song called 'This Is My Life' (with 90,000 views on YouTube) in late 2021. Singer Ken McLellan, heavily tattooed, including all over his skull, spoke of pain, anger, regret, desolation and despair as his key driving forces. Deptford John said McLellan had eleven kids. 'Some of these people are like tribal elders,' John added.

Of the newer UK bands, the main one appears to be Whitelaw. Deptford John asked if I'd looked into them. From the east Midlands, formed in the late nineties, signed to Midgard, they agreed to be featured in the 2006 Channel 5 *A MacIntyre Investigation* documentary *Nazi Hate Rock*, alongside America's Max Resist.

In this documentary there was mention of Whitelaw's links to the BNP and talk of the controversial German Project Schoolyard, where 25,000 copies of a compilation of 'nationalist rock' had been distributed free to schoolkids. B&H, under the banner 'Britain Awake', claimed they had done one better and produced 50,000 copies of two compilations for distribution.

The 2013 B&H weekend in Oxfordshire, which Whitelaw played at, seems to have been the last significant gathering in the UK, although B&H claim despite 'state security operations, Red bleating and media witch hunts' they have managed to stage an ISD memorial gig in the UK every year since.

Whitelaw are still active: HOPE Not Hate targeted a 2019 gig in Newcastle. The band's latest album was released by Midgard in 2022. 'They invited me up to their radio station,' Deptford John said. 'I went, thanks but no. I know people who go to those things [gigs]. That's why I know they go camping together; they have secret events. I don't like the intensity and secrecy of it all. Also, by going you're condoning something, you've joined it inadvertently by being there.'

I kept an eye out throughout 2022 for what may have been B&H events in the UK but didn't see anything significant happening. However, something else had risen on the UK Oi! scene and was said to attract a similar audience. It was far less easy to identify (no Swastika capes!), making it less easy to police, and it became identified as the 'grey zone'. It was first reported on in 2013, when *Vice* went to town on an event called 'Monsters of Oi!' taking place at the Boleyn Tavern in east London. They headlined the piece: 'Britain's Nazi Punk Scene Is Alive and Limping: Bald fascists with guitars are still playing awful, hateful music in Britain's pubs.'

The bands listed as playing were: I.C.1 (police code for 'white male); Last Orders (the eighties band from Grimsby who had featured on the NF's White Noise Records compilation *No Surrender!*) and Citizen Keyne. Unite Against Fascism rallied to have the gig cancelled, and it was. *Vice* said the gig and bands, particularly I.C.1, were an example of what was then being dubbed 'patriotic Oi!'.

I.C.1 might have been slightly more than that: an English/German collaboration from the singer in UK RAC/B&H band Razors Edge. They'd played Skrewdriver's White Christmas gig in 1992, and been a mainstay of the short-lived ISD Records, releasing an ISD Memorial album split with No Remorse. I.C.1 also appeared on a 2014 British compilation *Bathgate Belongs To Us!* produced by 100% British Oi! Productions, which is a fascinating snapshot of this burgeoning 'patriotic Oi!' movement. Among the bands included on the comp were: Tattooed Mother Fuckers (TMF), No Quarter, Citizen Keyne, Pressure 28, Code 1, Last Orders, Bakers Dozen plus The Glory Boys from Spain and Heroes who featured members of Swedish RAC band Dirlewanger.

Vice singled out two of these bands as being suspect: Tattooed Mother Fuckers and Pressure 28. TMF featured the former singer of English Rose, the RAC band from Leicestershire who had been signed to Rebelles Européens, played B&H gigs in '93 and subsequently been released by ISD Records. I watched them do a couple of gigs circa 2013 that have been uploaded to YouTube. One was a Blackpool pub gig that happened to coincide with Rebellion. The singer said: 'This one's dedicated to a man called Ian. Cheers. You do your homework.' Then they played 'I Don't Like You' by Skrewdriver. Gary Hodges also appeared on stage with them to do 'Wonderful World', 'Evil' and 'Chaos', his first appearance as far as I could tell since the controversy of his 4-Skins *The Return* album.

I read somewhere that the TMF singer has abandoned the far-right scene. In an online interview he explained that he dreamed of playing with Sparrer or the Rejects, but knew 'with the stigma of my past that it will never become a reality'.

There was a Pressure 28 gig in Widnes, September 2022, at a pub called the Snig, that I planned to attend. Also on the bill were two new wave of British Oi! bands, Tear Up from Watford, who I'd seen play with Lion's Law and The Templars at the

100 Club, and the formidable B-Squadron. I'd seen them play at Cream of the Crop. They were said to be linked to Leicester's famous Baby Squad football hooligan firm. The singer's roar was incredible. I could see why many in Oi! rated them. Their 2021 album *Everything You Hate* was released by Rebellion and featured the standout 'Do You Know Stanley'.

I was bemused then when B-Squadron, prior to the Widnes show, announced on their Facebook page that they were fed up of getting accused of being Nazis by people on the internet and were splitting up. They copied-and-pasted a comment someone had made about a gig they were due to play in November in Staffordshire, 'A Night of Pure Oi!', alongside Code 1, Citizen Keyne and Ragged Glory. It had been dubbed a 'Nazi gig'. I searched a recent Ragged Glory gig online, which also took place in Widnes. They started off with a song dedicated to someone who they said had been Skrewdriver Security: 'We were all there, I don't know if you were, but we were'.

The Pressure 28 gig in Widnes was cancelled. HOPE Not Hate claimed '200 skinheads and Nazis' were set to attend, made serious accusations against the gig's promoter, petitioned the council, the police and the local MP. What I found odd is Pressure 28's entire catalogue is on Spotify. They are from Manchester, claim the 28 in their name is not a Blood & Honour signifier but related to the correct tyre pressure for a type of scooter.

Mike Josephson at Longshot had released a single by them in 2010. I'd asked him about that. 'I've had many conversations with [singer] Kev,' Josephson said. 'I was interested in doing a follow-up release, a full-length, and he was the one who said, no you shouldn't do it. He said, I appreciate it, mate, but there's just a little bit of stuff blowing up with us online again. I personally still think they're a great band and I don't know what they've done [that's] so egregious as a band, but it's the old saying: If you lay with dogs you'll get fleas. That's sort of where Kev's at. In my personal conversations with him I get the impression he is personally not politically motivated, but he's had a history that sort of lumps him [in] with some pretty questionable people. I don't have any regret about doing that single ['Spirit of 69']. I think it's a great song, the message in the song is amazing, it's probably one of the more Oi! releases I have. I can understand and respect as well that some people have issues with that band.'

I watched online a small pub gig Pressure 28 played in Blackpool in 2015, again coinciding with Rebellion, dubbed 'The End Is Nigh – Oi! Ain't Dead'. Also on the bill were Indecent Exposure and No Quarter. The night was promoted by Unstoppable Hate Distribution, and said to have attracted faces from anti-Muslim group, the Pie and Mash Squad, B&H, the National Front and North West Infidels.

Unstoppable Hate had organised another pub gig in Blackpool to coincide with Rebellion the following year, 2016, under the title 'The Real Rebellion'. It was held in a club that had previously hosted the BNP's national conference. Bands billed to appear included Tattooed Mother Fuckers, Sweden's Pitbullfarm, Indecent Exposure and No Quarter.

No Quarter had a memorable song, 'Ain't What I Call Oi!' ('Politically correct, watered down, this ain't what I call Oi!') released on the Rebellion Records' 2014 album *New Breed Rising – 100% British Oi!*. They featured a youngish singer who also played in Close Shave, the band who had attached themselves to the B&H scene in the early nineties. I watched a recent gig online that they did with Pressure 28 in Tamworth and they had some lads lined up in 'No Quarter Security' Ts, an obvious Skrewdriver touch.

Many of these 'patriotic Oi!' bands were released by Grey Zone Records (active from 2014–19) – and I wasn't sure which had come first, the 'grey zone' term or the label name. I suspected the bands had decided it would be funny to adopt the moniker. Citizen Keyne were also signed to Grey Zone. They were from Milton Keynes, kept popping up at these gigs, and were another of the bands *Vice* had first highlighted as being 'patriotic Oi!'. I watched a 2021 gig they did in Pontefract. The singer ranted against footballers taking the knee in support of anti-racism: 'We don't take the knee for no one, if you don't like it, fuck off.' Their most recent album [2014], called *White Collar Hooligan* had titles such as: 'Paedo Scum', 'Keyboard Militia' and 'Stand Proud'. Paul Swain, the former 4-Skins and Skrewdriver guitarist, plays guitar with the band. I saw him at the Cream of the Crop gig I attended in Bedford. Although they weren't playing, another band he was in, Stronghold, had a prominent merchandise stall selling T-shirts and CDs at the festival. Stronghold were a fairly new band but classic 'grey zone': featuring members who had pasts in RAC bands such as Bulldog Breed and Indecent Exposure and some who came from other 'grey zone bands' such as Retaliator and TMF. Swain also had a third band, the newish Tank Turret, who featured Deptford John's old pal Frenchie, another early member of Skrewdriver. They were signed to Midgard.

Code 1 played with many of the above names and were another band signed to Grey Zone Records. They were on the bill at the 'A Night of Pure Oi!' with B-Squadron. I watched a Pontefract gig of theirs posted for posterity online. They had a portly older fella doing the shouting. He was wearing the Fred Perry polo popularised by the American far-right organisation the Proud Boys, black with yellow trim. The band had album titles such as *Telling It Like It Is*, *You Won't Beat Us* and *Outlaws of Oi!*.

Retaliator were another band signed to Grey Zone Records and often featured on the bill with acts such as Tank Turret, Citizen Keyne and Pressure 28. They were an Oi! band from East Anglia, formed in 1996. Their bassist and songwriter Pete Roper wrote a book: *Crucified: Life in a Skinhead Band* (self-published in 2016). He has also played in Condemned 84, the biggest of all the 'grey zone' bands, and it was a side project of Roper's called Balefire that Mensi kicked up a storm about when a member of Infa Riot joined.

At the time Roper wrote the book he said Retaliator had gone through about fourteen members, and a fair few of them had convictions, mainly for violence. He said that the 'grey zone' bands had 'few friends in the Oi! scene' on account of their 'belligerent patriotic stance'. He also mentioned writing a song that he described as 'very RAC', directed against the 'politically correct thought police'. There was a theme of waging war with the politically correct running through the book and the 'grey zone' scene in general.

Roper admitted it had been a mistake for the band to play the Skinhouse in Milan run by Hammerskins (the Skinhouse Milano made waves in 2014 hosting a Hammerfest in their city). It had been poorly attended he said, and an easy point of attack for the band's critics. As a counterbalance he said the band had also played Rebellion (Holidays in the Sun as it was then called) in 2001.

In the book Roper protested that Retaliator were not racist, but he did talk about the 'threat of Islam swamping everything'. A single called 'Armed and Ready' was Retaliator's response to the 2005 London terror attacks. Also, he described their album *Lionhearted* as part of a 'long overdue fightback' as the country had been 'brought to its knees by cultural Marxism and political correctness'. He went on to mention the warrior race, a holy war spreading in Europe. One song on the album, he said, was a manifesto for all the 'grey zone' bands excluded from the Oi! mainstream by politically correct bands, labels and promoters. Roper ended his book by saying the Oi! scene (in 2012–13) was a disgrace, full of 'cowards and traitors'. He singled out two names: Daryl Smith from Argy Bargy and Cock Sparrer for being 'squeaky clean' (see next chapter), and Mensi – not just his 'extreme far-left frothing at the mouth' anti-fascist 'bully boy' stance but also because of all the bands who were attracted to play with the Upstarts at 'Antifa gigs' but wouldn't play with the 'likes of us'. This, Roper stated, was because they were too afraid to show their 'true colours' and hoped they might get put on the line-up for the next Rebellion festival.

Retaliator had a band member called ASBO who also cropped up in line-ups of TMF, Indecent Exposure and The London Diehards. Maybe it was coincidence, but the latter name immediately brought to mind, the Diehards, one of the earliest NF/RAC Oi! bands. The London Diehards had formed in 2014, done a split with TMF, and included a former member of contemporary B&H band Avalon as well as Terry Hayes from the obscure early eighties Oi! band, East End Badoes.

Hayes was a good barometer. He had been vocal in his support for Hodges' 2009/10 4-Skins comeback with Indecent Exposure.

East End Badoes had reformed at the same time. 'It's great to have Milky [Indecent Exposure's singer] back on the scene,' Hayes said. 'He got Hodges back on stage. The Index [as Indecent Exposure are sometimes referred to] lads are great, although they do have a bit of a rocky past.'

I'd hoped to see East End Badoes play at Cream of the Crop but they had to cancel because Hayes had just had a hip operation. I mentioned I'd been looking forward to seeing them to The Business drummer Chris Mundie and he said: 'They are great, lovely guys. Terry's really good mates with all the Dropkick Murphy guys and they're, like, massively anti-fascists. He's a Millwall fan, got that hooligan background but you couldn't ask for a nicer guy to meet than Terry Hayes.'

In an online interview with a Czech site (they were playing a gig in Vyškov) The London Diehards said: 'The scene in Britain is a strange one, in many ways similar to Europe with the big divide regarding politics. We've always tried to stay out of that yet somehow we have been dragged into it by various political extremists and keyboard warriors who think that if you play with X band you are Nazi / communist / grey zone, etc.'

Before joining The Business, Mundie himself had briefly played drums with the reformed early/mid-eighties Oi! band from Stoke called Section 5, who I'd also seen described as 'grey zone'. Mensi had an issue with them, and they had played gigs with RAC bands such as English Rose, Lionheart and Battle Zone in the late eighties. They had, conversely, also featured on Roddy Moreno's Oi! Records. Mundie had accompanied them on a short 2005 tour of Serbia they were doing with The Last Resort.

'It was a weird one,' Mundie said. 'I had an idea Section 5 might be a bit dodgy.' He'd been asked to do the gigs by the band's new guitarist Stephen 'Fish' Brooks, who had previously played in Discharge. 'I said to Fish, I don't want to be playing drums for some bonehead band. Fish said, course it's not, I wouldn't be in the band if it was like that. The tour was organised by Darren Russell who does Rebellion, who is about as left wing as it gets.'

Mundie said that, although the gigs were sometimes violent (there was a stabbing at one and police in riot vans were called to another) there was no neo-Nazi stuff. 'When we started playing in Belgrade someone in the front row stuck the right arm up almost instantly and Tosh [Section 5 guitarist/singer] stopped playing and looked him dead in the eye and said, if you put your arm up like that again I'm gonna come down there and rip it off and shove it up your arse.'

He added that Tosh, who was also playing guitar in The Business at the time, 'went very left wing' and 'fell out with quite a lot of people because they were getting progressively right wing again.

'Back then when The Business did UK gigs, there were a few people who were on the right-wing side of things, nothing extreme, but sort of Queen and country and all the rest of it, almost like a caricature,' Mundie said. 'It wasn't taken as a serious thing – we didn't have this division that we've got now. Everyone got on back then, everyone was going to the gigs, people who maybe did have unsavoury views kind of kept it to themselves, almost embarrassed to bring it up, it was very much hidden away and it never really came into it.'

The Brexit campaign in 2016, he said, had changed that.

'For me Brexit was the big one,' Mundie said. 'No matter what anyone says there was this rhetoric running through the whole campaign, coming from the UKIP side of things, which was that old, your life would be better if it wasn't for all these foreign people coming over here. Stuff that you thought had disappeared all came back: immigration became a big issue again. And all these people who kept their racist views to themselves became a lot more vocal about it. It was an easy card for some of the more right-wing people to say, we're not hating other people we're just being pro our own people. The Business were removed enough from that for it not to be an issue at our gigs, particularly, but you did see elements of it creeping back in before Mick [Fitz] died. I heard people talking about one of the "grey area" bands we were doing a gig with in the States. I don't think we would have been put on the same bill with them in England. I was like, aren't they a bit dodgy, a bit Nazi-ish? Mick said, no they're not proper boneheads they're just thick cunts who don't know any better. And they were nice enough guys. There's a lot of people who aren't that bright who get caught up in it and taken along for the ride. People would make excuses for their friends as well. He's an alright guy, I don't agree with him on X, Y, Z . . . a lot of that about.

'The horrible line, "we're telling it like it is", always made me feel uncomfortable,' Mundie added. 'This idea that their opinions aren't shitty opinions, it's just that they're being oppressed and not allowed to express themselves. And it's almost accepted now; there are people who have views that wouldn't have been tolerated ten or fifteen years ago. And you see more and more of it – people online saying we should be sending the navy to torpedo these boats in the channel. What the fuck is that?'

I mentioned Frankie Flame. I'd been following a thread online about an anti-Muslim rant he'd posted on his Facebook page in

2016 in the wake of the Paris attacks. 'Fuck them all – if we are attacked, we fight back,' was a top line. It had seemed to stir up quite a bit of feeling, support, among some in the Oi! community. 'Frank came to Norway with us [The Business], we were on same bill,' Mundie said. 'As a performer he does all this "Knees up Mother Brown" cockney stuff, it's great, and then you make friends with him on Facebook and you go, oh fucking hell . . . makes for pretty uncomfortable reading.'

Flame, one of the obscurer early eighties Oi! acts, revived his musical career via Hammer Records in the late nineties and is now playing as Superyob ('music under no political banner'). He too had been dragged into the 'grey zone' conversation, emblematic in many ways of acts with no obvious RAC connection that were being called out online. 'Our shows aren't political gatherings, they're entertainment for working-class people like ourselves,' Flame said. He'd worked with popular European bands such as Klasse Kriminale and Evil Conduct, and his latest album was released by the mainstream Oi! label Randale.

I read comments he made about immigration in interviews that could be interpreted as xenophobic. Critics also pointed to Superyob shows at contentious hardcore skinhead pubs such as De Kastelein in Bruges and Skinhouse Menfis in Thuringia, central Germany, and a collaboration with purported right-wing figure, Antonella, ex of Klasse Kriminale and RAC band Battle Zone. Another Hammer Records Oi! band, Straw Dogs, backed her on a track attributed to Antonella's Klasse Kriminale on the 'patriotic Oi!' comp *Bathgate Belongs to Us!*. Straw Dogs went on to release an album with an American Oi! label associated with the notorious Max Resist.

The notoriety of the 'grey zone' bands seemed to briefly threaten to engulf the whole Oi! scene. Phil Templar was the subject of much criticism circulated online. It was due to his involvement with German band Stomper 98. As a teenager the band's singer, Sebi, was in a German RAC band called Boots Brothers who released music via R-O-R. He had written in the German media about his regrets over his past. Approaching Stomper's tenth-anniversary show in Leipzig in 2008, which The Templars played at, a photo was published 'proving' Sebi was still a neo-Nazi. He was pictured hugging the singer of the notorious Endstufe at a recent, riotous 4-Skins/Indecent Exposure German gig put on by Bootboys Hildesheim who critics suggested were 'riddled with neo-Nazis' (they insisted they were 'non-political'). Sebi said the photo had been snapped among the excitement of a crazy gig.

Phil had also played twice in the mid-noughties with a new band put together by Alex Allui – who was also regretful of his past associations – former Battle Zone singer: at CBGB and in Boston with Klasse Kriminale. Allui was then approaching forty and stuck between a rock and a hard place. 'I am an ex-Nazi in the eyes of the left and I am a race traitor in the eyes of the right,' he said.

I didn't ask Phil directly about Sebi or Allui but when we were discussing bands The Templars had released splits with, I mentioned Crashed Out and said, their bass player Spin . . .

'Used to play for a far-right band in the past,' Phil shot back.

I felt like I'd hit a raw nerve . . . 'but has since abandoned that scene and Crashed Out gave him a second chance', I continued. I thought that was quite a positive story?

'That's 100 per cent a positive thing,' Phil said. 'I just turned 53. If someone can look at their past and say, I've made mistakes, and move forward, put that weirdo shit aside and give themselves a second chance then I don't have a problem with that. It's when I see older people, my age or older, still doing the same stupid shit they were doing as a teenager, then I'm like, you're still believing in that garbage? Really? If someone did stupid shit in their past and they have enough common sense to leave all that garbage alone and live their life properly I have no problem with that person. People can make mistakes, that's all I'm saying. If you have the wherewithal to know that you made mistakes and correct them then I'd say, good for that person.'

Chris Wright had mentioned to me Crashed Out had also been labelled 'grey zone' online in their past. I naturally presumed this was because of Spin. 'It was more the Hammer Records thing [Crashed Out had released two albums with the label in the nineties],' Chris said. 'The odd thing was said [about Spin] but nothing that bad where you think, I'm gonna wrap the band in – there's more positives than negatives. We play anti-fascist gigs, we toured and released songs with the Upstarts. Spin joined the band after he'd already denounced his past. Like Mensi said, everyone deserves a second chance.'

Wright said his younger brother Lee had sent Crashed Out's first demo tapes to record label addresses he found in punk fanzines and Hammer Records offered him an album deal. 'Unbeknown to Lee the label had a name for being grey zone,' Wright said. 'Lee was 15 and he said at that time he thought "left and right wings were things on aeroplanes".'

He added that in the north-east they referred to 'grey zone' bands as 'fence sitters', bands who say they want nothing to do with politics either right or left. 'I understand from a band's point of view that they just want to play music,' he said. 'I also understand that people want to keep the scene free of right-wing bullshit. I personally find it a bit weird that a band would want to play punk rock but not denounce right-wing racist shit!'

I pencilled in going to see Condemned 84 play. From Ipswich, their 1986, *Oi! Ain't Dead* EP is something of a classic. I'd seen Tear Up doing a rousing version of the title track live. Since then, they had released music via labels as diverse as Roddy Moreno's Oi! Records, Rock-O-Rama, Hammer Records and most recently Sweden's Pretty Shitty Records (home to a new band from the former singer in Agent Bullogg, one of Sweden's biggest eighties RAC acts). I was impressed that Condemned 84 currently feature a guitarist who had also at one time played with the American Oi! band, Anti-Heros. They gig under a 'No Bullshit – No Politics' banner and among their output is an album called *No One Like Us . . . We Don't Care* and a single called 'The Real Oi!'.

They were one of a handful of UK Oi! bands among the slew of NSBM bands featured in an article written in 2017 by Paul Resnikoff, founder and publisher of Digital Music News, under the headline: 'I Just Found 37 White Supremacist Hate Bands on Spotify'.

Resnikoff referenced a 2014 list of 'white supremacist hate' bands compiled by the American civil rights organisation, Southern Poverty Law Center. The other Oi! acts named included: Bakers Dozen from Scotland (formed in 1995, also on Grey Zone Records, with a song called 'British Oi! Is Fighting Back' and a documentary in the making called, *Still Divided From the Masses*), Brutal Attack, Legion of St. George (formed late nineties), Ravens Wing (who featured No Remorse members), Skinfull (Oi! band from Coventry who also appeared on the *Bathgate Belongs To Us!* compilation), Skullhead and Tattooed Mother Fuckers.

'When we split up, Condemned 84 formed,' Deptford John said. 'Uncanny almost. I've never seen them but I've heard they're a white power band; but then again they've probably heard I'm a white power bloke! It's like the things people write on Facebook [attacking Oi! bands] – it's a small-town, twitching-curtains approach to everything.'

The Condemned 84 gig was in Peterborough on Bonfire Night with Superyob in support. Three days before, the band announced on their Facebook page – under a headline that read 'DEMOCRACY IS DEAD IN THE UK' – that the venue had cancelled the show due to 'pressure from the local police licensing department'.

There are only three Condemned 84 songs on Spotify currently, all from Link Records' eighties Oi! compilations. I watched online a gig they played at Bedford Esquires in 2019. It was under the banner of the 'Main Event', which seemed a deliberate reference to the two controversial B&H gigs in '88 and '92. They looked to be a youngish band backing the original singer, another Kev. I read at a recent gig of theirs in Denmark a minor riot between neo-Nazis and anti-fascists broke out but the Bedford gig passed untroubled.

I noted Condemned 84 played a gig with RAC band English Rose and had released a split single with Indecent Exposure in 2009. I also found a track of theirs on a 2000 Nordland Records compilation alongside a slew of German and UK RAC bands.

Skinfull, who Resnikoff also named as white supremacists, had played (alongside other UK 'grey zone' bands) at the controversial two-day 'NYC Oi! Fest' in 2015. Among the American bands on the bill were Brassic, who bragged of sharing a stage with neo-Nazi band Youngland, one of the several the Sikh temple shooter, Wade Michael Page, played in. The following year, the

'NYC Oi! Fest', featuring many of the same bands, drew even more heat. Offensive Weapon, an American band said to have links to the white supremacist prison gang 211 Crew, were singled out as they included in their set a song called 'New Glory' by Youth Defense League. Nick Solares, a British food writer for popular website *Eater*, was 'outed' and forced to apologise for being involved in YDL in the eighties.

A July 2022 gig in Leeds seemed to bear some of the classic hallmarks of a B&H gig – 'Oi! The Resurrection 2'. A period photo of a phalanx of young skins in Union Jack Ts with one throwing what might be a Sieg Heil featured on the flyer and there was no venue specified. The bands advertised to play included Code 1, Queensbury Rules and Combat BC. The gig, surprisingly, went ahead, despite protests and a police visit. In a local newspaper report following the event, where the pub venue apologised for allowing the gig to happen, Combat BC, a female-fronted German band, were exposed for using Nazi imagery and had a song called 'Anti-Antifa'.

Queensbury Rules are from Bristol, started up about 2013, and were another band signed to Grey Zone Records. They had played the NYC Oi! Fest in 2016 and featured on Rebellion's *New Breed Rising – 100% British Oi!* compilation. In fact, they had supplied the title track, 'New Breed Rising'. I watched a taster of their set online at the 'Best of British Bulldog Oi! Fest' taking place in a pub back room in 2016. The singer, young and angry, had a voice similar to prime Gary Hodges. You can listen to them on Spotify.

Having encountered a lot of Oi! bands who have denounced their neo-Nazi past, I wanted to offer the same opportunity to

Indecent Exposure. I had enjoyed the music on their first cassette, and listened to their two eighties albums on Rock-O-Rama repeatedly, plus even given a couple of listens to a live album. There were tracks from the albums that I felt uncomfortable with. I mentioned this to Crown Court's Trevor Taylor, seen sporting an Index T-shirt circa 2013 but not since. He asked if I was referencing their inclusion on the notorious 1985 White Noise Records compilation *No Surrender!* I wasn't sure how far to push him on this. I knew he felt the hoopla around B-Squadron undeserved and a bit wet. I mumbled lyrics, unsure myself as to the way I was interpreting them, the conversation ran dry. Afterwards I questioned the words I thought I'd heard on the tracks I found offensive and came to the conclusion, first cassette aside, that the band's output was unpalatable. I had hoped to discuss the subject further with Phil Templar, who I knew liked the band's first cassette too, as he included 'A Matter of Time' in a list he was asked to compile of favourite Oi! tracks, but forgot.

Professor Matt Worley, however, did speak to me about a sense of ambiguity he perceived was attached to the band. Link included another of Indecent Exposure's first cassette tracks, 'Bank Holiday', on the 1987 compilation album *Oi! Glorious Oi!*, which is available on Spotify. The band's drummer, Swatton, was also supporting Rise Up, the newest, youngest UK Oi! band. I'd kept an eye on them since seeing them at Cream of the Crop. Singer Joe Worthington was in his late teens.

Mike Josephson told me: 'I've talked to Milky from Indecent Exposure and I'm going to give him my agreement and sympathy. At the time, in the eighties, one weekend he was playing a gig with a B&H band, like actual neo-Nazi bands, and another weekend he was playing with Desmond Dekker [a Ska artist]. For him and a lot of people on the skinhead scene of that time I don't think politics was the focal point. He told me within one band you maybe had one guy who supported the NF or the BM, another guy who was like, fuck that, my best mate is black. When he told me this, I said, I understand, I can see how that can be the case, but I said, knowing what you know now hopefully you're not going to make the choice to go and play with band X, Y and Z on a weekend and say that you're not political. At the time in the eighties they didn't care who they played with, they were like, we're just skinheads, we're playing music, having fun.'

Since they'd backed Hodges on the 4-Skins comeback, the only gigs I'd seen Indecent Exposure advertised to play were the Unstoppable Hate pub shows in Blackpool. They hadn't released any new music since the eighties. I joined their private Facebook group, which had 4,500 members. That's where I saw them announce a 'private gig' for September 2023 in the west of France with Condemned 84 and Close Shave, plus Dutch band Haymaker and Shorbut from Germany. There was no venue specified. As I was finishing writing a draft of this chapter, I checked again on the details of the gig. It was taking place on Saturday the 23rd, the third weekend in the month. The anniversary of Ian Stuart's death is the 24th. 'There you go,' said Taylor.

Chapter 13

Runnin' Riot:
Cock Sparrer/Roi/Oi Oi The Shop

It was a slog. A sweaty, back-room kind of journey. Often unpleasant. Sometimes violent. To get to where we are now: 2023. A happy new Oi! world of 3,000 people singing along to Sparrer, Sham, the Resorts and Rejects in the Empress Ballroom in Blackpool, the Court in the *Guardian*, Chubby signed to Partisan, Grade 2 on the cusp of the mainstream, new hip boutique Oi! labels worldwide, a trendy London Oi! shop, scores of sharp, modern new bands on a thriving scene, free from the far-right associations and reaching new audiences, and 6,000 tickets flying out the window for the Cock Sparrer's two sold-out nights at the Roundhouse to celebrate their fiftieth anniversary.

Roddy Moreno's Oi! Records packed up in '89, Lol Pryor and Mark Brennan closed down Link Records in '92, ending with another volume of their *Oi! Chartbusters* comps. Link had kept The Business going for a period and repackaged all the best of eighties Oi!. They'd also put out releases from bands now considered 'grey zone', such as Close Shave.

Brennan immediately created a new label, Captain Oi!, and it started the way it meant to go on, with reissues of eighties albums by Last Resort, Business, 4-Skins and Sparrer. It was Link all over again. And over the next thirty years, Captain Oi! scraped every cupboard clean, compilations included: *Oi! The Demos*, *Oi! The Rarities* (a five-volume series) and *100% British Oi!*. In the noughties, however, alongside releasing new stuff from old hands such as The Gonads and Upstarts, the label did support a couple of bands who started a new churn of Oi!, what would essentially become UK 'streetpunk'.

The most significant of these was Argy Bargy. They'd actually started about '92. Chiefly the band was Watford Jon, who worked for Captain Oi!, and Daryl Smith, who went on to become a member and then guiding force in Cock Sparrer. Jon and Daryl idolised Sparrer and had taken their name from a Sparrer song. They were both just out of their teens when they started Argy Bargy. 'There were hardly any other bands around, or at least there were no gigs going on,' Jon said in an online interview with *S.C.A.B.* in 2003. 'I wanted to kick things off again and hopefully inspire people to form new bands.'

They were the first hint of what was to come: a bit cheeky, punky pop Oi! with lyrics that clearly set them apart from the RAC scene. On one song, 'Bothering Me', they sang: 'All I want is a beer and a laugh, I don't want to preach on your behalf'.

Daryl was also in another Oi! band in the early nineties called The Elite (a different Elite to the obscure early eighties skinhead band). They were signed to a then-new Oi! label called Helen of Oi! based on the Isle of Wight. Between 1993–2003, Helen of Oi! released material by quite a few of the bands who'd go on to be labelled 'grey zone' such as Close

Shave, Frankie Flame, Pressure 28 and Another Man's Poison, gathering many of these bands for a '94 comp called *Oi! . . . It's Streetpunk.* The label also released five volumes of a compilation called *Punks, Skins & Herberts* featuring promising new homegrown Oi!, namely from Dundee's On File and Belfast's Runnin' Riot.

The audience was tiny. Watford Jon and Daryl played regular gigs at the Stick of Rock pub on Bethnal Green Road. It was run by the drummer in Cock Sparrer, Steve Bruce. Jon and Daryl pestered him to reform Cock Sparrer and helped organise a gig for them at the London Astoria in '93, the biggest Oi! gig for many years. The band have a remarkable story: a 1977 east London 'hooligan' rock band who'd cut two singles for Decca, made little impact and split up. Daryl's father, Mike Smith, had actually signed the band to Decca.

Bushell had saved them from the scrapheap when, influenced by Poplar lads such as East End Badoes' Terry Hayes who'd made up the band's '77 fanbase, he included an old unreleased Cock Sparrer song 'Sunday Stripper' on *Oi! The Album.* The band reformed for a one-off gig at his birthday party at the Bridgehouse and he then included two more of their tracks on *Strength Thru Oi!* including the long-lost gem, 'Runnin' Riot' (the band's debut '77 single: 'I can't stand the peace and quiet, I just want a running riot'). They became something of an Oi! cause célèbre even though they were never skinheads.

Gary Lammin wrote 'Runnin' Riot' when he was 18 in 1974, when he first joined the band. His dad was a docker, trade unionist and a shop steward, friends with Jack Dash (militant and celebrated trade union leader). Lammin worked on a building site and was sold on high-energy proto-punk rock, particularly the New York Dolls. He said the rest of the band preferred prog: Genesis, Yes, Wishbone Ash, King Crimson. He pushed his own songs on them and made them change their name: the original, Janus, he said, 'stunk the room out'. Bassist Steve Burgess, the band's head honcho, eventually relented but Lammin remained an uneasy fit in the band.

There is one Cock Sparrer story that became apocryphal from this period. It relates to Malcolm McLaren wanting to become their manager when he was looking for his own New York Dolls. The story goes that Cock Sparrer turned him down because he wouldn't get a round of beers in – they could have been the Pistols but were not bovvered, sort-of vibe. Not true, said Lammin, when I spoke to him. Yes, McLaren came to see them rehearse, in an east London pub, in 1975, just before he put the Pistols together. Lammin had been bugging the impresario at his Sex boutique on the King's Road for some time.

'East London in them days wasn't a trendy area and Malcolm came one Friday about 6.30 p.m., tottering through the doors dressed up in all gay bondage gear,' Lammin said with a smile. 'I was actually frightened at the reaction. This pub was predominantly white-male working class. Everybody was in there getting oiled up after a hard day's work, eating steak-and-kidney pies and boshing down loads of beer. And in comes Malcolm, on a pair of women's platform shoes, tight bondage trousers with a zip that looked like it went from his crotch to his arse, a little Bolero jacket, tartan beret and a women's handbag over his shoulder. I can still see one geezer's face now, eating a steak-and-kidney pie in the corner – stopped in suspended animation with his mouth open. I looked at this bloke and I thought, he's going to come over here any minute and stab that fork in Malcolm or one of us. I said to Malcolm, let's get upstairs, and he'd copped the atmosphere – he was absolutely fearless – and he looked around and he went, actually no, Gary, I think I'll stay down here, I'm quite enjoying the ambience and you can get me a gin and tonic, make that pink gin and tonic please; really stepping up to the plate.

'We got him upstairs in the end but Cock Sparrer wouldn't play any of the songs I'd written and were doing these long-winded, dirgy, prog rock-type numbers. Malcolm, said, but where are all the songs Gary's been showing me at the shop? It was Colin [the band's singer] who said, you gonna get a round of beers in? And Malcolm said, no I'm not, I don't like what I've heard. And he added this: I have come all the way over from the King's Road, you should be buying me a beer. I said to Malcolm, I'll go and get you another drink, and he said to me, Gary, I've always thought you looked like a bit of a football hooligan, you should work on that. We didn't turn him down – he turned us down.'

At some point soon after, Lammin said Burgess agreed to include his songs in the band's set. 'As long as I made him co-writer,' he said. 'So I agreed to that.' When the band signed to Decca in the wake of the punk explosion, the label appointed Keith Altham to act as their PR. The ex-*NME* writer, so-called 'Godfather of music PR,' was known for his work with the Stones, The Who, The Beach Boys and many more. 'We're in his office and he's tearing his hair out because I've got this football-terrace lad "bootboy" look, but everyone else to all intents and purposes are dressed in flared denims, that sort of hippy look,' Lammin said. 'Cock Sparrer refused to get on the punk imagery thing – I didn't do that either but what I'd been doing was wearing tartan baggy trousers – "Oxford bags" we called them – and a sort of tank top with a Rod Stewart style of haircut. That was your generic football lad look.'

'Keith said, so if you're not punks, you've got to be something, what are you? I remembered what Malcolm said, and I said, we're football hooligans. He said, great, I can work with that. What team will it be? I said, we'll all be our own different sides. I'm Millwall, I was going to matches at the time. [Guitarist] Mickey's Arsenal. Keith went, no, football fans don't mix with each other, unless you choose one specific team then we're not going with that football idea. I think it was Colin who said West Ham. That's how we became known as a West Ham band. Steve Burgess didn't even like football . . . he liked cricket. And let me tell you, we weren't football hooligans – we were never violent thugs on the football terraces. We were really only using it as a vehicle for an image. I got to make that clear – we were all pretty nice lads.'

It was the hooligan image that had captured the Oi! imagination. Altham hyped it relentlessly to little success. When I'd asked bands like Sham and Menace about Sparrer, they said they never came across them on the scene. It seemed only the so-called 'Poplar Boys' were fans. 'We met them after they saw an article in the *East London Advertiser* that I'd got for the band,' Lammin said. 'The Poplar Boys were very funny lads and real characters; very mischievous but not violent at all. They really helped create a great atmosphere at our gigs with loads of jumping about. It was the first time I'd ever seen stage-diving. They were not skinheads, just good geezers that loved punk but were also knowledgeable about art and fashion.'

After Sparrer split, Lammin formed a new band, The Little Roosters, with him up front. Steve Bruce was on drums and

Steve Burgess also joined the band. They'd actually played at Sham's 'Last Stand' gig at the Rainbow in '79. 'Cor, that was a night,' Lammin said. 'I made a lot of money out of that gig. We were coined off the stage. When the curtain came down, I went back and hoovered up about sixty or seventy quid in coins. It was frightening when Sham played, dangerous.' And the Rejects first proper gig was supporting the Roosters at the Bridgehouse. 'I got them that gig,' said Lammin. 'I saw them as genuine working-class lads with a burning ambition just like myself. They needed a favour like I always needed a favour.'

By 1981, when Bushell was hyping Cock Sparrer as a key proto-Oi! band, the Roosters were nowhere near it. All new-wave leather jackets, skinny ties, striped trousers, blouses and bouffant hairdos. They released an album on Polydor produced by Joe Strummer no less. It sank. Lammin focused on a promising new career in acting.

'I distanced myself from Oi! because I didn't think the Oi! people, those who were prominent, spearheading the movement . . . I'm not saying they themselves had any dodgy right-wing connotations but my feeling at the time was people who could have were not distancing themselves from the more undesirable elements that were being attracted to the situation,' Lammin said.

The rest of Cock Sparrer decided to reform in 1982. They were all now pushing 30. They got a deal with a French label called Carrere, who'd had a recent UK Top 10 with Black Lace's novelty hit 'Superman' but also worked with bands such as Sparks, Saxon and Rose Tattoo, and cut a new single, 'England Belongs to Me'. 'A song that took twenty-five minutes to write and twenty-five years to defend,' Burgess is quoted as saying in

Bruce's 2010 book *The Best Seat in the House: A Cock Sparrer Story*. Bruce called the song our 'nemesis and salvation'.

Lammin said Steve Burgess had asked him to be involved in the reunion and play on 'England Belongs to Me'. 'He said, it's about the Falklands conflict,' Lammin told me. 'I said, do what? "England Belongs to Me"? You're having a bubble bath, aren't you? I said, actually I think England belongs to everybody, man. I'm not playing on that. I said, England's a free state, it's what makes us great, you can't come out with statements like that. In their defence and to my detriment, I just heard the title and I didn't go past the title . . . as a staunch socialist that was my reaction, my gut instinct.'

There was no denying 'England Belongs to Me' could be read as problematic. It was a confusing song; seemed to be anti-war, about working-class lads being put on the front line in the first verse, but then gets chest-beating. 'Heads held high, fighting all the way, for the red, white and blue.'

The album they cut for Carrere was a straight-up classic. 'Where Are They Now', 'Riot Squad', 'Working', 'Take 'Em All', 'Watch Your Back' – it would be easier to list the songs from the album that didn't feature on the set list for their Roundhouse fiftieth anniversary gigs. Carrere, however, refused to release it. The band had tried to play a few comeback gigs in London and these had all been marred by violence, stage invasions and Sieg Heils, as the same skinhead crowd that was beginning to follow Skrewdriver was drawn to the band, following the release of 'England Belongs to Me'. The song was adopted as something of a RAC anthem with both Skullhead and English Rose including covers in their live sets.

Carrere saw problems with the album content: working while

signing on, shooting enemies, and a song that matched the lyrics from Vera Lynn's 'There'll Always Be an England' to the Colonel Bogey tune. It was picked up by Razor Records, an indie label that was home to Splodge, Red London and later the Upstarts. It sank. The band didn't want to play live, couldn't really. Another of Lammin's original songs, 'Chip on My Shoulder', was included on the *Son of Oi!* comp in '83 and the band cut another album, *Runnin' Riot*, in '84, that was half-hearted, half-baked, released by Syndicate. That was it, what Daryl picked up in '93 and ran with; a sort of truncated Sham story without the hits.

Link, of course, had kept the Cock Sparrer name au courant, often including them on their endless eighties Oi! compilations and the label had even had Sparrer cut a live album (a cash-in policy adopted by Link and applied to many bands). Sparrer had to record theirs in the studio, the band still too worried about attracting the wrong crowd in 1987 to actually perform live.

Daryl from Argy Bargy joined the band as a second guitarist for the gig at the Astoria (essentially replacing Lammin – the rest of the line-up was the same). That they could play such a large venue, when Oi! was barely filling pub back rooms, was encouraging, but when the gig ended in the sort of violence that had blighted their career so far, the way forward was uncertain.

Argy Bargy signed with a new UK Oi! label called Step-1 in 1995. Kent-based, the label was as interested in releasing contemporary Oi! as they were repackaging the old stuff, via their subsidiary 84 Records. Argy Bargy's debut album was called *Drink, Drugs and Football Thugs*. Step-1 also released a compilation called *Oi! . . . The Next Generation* that featured Argy Bargy alongside Close Shave, Straw Dogs and Pressure 28. The label also released Condemned 84, Code 1 and Bakers Dozen. This was the era before the 'grey zone' existed, but the dire present reputations of the bulk of Step-1's roster of acts is a good marker of how Daryl Smith and Watford Jon became their generation's chief success story.

There were other green shoots. Crashed Out were filmed in their hometown of Hebburn (near Jarrow), for a documentary called *World of Skinhead* (Channel 4, 1995) made by George Marshall. Marshall was from Glasgow and had coined the still-used-today term 'spirit of '69' in the late eighties when he was running a fanzine called *Zoot*. 'We coined the catchphrase because the image of Nazi boneheads had nothing to do with what skinheads were about,' Marshall told the *Independent* in 1992.

Zoot had developed into *Skinhead Times* with its slogan 'Pride not Prejudice', a popular fanzine with a 5,000-copy circulation that ran for six years up until 1995. *Spirit of '69* became the title of a book (subhead: *A Skinhead Bible*), published in 1991 by Marshall's own company, ST Publishing (the book Luis of the Rotten Boys said was so important to the scene in Brazil). Marshall hung up his boots in 1995 aged 29, stopped being a skinhead. In 2011 he published another book, *Skinhead Nation*, which updated and complemented *Spirit of '69*. Both make for illuminating, if at times uncomfortable, reading, in terms of chronicling this transitional period for Oi! in the nineties and noughties.

'The scene was crap back then,' Lee Wright of Crashed Out said with admirable honesty. After their two albums on Hammer, Lee took a long sabbatical before returning in 2005 with his brother Chris on vocals and an album on Captain Oi!. The following year, 2006, a tiny snippet of Lee from the Marshall documentary was featured at the start of the acclaimed film,

This Is England, directed by Shane Meadows and set among a gang of skinheads in 1983.

The best example of where Oi! was then and is now comes from a look at the history of the annual Rebellion Festival. It started as a small punk festival in 1996, in Blackpool, called Holidays in the Sun [HITS]. The organisers actually approached Daryl that year, keen to have Cock Sparrer play alongside Sham 69, Stiff Little Fingers, U.K. Subs, The Damned and Slaughter & the Dogs. Daryl rebuffed the offer for fear the band would only attract trouble at the gig. The festival, however, was a minor success. Co-organiser Jennie Russell-Smith told me attendances for gigs by vintage punk bands at the time was then 'down to about one hundred' so it made sense to gather everyone together for a weekend.

HITS moved to Morecambe in 1997 where it largely stayed for almost a decade, incrementally expanding in size. There were 15,000 at the festival I attended in Blackpool in 2022. Initially, Jennie and festival partner, Darren, who had started out promoting hardcore gigs as a teenager in Birmingham in the mid-eighties, namely Napalm Death, steered clear of UK Oi!. . . bands. As the festival grew, however, they began to incorporate bands such as Menace, The Business and Red Alert and Oi! bands from Europe and America such as Oxymoron and Anti-Heros.

From 2000, Argy Bargy's name began to appear regularly on the festival bill alongside another notable new UK Oi!/streetpunk band Beerzone (who released an album called *British Streetpunk* in 2003 on Captain Oi!). This was a new beginning in the UK, Oi! carving out a reputation free from far-right or 'grey zone' band associations and presented as punky fun entertainment.

Cock Sparrer, with Daryl as a member, played the festival for the first time in 2001. Billed as their only UK gig of the year, their performance was free of significant trouble. It was the start of the glorious Sparrer renaissance in the UK, one which would become inextricably linked with the influence of Darren and Jennie's festival. The pair had hooked up with M.A.D. promotions in Berlin and developed their brand to include similar festivals in Spain's Basque Country and Berlin. There were also one-off gigs in other UK venues, and events in Japan, America and the Netherlands.

Darren and Jennie required more bands as they expanded their operations and a clutch of UK Oi! bands reformed such as Vicious Rumours, Section 5, Infa Riot and The Oppressed to play for them. Older bands such as the Upstarts, Rejects and The Business became regulars alongside UK82 bands such as The Exploited and GBH and heritage American hardcore acts such as Dead Kennedys.

Daryl became a part of the festival team around 2005 when it moved permanently to Blackpool, changing its name to Rebellion in 2007. A new Cock Sparrer album, *Here We Stand*, was released that year by Captain Oi!. It was mixed by Lars Frederiksen, who'd become a key supporter of the band.

There was a drive in the noughties, under the influence of the American scene and bands such as Dropkick Murphys, to rebrand Oi! as 'streetpunk'. Alongside Cock Sparrer, Argy Bargy, Crashed Out and Beerzone, a handful of new emerging acts joined up. Booze & Glory were perhaps the best known. Formed in London in 2009, all the band members were originally from Poland, known in the Oi! scene over there. They signed to Step-1 and loudly proclaimed they were West Ham fans. Micky Fitz guested with them. The band claim the 2012 video for their song 'London Skinhead Crew' is the most watched skinhead-related vid on YouTube ever with 27 million views. I saw them at Rebellion. People said they were good guys, a key step toward establishing the modern UK Oi! scene. Another 'street-punk' band that helped in this decisive shift were Gimp Fist, from Newcastle, formed circa 2007. I also saw them at Rebellion. The singer, I was told, was an ambulance driver and the band were all 'left-leaning' types.

Bushell was never far from the action, watched it all. His baby. In 2011, he put his name to a new Oi! compilation, *30 Years Of Oi!. . . Never Surrender* released by Holland's Contra Records. The two-CD package was a good indication of the relative health of the scene, a mix of old hands such as the Rejects, Sparrer, Resort and Business plus newer bands such as Argy Bargy and Booze & Glory, alongside acts from around the world such as Stomper 98, Marching Orders and Evil Conduct. The latter were an eighties Oi! band from Holland who'd reformed in '99, released splits with Old Firm Casuals and Gimp Fist, and adopted the 'streetpunk' stance (*Working Class Anthems* was the name of their 2012 album on Randale).

Hard Skin, a sort of music biz insiders' Oi!/skinhead parody band whose debut album, *Hard Nuts and Hard Cunts,* featured the drummer from indie band Lush (Chris Acland RIP), came back in 2013 and released an album of Oi! songs with guest female vocalists such as Alison Mosshart from The Kills, Joanna Newsom and Miki Berenyi (also of Lush). Knock Off also formed in 2013 and they became another popular, modernising Oi!/'streetpunk' band, cut in the image of Argy Bargy. The swell was becoming a wave. Arch Rivals, formed in the early teens, were perhaps the first UK band to suggest this music had some modern relevance. The band's guitarist, Tom Murphy, went on to form Hard Wax, whose 2022 album *Don't Stop the Beat* bore that out.

In 2016, Rebellion was advertising bands under the category of 'Oi! worldwide streetpunk'. There'd been a transformation. Sparrer were the figureheads and still today refer to themselves as 'streetpunk' in all their marketing. They'd gone from strength to strength, led the way, held the torch. They'd headlined the Kentish Town Forum in 2010, their first London gig since the Astoria in '93 and signed to American label Pirates Press, also home to Rancid. The two bands toured America together in 2012, a joint fortieth/twentieth anniversary tour. A prominent UK MMA and UFC cage fighter used 'England Belongs to Me' as walk-on music as their reputation was rehabilitated. In America, they were popular among hardcore fans of the New York Red Bulls football team who adopted 'Take 'em All' as their anthem. Their 'Fifty' shows at the Roundhouse in 2022 may have been largely ignored by the mainstream media, but there was no underestimating their significance: a celebration of fortitude, a culmination of years of assiduous planning from Daryl and Rebellion, a vindication and validation, two fingers from Oi! to the world, albeit under the cloak of 'streetpunk'.

The Last Resort initially resurfaced in 1989. Link released a half Resort/half Combat 84 album and were talking to Roi about re-releasing the band's classic *Skinhead Anthems* album. He suggested recording new material. Graham Saxby said Arthur Kay was involved but not for long. 'Arthur wanted to do it more the old Resort and Roi wanted to do it a bit more rock,' he said. 'Roi had started getting into heavy metal and if you listen [to the comeback album, released under the name The Resort] he's singing in a different way. I mean he's the voice of Oi! in a lot of ways but Roi was getting singing lessons at the time because he wanted to be more like AC/DC, Rose Tattoo and Guns N' Roses.'

The album went largely un-noticed and Roi, with Steve Whale from The Business, actually did form a heavy metal band, Heavy Metal Outlaws, and released an album, *Sex For Sexisms Sake*, in 1992 on Link. During this heavy metal phase, Roi spent time in America. 'Used to run about with bands like Warrant, Love/Hate . . . we did a little thing called Horrorshow, it was between AC/DC and The Cult, we did a stonking version of 'King of the Jungle',' he said during his Rebellion Q&A.

In 1995, Roi was interviewed for *Oi! The Video*, an almost two-hour long documentary made by Stuart Newman that has since been uploaded to YouTube (quarter of a million views and counting). It also features interviews with the Sparrer, Argy Bargy, Bushell, Mark Brennan, the Rejects and The Business. Roi was sat in what looked like a suburban back garden, bare-chested bar a leather waistcoat, with this long heavy metal mane of hair. 'I could sit on my hair at one time,' he said at Rebellion. 'I didn't have it cut for over twenty years.'

It was Saxby who then got The Last Resort reunion rolling proper, in 1996, initially for a gig in Belgium. Roi again fell out with Kay and Saxby stepped in on vocals. 'Roi wanted to do more like a rock thing,' Saxby said. 'Arthur wanted to do it more "take the money and run" sort of thing.' Kay enrolled Daryl and 'Dustbin' Burgess from Argy Bargy. 'The Belgium people wanted Roi but Arthur said, look I've got Saxby the original singer, and they accepted it,' Saxby said. 'I always regretted leaving The Last Resort.'

This line-up made an album, the excellent *The Full Monty*, released by Step-1. 'That was pretty much all Arthur's songs, and the early copies do say The Last Resort,' Saxby said. 'Then Roi says he owns the rights to use the name, so we just started going out as The Warriors. We played on and off between '96 to 2003, doing a load of Last Resort numbers. People used to come to see us because it was the nearest thing to The Last Resort because Roi wasn't going at the time.' They also included a few Cock Sparrer songs in the set. 'Daryl was also in Cock Sparrer,' Saxby laughed. 'So we did 'Runnin' Riot', 'Chip on my Shoulder' and 'Watch Your Back'. We all love Cock Sparrer.'

They made two more albums as The Warriors then took a break. Arthur retired. In 2009 The Warriors, with a new line-up, started back up and have been going ever since, recording six more albums – one of Oi!'s understated successes. They also got dragged into the 'grey zone' debate. Listening to their material I'd say they were socialists if anything. 'The worst thing of all is association,' Saxby told me. 'I think that's what we were dealing with, being associated with people, not deliberately but unintentionally, and that's how you can get it. So in the last few years we've tried to avoid certain bands; we can't play with them, even though they're not Nazis, but they've played with that band and that band is, so because they've played with them we can't play with them! That's what it's like. I do agree with it in a lot of ways but it can get taken to an extreme.'

The Warriors were about to tour America, when I spoke to Saxby, and he said they were going to throw some of the old Resort classics into the set: 'Violence in Our Minds' and

'King of the Jungle'. 'Roi's not allowed in America so when we go out there they like to hear them. In 2012 we did a gig out there and it was all Last Resort songs.'

Roi came back in 2002 and played a few festivals in Europe. He was surprised by the size of the audience and the appetite for The Last Resort. He cut a song, 'We're Gonna Get You', as Millwall Roi's Last Resort, which was included on the Bushell-compiled *Addicted to Oi!* compilation album released by Captain Oi!. In 2003 he did his first gig as The Last Resort in twenty-one years. I got the impression it was a bit of a bumpy take off. He still had the long hair and at Punk & Disorderly in Berlin someone shouted out 'Oi, skinhead get your hair cut!' and he may even have been assaulted.

At Rebellion during his short Q&A he was asked what the motivation was for reforming the band. 'That was Lol Pryor,' he said. 'Lol said, everyone else is out there having fun, why don't you do it . . . he had more faith in me than I had in myself at the time. I'd known Lol since I was about 20, we go back a long way.' The Last Resort first played for Jennie and Darren in 2005, releasing a new album the same year, *Resurrection,* on Captain Oi!. The band then fell quiet for a period before returning with the hard-hitting *You'll Never Take Us (Skinhead Anthems II)* in 2009. Furbank's skinhead graphic was updated for a cover that echoed the 1982 original. The album was angry, violent, with strident songs about war widows left to rot, abused single mums, the underclass essentially, always anti-Tory. 'A lot of people now feel the same way we used to feel,' Roi said at the time. 'Especially the kids living in the blocks where I live.'

He added, in 2017: 'There is still a massive divide between rich and poor. They continue to sell off our national assets in order to line their own pockets, while nurses and teachers and the like are struggling every day to make ends meet.' There was also a real sense of unapologetic patriotic pride in the band's songs. 'And you're not proud of your country? I'm proud of my roots, the place where I come from,' Roi said. 'Not the government or the politics: I hate politics.'

The band, Beefy on guitar and JJ (formerly of the Anti-Nowhere League and The Business) on bass, might have swung a little towards the 'streetpunk' sound but Roi was all Oi!, his cockney voice deeper than ever, full of menace, blood-curdling. People started to call him 'the king of Oi!' and it was richly deserved. A video the band made in 2013 for a song called 'Never Get a Job', from a new album, *This Is My England: Skinhead Anthems III* blew up on YouTube. Take a look. It's peak Roi. He has this reputation. A Millwall football face; football violence another strong theme running through the Resort's catalogue. He also appears to have lost an eye. He hasn't but it's sort of whited out, and every inch of his torso and arms are covered in tattoos.

The eye was something of a taboo subject, but I asked Saxby anyway. They both still live in Herne Bay, bumped into one another now and again for a chat. 'He's always worn glasses since I've known him – forty-five years now,' Saxby said. 'He might have had a bad eye, a cataract or something was forming, and then at football one time there was a fight and it made it worse.'

Roi had seemed ill at ease at the Rebellion Q&A, not a natural public speaker like Jeff Geggus. When he was asked, how is the book coming along? He answered: 'I don't know where to start with it. I don't know what I can let out and what I can't let out . . . you know what I mean?'

'He's a lovely fella if he knows you,' Deptford John told me. 'He's a really nice bloke. I've never seen Roi punch anyone.'

I stood next to him at Cream of the Crop where The Last Resort were headliners. He wasn't as tall as I imagined, or as broad. Adidas old-school trainers, tight Levi's jeans. He looked younger than his years. He was in the courtyard chatting with friends. Had on the most amazing T-shirt, 'Borstal' it read. A new UK hardcore band I later learned.

The Resort played all the old songs at Cream of the Crop: 'Rebels With a Cause', 'Resort Boot Boys', 'Working Class Kids', 'Skinheads in Sta Press', 'King of the Jungle' and as a finale, 'Violence in Our Minds'. I was surprised by the Sieg Heil, the only one I saw in 2022. It came midway through 'String 'Em All Up' from *Anthems II* about twenty minutes into the set. I heard JJ introduce the song one time as 'politically incorrect'. It concerned rapists and wife-beaters ('string 'em all up by the balls, line 'em all up against the wall, load up the guns, aim for the face and make the world a better place').

JJ saw the Nazi salute and immediately halted the music and pointed at someone in the crowd. 'You can't do that here mate,' he said over the mic. There was another salute during 'Skinheads in Sta Press', this time they played on. I thought at one point there was a chant of 'Sieg Heil, Sieg Heil' but it was 'skinhead, skinhead'. The atmosphere was quite intense, heavy – there was an edge rarely associated with a band forty-odd years into their career.

They also played songs from their new album, *Anthems VI*, released by Randale in 2021: 'Boots on the Ground', 'The Devil You Know' and the intimidating 'Psychopath', where Roi quite convincingly inhabits the mind of a killer. It starts with the line,

'I'll rip your heart right from your chest, I'll smash your skull and make a mess.'

Beefy, Keith Hillyer, who'd released a book *You Are The Beef! The autobiography of Beef – guitarist of The Last Resort* in 2013, was back in the band for this gig. It hadn't been cost effective for Lars Frederiksen, who had taken over from him around 2018, to fly over from America.

Lars joining the band had given The Last Resort a major boost. Rancid after all remain a draw, their most recent album, released in 2017, reached number twenty-three in the US charts. Lars had been a long-time fan. He'd formed his own Oi! band in 2010, The Old Firm Casuals, and they'd recorded a split single with the Resort in 2011. He'd even started to follow Millwall.

At Rebellion, Roi explained how JJ had sorted Lars joining the band. 'He said he's got this geezer coming down from London to audition, his name's Dave,' Roi said. 'I should have twigged. Soon as I seen Lars, I went, oh you cunt.' He added: 'Lars brought his sound to our unit. And he complements it.'

Lars had contributed much to *Anthems VI* and it was as vital as anything the band had released, among the best Oi! music ever recorded. At Rebellion it was suggested the band now sounded like 'the Black Sabbath of Oi!'.

'Can't get a better compliment than that can you?' Roi said. 'I love it [the album]. I've always liked that harder side and I've never hid that from nobody.' He mentioned one track he was particularly happy with, 'Freedom Pt.2', a reworked version of 'Freedom', the very un-Oi!-like almost five-minute epic opening track on *Skinhead Anthems*. They were always a little leftfield, so was Roi.

In recent times the Resort have played gigs all around the world. Japan twice. 'We've been extremely lucky,' Roi said at

Rebellion. 'It gives me that uplift, the buzz I get from it is unbelievable.' He was asked specifically about playing in Indonesia. 'I couldn't believe the way the crowd reacted, the one in Jakarta especially, they went absolute nuts and they were all kids, 600 of them,' he said.

Asked what was in the future for the band, he looked to JJ, sat in the front row beside Bushell, for help. JJ said there were more gigs lined up. 'We'll do another record at least,' Roi said.

Anywhere you'd like to go, he was asked?

'America, if I can get in,' he said.

I watched them play to a packed crowd, over three thousand, on the main stage at Rebellion on the Saturday night. With Lars on guitar, the chug and chant of the Resort songs filled the Empress Ballroom, hundreds in a massive scrum of Oi! frenzy down the front.

The last stop has to be the shop: Oi Oi The Shop. Roi sang about it on *Skinhead Anthems III*, on the song 'Resort Boot Boys II'. It's situated in north London's popular Camden Market and is currently the most positive and thriving advert for the Oi! scene worldwide. Go up the famous 'Clash steps' (where The Clash shot the cover image for their debut album) and you can't miss it. Inside it is bright, clean, very smart. Rails of band Ts, flight jackets, Harringtons, button-down shirts, slacks, braces, books, records.

Bill Bennett and his wife Sarah McCauley started the shop in the late noughties, and have been in their current location since June 2021. Bennett is 61, had been a skinhead in the seventies as a schoolkid but now had a big bushy beard. His enthusiasm for Oi! was obvious from the get-go. He was raving about a new band, Clobber. 'Proper kick-you-in-the-bollocks music,' he said. 'The singer's a skinhead and they mix their stuff with punk and hardcore. They remind me of the old-school days, rough and ready, Crown Court style; they're that breed that is coming in now. A lot of bands are now crossing over hardcore and Oi! and the scenes are coming together. You're even getting "straight" people going to the Oi! gigs – back in the eighties you'd never see that.

'Also bands like Grade 2 are bringing in the younger side,' Bill added. 'People that wouldn't have necessarily come to the gigs. The music has changed a bit as well. It's a lot more melodic. It's bringing in a new audience.'

Clobber. I looked into them and liked them, mentioned them in the *Guardian* piece. 'Tottenham Court Road' from their debut EP *Tribal Rites of the New Friday Night* instantly got to me. 'You have to really go to gigs and experience this stuff,' Bennett said.

The shop started small, a hobby really, just a place for people to meet. 'I wanted there to be a skinhead presence in north London,' Bennett said. 'We were probably the first people to call the shop a skinhead shop because people were too scared to say that.'

'You were laughed at,' his wife said.

'I had one guy who came over to me in the pub and said, Oi Oi The Shop my arse, you won't last ten minutes with a name like that.'

'That was somebody on the scene as well,' McCauley said.

You were probably advised to call it a 'streetpunk' shop, I joked.

'Streetpunk was the soft version of Oi!,' Bennett said. 'That's an Oi! band trying to get away from the Oi! but still playing Oi!; it's a get out clause. That annoyed me a bit.'

When you started the shop was Oi! still a dirty word then, I asked?

'I got a hell of a lot of stick,' Bennett said. 'I got people coming up to me in the shop and spitting at me, giving me abuse.'

I was taken aback by this, still am. People came in the shop and spat at you simply because the shop was an Oi! shop?

'For years we also used to get groups of Antifa coming up and checking out what we had,' said McCauley. 'They'd always come up in gangs. We'd recognise them because they were always wearing black and it was like an intimidation thing. They'd say nothing, flick through the records and the books. It went on a while, for years, with different groups of people. At the end of the day we want to flog clothes, book, records – we're not interested in politics.'

'The scene is completely different now,' Bennett said. 'All that shit has gone. There's some great bands that should be out there headlining big shows but they don't get a chance because they're linked with the Oi!. This is why we have to tell people Oi! is not a dirty word. That's why we chose the name Oi Oi The Shop: we stick behind that. Me and Sarah.'

Cock Sparrer were early supporters. 'It was actually Colin we met first, the singer, when we were in the shop on the High Street where Urban Outfitters is now,' McCauley said. 'He came down with a signed poster and this was the crappiest little shop, it was almost embarrassing. I love them but they've been Bill's favourite band since he was a kid and they've supported us all along. We've become really friendly with Steve the drummer and his family. They're like a gang of schoolmates on the stage, they all genuinely like each other. The songs are sing-along, kind of anthems, and people can relate to their lyrics.'

'They are down-to-earth people, working-class people like us, doing a job, going out there earning money, and they go and do gigs,' said Bill. 'They came from nothing and worked their way up to where they are today and that's why people respect them because they worked hard; they've done themselves proud. Can't fault them, they are fantastic.'

Oi Oi The Shop was particularly popular with the new wave of Oi! bands in Europe. 'They used to bring their new records or just stickers to give out, spread the word about the music and what was going on, and it just built up and up from there,' Bennett said. 'The shop became a pretty big name abroad because people respected us for doing what we'd done. They knew that other people would not use that name Oi!.'

'Probably over half our sales are international now, if not more,' McCauley said.

'You go on our website or Instagram and you see the photos – you'll see all different nationalities,' said Bennett. 'And when people come here, they're so happy to be here. People say we chucked our luggage down and we came to the shop as quick as we could . . . that's how crazy it is. They love it.'

The pair also started running Oi! gigs in London around 2013, chiefly at the Fiddler's Elbow venue in Camden, mostly European and American bands. 'They would come over for a gig, they'd come down the shop, we might do a DJ night the night before,' said McCauley. 'When The Templars played, Phil DJed at the venue the night before and it was heaving.'

'It was mostly bands from abroad we put on,' said Bennett. 'Bands like Evil Conduct; some of them were fantastic.'

'We put Crown Court on for their first gig at Fiddler's Elbow,' McCauley said.

'They weren't called Crown Court then,' Bennett corrected. 'It was Trev's first band, Stomping Ground.'

This is, ultimately, where we came in. Back to the rebirth of Oi! as a modern, relevant force. Violent. Tough. Ugly.

Sarah said they were now planning on expanding their own brand of clothing and merchandise. 'We have to do that because some brands wouldn't supply us,' said Bennett. 'Some well-known names have totally blanked us.'

Brands who have been given kudos because of skinheads wearing it? I'd read a 2018 article in the *Guardian* about how Dr. Martens 'stomps to strong profit on back of nineties fashion revival'. It said sales of the 'British bovver boot brand' were up by a fifth to almost £350 million that year, led by a surge in demand across Europe, where the company opened sixteen new stores. The article did mention the impact skinheads had had on the brand: 'Dr. Martens first set trends when it was adopted by skinheads, a sixties youth subculture whose style expressed working-class solidarity'. But, of course, there was no mention of the second wave of late seventies/early eighties skins, who were the ones who actually had started the trend, no mention of Oi!.

'Brands who are now having a dedicated area in their shop, they're promoting the whole subculture thing and yet they don't want to supply to us,' said Bennett. 'At one time they wouldn't even look at a skinhead, now they're using it because of people like us. But our intention wasn't to turn around the reputation of Oi! or skinheads, it was just somewhere for people to meet and to say Oi! isn't a dirty word – if someone's got the bollocks to do it, what we did, things will happen and you get respect for that.

'We're just out there telling people, we're a skinhead, punk and hardcore shop; come and see us, we're not going to bite your head off,' Bennett added. 'We're not going to give you a good kicking and tell you to fuck off. Come and see what it's all about, talk to us. A lot of people come in with negative thoughts and go out completely different; they see a different side of what's going on. It just needs that gate to open up a bit more to show people what the Oi! scene is all about because it's still closed a bit. It needs to be opened fully up to these young kids, especially in the fashion scene – Oi! has got a lot to offer fashion, a lot to tap into, to experiment with. But people don't because of this little tick next to it saying, don't go near that, they're a bit dodgy.'

'People do come in sometimes, especially Europeans and Americans, and they assume the worst,' said McCauley. 'They'll ask about it and we'll take time, if we're not busy, and explain. Just a couple of months ago I had the [celebrated NY punk rock] band Gogol Bordello in, the singer Eugene [Hütz], Sunday afternoon. While he was in the shop, this guy comes in, young Spanish kid, and he says, Oh, is this a Nazi shop? I did the usual spiel and he left. Eugene was outraged. He said, What? You have to put up with that? How do you stick that? I said, it happens all the time, you get used to it. It's just people who don't know what they're talking about, but if they ask nicely then we talk to them about it and they'll go out and have a completely different opinion of the scene.'

Acknowledgements

Thanks to all those that took the time to speak (and listen) to me: Dave Parsons, Chris Wright, Gaz Stoker, John Foster, Patty Smith, Gaz Douglass, Neil 'Newts' Newton, John Woodward, Neil McLennan, Paul Sham, Markus Erling, Garry Bushell, Chris Mundie, John Armitage, Jo Barnett, Trevor Taylor, Danny Swan, Ralph Orton, Dave Bianchi, JJ Pearce, Noel Martin, Matthew Worley, Jennie Russell-Smith, Phil Templar, Graham Saxby, Jeff Geggus, Mike Josephson, Derek Ridgers, Tommy 'Mensi' Mensforth[1] [RIP], Bryan Zimmerman, Bill Bennett, Sarah McCauley, Al White, Doug Kane, Greg Huff, Victor Lapprend, Luis Português, Karl Kahl and Gary Lammin.

Also thanks to *Creases Like Knives* for permission to use Trev's epigraph quote, and a good general grounding. Other websites I returned to regularly for information during 2022 were: american-oi!.com, standupandspit.wordpress.com and Oi! The Archives on Facebook. Further thanks to Claudia Zrycki, Henrike Baliu and Alexandre de Almeida for help with the Luis Português interview and to Cristian Dentone for facilitating and translating the Osvaldo González interview.

---

[1] I interviewed Tommy 'Mensi' Mensforth in 2011 for *The Stone Roses: War and Peace* (Penguin, 2012).